P9-DHQ-510

GOD'S
NOT
DEAD

GOD'S NOT DEAD

EVIDENCE FOR GOD
IN AN AGE OF UNCERTAINTY

RICE BROOCKS

W PUBLISHING GROUP

AN IMPRINT OF THOMAS NELSON

© 2013 Rice Broocks

All rights reserved. No portion of this book may be reproduced, stored in a retrieval system, or transmitted in any form or by any means— electronic, mechanical, photocopy, recording, scanning, or other—except for brief quotations in critical reviews or articles, without the prior written permission of the publisher.

Published in Nashville, Tennessee, by W Publishing Group, an imprint of Thomas Nelson.

Thomas Nelson titles may be purchased in bulk for educational, business, fund-raising, or sales promotional use. For information, please e-mail SpecialMarkets@ThomasNelson.com.

Unless otherwise noted, Scripture quotations are taken from the New King James Version®. © 1982 by Thomas Nelson, Inc. Used by permission. All rights reserved.

Scripture quotations marked NIV are from the Holy Bible, New International Version®, NIV®. © 1973, 1978, 1984 by Biblica, Inc.™ Used by permission of Zondervan. All rights reserved worldwide.

Scripture quotations marked KJV are from the King James Version of the Bible.

ISBN 978-0-7180-3701-7 (TP)
ISBN 978-0-7852-3833-1 (IE)

Library of Congress Control Number: 2012954165
ISBN 978-0-8499-4853-4

Printed in the United States of America
17 18 19 RRD 11

To my children's children

So the next generation would know them,
  even the children yet to be born,
  and they in turn would tell their children.

—PSALM 78:6 NIV

CONTENTS

PREFACE

WHILE VISITING THE CITY OF NEW ORLEANS, I CASUALLY mentioned to a friend that I was writing a book titled *God's Not Dead: Evidence for God in an Age of Uncertainty*. I explained that my motivation was a desire to help people defend their faith against the rising tide of skepticism and atheism—particularly on university and college campuses. I also described how more than 50 percent of young people who finish high school and attend a university abandon their faith—primarily because they were never taught the reasons that undergird their beliefs.

"This needs to be a movie," he immediately shot back. Within a few weeks the owners of PureFlix, a faith-based movie company, flew to Nashville to discuss how to bring this issue to the big screen. The result of our dialogues was production of the movie *God's Not Dead*. The plot centers on a university freshman who is challenged by his atheist philosophy professor to defend his faith that God exists in front of the class. The drama that unfolds has caused audiences from Los Angeles to London to cheer and clap as well as shed tears.

The movie's box office success shocked not only the critics but also all involved in making it happen. None of us would have dreamed that this production would top 60 million dollars in US theaters and spread as a global phenomenon. Because of its popularity, the movie has been discussed, debated, and dissected to try and analyze why it made such an impact. The storyline resonated with people of all ages who have been challenged to defend the reasons behind their faith beyond their own subjective experience. The simple, straightforward answers offered in the movie have inspired millions of people who watched it in theaters or later on DVD.

This book, however, is not a novelization of the screenplay but an overview of the evidence for God's existence. What you are about to read has been translated into several languages and has helped people who were motivated by the dramatization to become defenders of the faith. Our initial goal, to see millions of people grasp a rational defense of the truth of the Christian faith, is being realized.

One of the most important aspects in examining the evidence for God is to know what you are looking for. God is not a physical element that you can measure in a test tube or a particle you can find at the Large Hadron Collider in Switzerland. He is the intelligent mind behind the universe. Put simply, if you are looking for Bill Gates, you won't find him by breaking down a computer.

If there is an overarching theme to this book as well as the movie, it is the fact that real faith in God is not a blind leap in the dark but a result of considering the evidence and making a rational step of faith in the direction the evidence is pointing. If we are open-minded, we will be willing to follow the evidence wherever it leads—even if it leads to God.

The stories of those who have been affected by the movie have poured in from around the world—not only of those who found the reasons they needed to believe, but also those who faced severe challenges and ridicule because of their faith in God. It is important to note that these people were not suffering from a "persecution complex" but were in essence expressing their desires to give reasonable responses to the criticisms and objections to the Christian faith. For the most part, they expressed gratitude for the answers they are now able to give in response. This is the primary motivation in offering this book to you—so you are able to know God is real and simply and clearly explain that faith to others.

INTRODUCTION

GROUND ZERO OF FAITH

Christianity has been successfully attacked and
marginalized . . . because those who professed belief
were unable to defend the faith from attack, even
though its attackers' arguments were deeply flawed.

—WILLIAM WILBERFORCE, *REAL CHRISTIANITY*[1]

"GOD, I JUST CAN'T BELIEVE IN YOU ANYMORE." THIS WAS
the frustrated conclusion of Dean, an executive in the music business in Nashville, as he drove down the highway thinking of a
conversation he had recently with an atheist—a conversation that
rocked his world. He had been deeply challenged by this person's
questions and objections to the existence of God. What was most
upsetting to Dean was that he had no answers. Frustrated and
embarrassed by his own inability to answer this skeptical barrage,
he decided to verbalize his decision to stop believing.

What happened next was the last thing he expected. After
making his declaration that he would no longer believe, he heard
an inner voice: *Who do you think you're talking to?*

He immediately pulled his car over to the side of the road and retracted his unwarranted decision. However, he determined not to bury his doubts any longer but deal with them head-on. After studying the issues and evidence, he received the answers he needed. He says he is now able to answer the skeptic's challenges as well as help the doubter who is struggling to find faith.

Stories like Dean's have led me to write this book. All believers should be able to give the reasons for their faith. This is the charge given to us from one of history's greatest examples of someone who recovered from the dark night of unbelief: the apostle Peter. "Always be prepared to give an answer to everyone who asks you to give the reason for the hope that you have" (1 Peter 3:15 NIV). There are straightforward answers for the skeptics' questions, but most believers aren't familiar enough with them to be able to explain those reasons to others. I hope this book changes that for those who read it.

The bluster from the ranks of the unbelieving is summed up in the words of musician and zoologist Greg Graffin of the group Bad Religion, who asserts that those who suggest life was intelligently designed have "not produced a single shred of data" to back up their claims.[2] To say there is no evidence for this Creator is like saying the thousands of paintings in an art museum couldn't have been painted because there are no artists visible in the gallery. The evidence of an intelligent mind behind the universe is so overwhelming that it has "shredded" the notion that everything was produced by nature alone. This evidence cannot be dismissed by merely the discovery of another obscure fossil or an untestable hypothesis of a theoretical physicist.

In the name of science and reason, faith is being framed as irrational and illogical. The metanarrative of Darwinian evolution has turned many minds and hearts, teaching that life arose spontaneously from nothing, for no reason, and for no purpose, guided by the "blind watchmaker" of natural selection.[3] The belief that everything we see around us came about through natural causes is called *naturalism*. As Stephen Hawking concluded, "What place, then, for a creator?"[4]

I intend to show you the need for the Creator to explain the world around us as well as the world within us, that is, the human soul. To do this, I refer to some of the thousands of scholarly works written on the evidence for the existence of God. For centuries great minds have wrestled with the idea of an inspired creation and brilliantly answered doubts, quandaries, and accusations. And today we need the wisdom of history's giants of philosophy, theology, and science. I will refer to their arguments alongside my own comments as you absorb the genius of those who have already fought and won the great intellectual battles for faith. My own ideas and observations have come through years of study and discussions on these topics with skeptics as well as seekers. The reality is that people come to a place of faith not against reason but through it. That's why the first step of faith or *ground zero* is to believe God exists.

Make no mistake; radical atheists present their case with great fervor. They assert there is no rational proof for the existence of God, the Bible is a book of fairy tales and contradictions, and religion in general is a bad thing. Furthermore, they charge that anyone who is rational and not delusional will come to the same conclusions. They feast on unprepared religious people who unintelligently hold to beliefs they've merely inherited, who have only a secondhand faith. But these skeptics are seldom willing to take a second look at the faith assumptions behind their own worldview. With almost religious zeal they believe it's only a matter of time until everyone sees things their way. Their strategy is simple:

1. Use ridicule and mockery to label people of faith as anti-intellectual or irrational.
2. Set up a false dichotomy between science and faith, telling people to choose one or the other.
3. Keep the debate one-sided by not allowing a dissenting opinion in the public arena, making sure the only places where expressions of faith are allowed are in strictly religious settings.

The sad reality is that this strategy is working. According to the Pew Research Center, in 2007, 83 percent of millennials said they never doubted God's existence. In 2012, the number dropped to 68 percent. That is a fifteen-point drop in five years.[5] Other studies have shown that more than half of the young people in America who attended church will drop out after they leave high school for college.[6] While there are a variety of reasons for this, one of them is that these students have never been prepared to handle the objections the skeptics raise. Young people must have more than a religious experience if they're going to withstand the intellectual onslaught that awaits them in college.

As a Christian minister my passion is to teach the truths believers need not only to defend themselves from getting robbed of their faith but also to go on the offensive with the unbelieving world around them, demonstrating that God exists. Once that truth is firmly grasped, it becomes a logical necessity to seek out the nature and character of this Creator.

One of my great joys has been watching people find a faith in God that is both intellectually satisfying and spiritually fulfilling. The good news is that there are encouraging signs of a spiritual awakening happening among young people. Though not as dramatic as the growth of the Christian faith in Africa, Asia, and South America, thousands of people in North America have come to faith in God for the first time or returned to a faith they once had; but the struggle is far from over. The new generation of skeptics is committed to its own nonbelieving agenda. Its mission is to see the elimination of all religious faith, or as atheist Sam Harris said, "the end of faith."[7]

People of faith cannot afford to be passive and disengaged. Many fall into the trap of thinking, *Maybe if we are nice enough, they will know we are true believers and God is real.* After all, doesn't the Bible say to "preach the gospel and if necessary use words"? Well, no, it doesn't. That phrase is usually attributed to Saint Francis of Assisi, but it is doubtful that he ever said it. While we must certainly treat those who express hostility toward God with dignity, we must also be prepared to speak the truth boldly. No one said it would be easy. Even the great evangelist and apostle of the early church Saul of Tarsus asked people to pray for him so he could "speak boldly, as I ought to speak" (Ephesians 6:20). We must, at least, be as bold in our witness for Christ as skeptics are in their attacks against the faith.

Those early believers grasped something we need to understand. Every worldview is in essence a story, a metanarrative that attempts to answer the real questions of our existence. As it has often been said by a wide range of authors, whoever tells the most believable story wins the age. The early Christians told their story and confirmed it with evidence: Jesus resurrected to fulfill the words of the ancient prophets. In our postmodern world people want to believe every story is equally valid, but all stories aren't equal. Once on an airplane I sat next to a strange woman who told me she believed she was God. After hearing this I smiled and said, "If you're God, I've got a lot of questions for you." Reason helps us dismiss absurd claims like this.

Similarly, skeptics make claims that are thin and easily dismissed as well, such as life was originally seeded on this planet by aliens, or Jesus Christ never existed. Other arguments require a much more thoughtful response, such as their claim that your religion depends on where you were born. If you were born in America, you would be a Christian. If you were born in India, you would be a Hindu. There's some truth to this, but it isn't the whole story. Just because you were born into a certain religion doesn't mean you will remain in that faith once you are old enough to think for yourself and consider other world views. As we will discuss later, much of the current, astounding growth of the Christian faith is coming in parts of the world where Christianity has not been the predominate belief system.

In fact, the lives of many of the skeptics themselves prove this point. Many of them were born into Christian families and cultures but left once they got older. The same is often true for people born in any culture. When later in life they are exposed to the free market of ideas, they change. They switch. They choose other options.

That's why I have spent the last thirty years focusing on university campuses around the world. The campus is an exciting place, a crossroads where a person's cultural upbringing meets the world of ideas. It can also be the place where the truth of Jesus Christ shines the brightest. The gospel of Jesus Christ doesn't prevail only when there are no competitors; it shines most brightly when it is held up to other faiths. Secular religions, like Darwinian naturalism, can't make the same boast. They don't do well when faced with competition. They try to eliminate rivals. That is why enormous energy is spent to keep any reference to the existence of intelligent design in nature out of the classroom. Real faith—particularly real faith in Jesus Christ—welcomes the challenge.

Remember that Christianity originally arose in the hostile culture of the Roman Empire, where to believe in Jesus Christ could cost you your life. Thousands of early believers were thrown to the lions, burned at the stake, or even crucified, as Christ was, for their faith. The experience of the early Christians wasn't a result of the culture they were born into or the way their parents raised them. Unlike more militant religions that force people to believe at the point of the sword, early Christianity spread by a force that was virtually unknown to men at the time—the force of divine love. This is what caused those who had grown up in the Roman Empire's culture of violence, subjugation, and fear to turn to Christianity. Christ commanded His followers to advance His message by the irresistible force of love and the power of truth.

True faith in God isn't coerced. It arises freely. The message of Christ transformed the Roman Empire because that message was based in love and truth and because it did not coerce obedience as other religions did. That's why skeptics, idolaters, and atheists turned to the message of Jesus in the early years of Christianity, regardless of where they were born. In places such as America, where the Christian faith has been practiced for generations, those born in the faith have an advantage that should not be ignored or dismissed as trivial.

My Story

Despite being born in America and raised in a family that attended church, I lived as if there was no God. As long as I didn't break any serious laws, I was okay. The notion of being religious was repulsive. Church was just a place to have weddings and funerals.

As a third-year university student, my personal problems became too big to ignore. As much as I tried to run from them or drown them with drugs and alcohol, they only grew larger. The turning point came when I began to doubt my doubts about God and I humbled myself by admitting I had deep needs. That step of humility put me in a position to listen when someone started talking to me about the reality of God and His incarnation as Jesus Christ. I'm grateful for the people who took the time to speak to me, answer my questions, and ultimately call my bluff by challenging my unbelief.

For the first time I understood something that was truly good news. What was that something? That God had foreseen my need and provided help, long before I knew I needed it. How long before? Try two thousand years before. At the right time in history, God became man in Jesus Christ.

I decided to believe God's story and accept it as true—not just true for me but really true for all humanity—the metanarrative that defines reality in this age of uncertainty. That fateful decision changed the course of my life. My questions were not all answered at once. In fact, following Christ has been a journey of continually finding the answers to the questions and quandaries of our existence. Yet time and time again, the answers have come. God isn't afraid of our questions, but we must ask them not out of hostility toward Him, but out of trust "that He is a rewarder of those who diligently seek Him" (Hebrews 11:6). Because God is real, humanity's search for Him will not be in vain. With this hope in mind, I write this book for three types of people:

The Seeker is attempting to believe but faces doubts about whether God is real. I offer the evidence in these pages hoping that person will be able to realize that it is indeed credible as well as fulfilling to believe in God. Even before understanding Christianity or the Bible, there is ample evidence that the world around us is no accident.

The Believer knows God is real subjectively but cannot easily articulate this faith to unbelievers. Hopefully these chapters will make the evidence for God clear so that it can be easily comprehended and then presented to others.

The Skeptic may be reading this book from a critical point of view and a predetermined mind-set that there is no God. My hope is that regardless of how attached this reader is to skepticism, the following evidence will ironically allow a seed of doubt to be planted, helping that person break free of the matrix of a godless worldview and embrace the real story that best corresponds to the evidence, the one that declares, "**God's not dead.**"

1

GOD'S NOT DEAD

What divides us is not science, we are both committed
to science, but our worldviews. No one wants to
base their life on a delusion, but which is a delusion?
Christianity or atheism?

—John Lennox[1]

When a Man stops believing in God he doesn't then
believe in nothing, he believes anything.

—attributed to G. K. Chesterton[2]

I WAS IN MY THIRD YEAR OF COLLEGE WHEN MY ATHEIST
older brother, Ben, decided to try to talk me out of my Christian
faith. I probably looked like an easy target. I had not been a
Christian that long, and Ben was in his third year of law school at
Southern Methodist University in Dallas. He was at the top of his
class, already had a master's degree in counseling, and had been
sharpening his disdain for Christianity for a while.

We arranged to meet over a weekend at our parents' house in
Dallas. Ben prepared as if he was going to be trying a legal case,

studying the Bible to get the ammunition he needed to blow me out of my new faith. He told one of his classmates, "I'm going home to get my little brother out of this born-again thing." He showed up with his prepared questions and finely tuned challenges, anticipating anything I might say. He was confident he could get me to abandon this whole notion of faith in God and belief in Jesus Christ.

I'd like to tell you that I had brilliant, learned answers for everything he brought up. But I never had the chance to respond. As I listened to and addressed Ben's doubts simply, the truth of God's Word began to soften his heart. I could see he was doubting his doubts. There was finally a moment when I told him, "Ben, it's not what you don't know about God that's keeping you from believing; it's what you do know. You know He is real and you know He is holy [meaning pure]." The apostle Paul wrote that people "suppress the truth in unrighteousness" (Romans 1:18). The reason? They don't like God's rules. The problem with this is that it's like trying to hold a beach ball under the water: the harder you push truth down, the more forcefully it resurfaces. This was definitely what my brother was doing. He was trying to escape from the pangs of conscience that were convicting him of his behavior.

At the end of the day—the day on which he intended to talk me out of my faith—he was baptized in a swimming pool. Not long after he came up out of the water he said, "I don't think you answered all my questions, but I think I was asking the wrong questions." Today, Ben is a successful trial attorney in Austin, Texas, and a formidable witness for Christ.

That weekend thirty years ago was a turning point for both Ben and me. He became a believer in Jesus Christ while he was trying to talk me out of "this born-again thing." And since that day, I've devoted my life to getting people out of "this atheist thing." I work primarily among university students around the world, and I have been joined by thousands of others who have found that faith in God is both spiritually revitalizing and intellectually satisfying. We've also seen the opposite: that atheism doesn't satisfy a man's heart or mind.

THE END OF FAITH?

More than forty years ago, the cover of *Time* magazine asked, "Is God Dead?"[3] The writers were reflecting upon the famous claim made by nineteenth-century German philosopher Friedrich Nietzsche that God is dead. Other voices from that century raised the same issue in different words. Followers of Charles Darwin had suggested that belief in God would soon disappear from a scientifically progressive society. Karl Marx had said that religion is a drug, "the opium of the people."[4] In 1999, *The Economist* magazine published an obituary for God.[5]

But a funny thing happened on the way to the funeral. In 2009, the senior editor of *The Economist* cowrote the book *God Is Back*,[6] which served as a retraction of the 1999 article. Christianity is experiencing astounding growth in Africa, Asia, and Latin America. In Europe, where there has been generations of religious decline, there are encouraging signs of spiritual growth, particularly in places such as London, Berlin, and Dublin that have a deep history of faith in God. This is due to an intellectual renaissance as well as a spiritual one. People are awakening from the dogmatic slumbers of secularism and naturalism. And in America the overwhelming majority still acknowledge the existence of God, and the nation is beginning to witness a spiritual awakening among youth. In spite of the fact that God has been virtually banished from the classroom, university and high school students are questioning what they've been taught—the naturalistic dogma that the universe and life are merely the product of blind, random forces—and they are acknowledging that there is rational grounds for believing in a Creator. The thick fog of unbelief that has hovered over academia is starting to burn off as more and more evidence for an intelligent Creator surfaces.

With this rise in faith worldwide has come a corresponding response. Over the last decade the secularist camp set out to stem the tide of renewed faith. The term *new atheists* has been given to a group of skeptics who have sought to revive the arguments against God and repackage them for a new generation. Ironically, very little is *new* about these atheistic arguments. In fact, the success of their claims is mostly due to the fact that the theistic responses to their claims—which are the truth about God—have not been widely circulated.

A generation ago, C. S. Lewis composed a set of lectures that were broadcast over the BBC and were transcribed and published as *Mere Christianity*. Formerly an atheist, Lewis realized that he had to ignore too much evidence to maintain his unbelief:

> If you are an atheist you do have to believe that the main point in all the religions of the whole world is simply one huge mistake. If you are a Christian, you are free to think that all those religions, even the queerest one, contain at least some hint of the truth. When I was an atheist I had

to try to persuade myself that most of the human race have always been wrong about the question that mattered to them most.[7]

The arguments atheists use against God quickly diminish when they are answered by learned believers such as Lewis. Atheists claim that the universe isn't what you would expect if a supernatural God existed. All this death and suffering, they say, are plain evidence that a loving, intelligent God could not be behind it all. The truth is that God has created a world where free moral agents are able to have real choices to do good or evil. If God had created a world without that fundamental choice and option to do evil, then we wouldn't be having this discussion. God made a world where choices are real and humanity is affected by the choices of other humans. Drunk drivers kill innocent people. Some murder and steal from their fellow men. Though God gave clear commandments to humanity, we have for the most part ignored these directives. The mess that results is not God's fault. It's ours.

We are called to follow God and love Him with all our hearts and minds. This means we have to think and investigate. Truth is another word for reality. When something is true it's true everywhere. The multiplication tables are just as true in China as they are in America. Gravity works in Africa the way it does in Asia. The fact that there are moral truths that are true everywhere points to a transcendent morality that we did not invent and from which we cannot escape.[8]

As Creator, God has placed not only natural laws in the earth but also spiritual laws. For instance, lying is wrong everywhere. So is stealing. Cruelty to children is wrong regardless of what culture you're in or country you're from. When these laws are broken, people are broken. Not only does violating these spiritual laws separate us from God, but it causes pain in our lives and in the lives of those around us. The big question becomes, what can be done about our condition? When we break these spiritual laws, whom can we call for help? How can we be reconciled to God as well as break free from this cycle of pain and dysfunction?

Is Atheism a Religion?

Religious belief is framed by skeptics as something you believe in without any evidence, while atheism is based on science. Ironically, atheism, in all its railings against God, also has intrinsic beliefs, dogmas, and tenets that supposedly can't be challenged. It is itself a belief system with all the markings of a religion. In an issue entitled "Forget the Church. Follow Jesus," *Newsweek* magazine agreed, calling atheism a "belief."[9] Atheism as a religion (a set of beliefs) is just as intolerant and closed-minded as the claims made against any faith system it assails.

With the fervor of the religious fundamentalists, these new atheists reject any competing ideas not just from religion, but also from philosophy. Stephen Hawking, in his book *The Grand Design*, declared that "philosophy is dead."[10] However Daniel Dennett, one of the so-called Four Horsemen of Atheism, has admited, "There is no such thing as philosophy-free science; there is only science whose philosophical baggage is taken on board without examination."[11] Therefore, in their minds, science becomes the only source of truth; like a ruthless dictator in a third-world country, atheists must eliminate all competition. No deviations from the atheistic, Darwinian dogma tolerated. Want to lose credibility in these secular citadels? Merely suggest that there might be something beyond nature that's responsible for our existence. This skeptical overreaction is simply . . . unreasonable.

DELUSION OF DISBELIEF

In his book *The God Delusion*, Richard Dawkins asserts that God must be a delusion because God couldn't exist. Dawkins, who is perhaps the world's most famous atheist, makes the claim that though the universe appears to be designed, it couldn't have been because we are still left with the question "Who designed the Designer?" This is itself an example of the irrational, unyielding position of the atheistic mind. The truth is you don't have to have an explanation for every explanation. Such a demand sets up an infinite regress where nothing would be knowable and science and reason would all break down (granted, that is a worse-case scenario).

If you were walking through the woods and found a turtle on top of a fence post, you could rationally conclude that it didn't get there by itself. Someone put it there. Even if you didn't have an explanation for who did it, you would be reasonable in assuming that time and chance wouldn't eventually place a turtle on a fence post.

Sigmund Freud spoke of religious belief as a *wish-fulfillment*, the desire to have some "father-figure in the sky" who can straighten things out for us and talk to us when we are lonely. David Aikman, a former senior correspondent for *Time* and author of *The Delusion of Disbelief*, put atheism in the same category as religion, saying, "Atheism is itself a delusion," the ultimate wish-fulfillment.[12] There are real reasons why unbelievers don't want

God to exist or at least seek to reduce Him to a blind impersonal force. No God—no accountability. No God—no real morals. "If God is dead," said Malcolm Muggeridge, "somebody is going to have to take his place,"[13] and that somebody else is usually man himself.

Think about it: the overwhelming majority of the planet believes that God exists. To maintain that those who believe in God are deluded means atheists (or radical skeptics as I call them) believe the majority of the world is under some kind of mass delusion. In order to maintain this position from an objective intellectual standpoint, they would have to dismiss all evidence of God and then explain how everything we see around us arose on its own—by chance.

The taunt of the skeptic is that those of us who have faith have no real proof for that faith. Skeptics say it's all based on feelings or delusions or due to our religious upbringings. One of the standard lines from atheists sounds like this: "When I'm asked to prove god doesn't exist, I ask believers to prove there are no fire-breathing dragons living in the center of the earth." Some of the other analogies commonly used are the tooth fairy and Richard Dawkins's personal favorite, the "Flying Spaghetti Monster."[14] They sit back as if this alone justifies their disbelief, but they are wrong. There are no good reasons to believe in a Flying Spaghetti Monster, the tooth fairy, or fire-breathing dragons in the center of the earth. There are good reasons to believe in God.

The real question is, how much proof is enough proof to convince you that God is real? Most of the time atheists haven't thought about what it would actually take to get them to believe. When Dawkins was asked this during a public debate, he said, "That's a very difficult and interesting question because, I mean,

I used to think that if somehow, you know, great big giant, nine-hundred-foot-high Jesus with a voice like Paul Robeson suddenly strode in and said 'I exist. Here I am,' but even that, I actually sometimes wonder whether that would . . . "[15] He doesn't appear to have given much thought to this trivial answer. In fact, if someone else claimed to see a nine-hundred-foot Jesus, he or she would be ridiculed. The truth is, if your mind is made up about what you don't believe and won't believe, then no amount of evidence will convince you. You will dismiss even the most devastating testimony against your position.

I have been challenged repeatedly on university campuses: "You're going to have to prove to me that God exists and Christianity is true." My response? "If I do, will you believe in Him and follow Christ?" When they say no I respond, "Your problem is not a lack of information. If you have all your questions answered and still don't believe, then your real problem is more emotional, not intellectual."

War of the Worldviews

No one comes to these discussions completely neutral or objective. In other words, reason isn't always reasonable. Our reason can be compromised by our own selfish motives. People who act corruptly or destructively may think they have reasons that justify their actions. On top of that, they have a way in which they view the world. Their *worldview* consists of a set of presuppositions that bias reason.

The theistic worldview centers on God. *Theos* is the Greek word meaning "god," therefore a theist believes in God and sees God as the creator and sustainer of life and the world around us.

The physical laws, the constants in nature, and the complexity of life all point to a rational intelligence. Theists push that logic, believing this intelligence isn't merely an impersonal force but is conscious and relational as humans are conscious and relational beings. Just as we desire intimacy, trust, and love from the relationships we value, so does our Creator.

The atheist worldview, also described as naturalistic, centers on nature. *A-* is the Greek prefix meaning "absence," therefore an atheist believes in the absence of God. Everything can be explained by natural causes and effects. As the lead singer for Bad Religion stated in his book *Anarchy Evolution*:

> If people ask me about my worldview, I say that I am a naturalist. When most people hear that word, they think of someone who spends a lot of time outdoors watching birds and admiring landscapes—and I suppose that description applies to me. But I think of naturalism as a philosophy rather than a lifestyle. From a philosophical perspective, naturalists believe that the physical universe *is* the universe. In other words, there are no *super*natural entities or forces acting on nature, because there is no empirical evidence for anything beyond or outside of nature.[16]

This worldview eliminates the possibility of God from the outset; therefore, no evidence for an intelligent Creator will ever be convincing.

The pretense of many atheists is that somehow they don't really possess any of these presuppositions. They project this air of objectivity, arguing with Socrates, "Scientists follow the evidence wherever it leads."[17] Unless, of course, it leads to God.

To say that nothing exists outside the physical world is a statement of faith. There is no way that anyone can prove that is true. Atheism and other worldviews are just ideas—big ideas—and as history has proven, ideas have consequences. For example, the naturalistic worldview stemming from Darwinian evolution has had disastrous repercussions when applied philosophically and ethically: millions died at the hands of atheist Communists and Nazis during the twentieth century.

"Imagine There's No Heaven"

If there is an anthem of unbelief, it is no doubt the song "Imagine" written by the late John Lennon: "Imagine there's no heaven . . ."[18] What if Lennon's song were true? Would the world be a better place if there were no God? Let's imagine.

If there is no heaven, then there is no God. If there is no God or heaven, then this life is all there is: when you're dead, you're dead. What John Lennon imagined, Vladimir Lenin had already built in the communist state of Russia. The godless world of *that* Lenin was a living nightmare of torture, genocide, and darkness. The twentieth century was the bloodiest century in history, thanks to the atheistic regimes of Hitler, Stalin, Pol Pot, and Mao Zedong.

If God is dead, then man is dead as well. Utopian dreams of humanistic paradise seem ideal until one fatal fact is recalled: man is the true cause of evil. Without the restraint of God and His law, humanity is free to act out any impulse, desire, or passion. Nothing would be ultimately right or wrong. Imagine an announcement was made in any major city of the world that the police were taking the week off. No crimes would be prosecuted, no laws enforced. What do you imagine would be the result? Peace and tranquility or lawlessness and chaos?

If there is no heaven, then there is no reward for any good deed done. Why sacrifice your life for your country or any other cause? If there is no hell, then there is no ultimate punishment for any crime. In other words, the terrorists who commit atrocities against their fellow men will, in the end, get away with it.

The experiment to build a society without God has been tried. It has failed. At the same time *religion* without God is equally disastrous. The prophets of old warned that people could worship with their lips while their hearts were far away from God. The warning is echoed in the writings of the New Testament, saying some people will be seen "having a form of godliness but denying its power" (2 Timothy 3:5). Looking back over our shoulders into history, it doesn't take long to realize that some Christians have given the critics of faith a lot of ammunition. Most of the failures resulted from disobeying the commands of Christ to love, serve, and forgive. Jesus was totally against powerless, compassionless religion and called it hypocrisy; but make no mistake: religion has no corner on the market of hypocrisy.

Un-Mahered

During the last century, arrogance and ignorance hurt Christianity in public discourse with skeptics. In this century, however, the roles have been reversed. One of atheists' favorite tactics is to use mockery and ridicule to attempt to discredit anything of a religious nature, particularly Christianity. Any baseless claim is given credibility if it serves to undermine faith in God. If believers aren't prepared, they can be wrongly influenced to think their faith is misplaced.

A student once told me he had heard this question in a philosophy class: If God is all-powerful, could He make a rock so big He couldn't move it? He told me that when he couldn't come up with the answer, he eventually backslid. My thought was, *If one riddle shook your faith, then you didn't have far to slide.* We shouldn't abandon truth when these *evangelists of unbelief* shout their confident lies at us. The question actually violates logic's "law of non-contradiction." And the answer to the philosopher's riddle is simple: because God is all-powerful, He could not create anything He could not handle.

Other challenges are much more absurd. Late-night comic and professional cynic Bill Maher (pronounced like the verb *mar*) regularly uses ridicule to denounce religion. Most of his arguments are what philosophy calls *straw men*: false pictures of something that have been created only so they can be easily confuted. Maher often takes the worst parts of anything associated with religion (suicide bombers, priests who abuse children, and especially anyone who refuses to accept evolution as fact) and paints them all in the worst possible light. He then announces, "Religion must die."[19]

While many bad things have been done in the name of religion, and even in the name of Jesus Christ, an honest inquiry can quickly separate truth from error, fact from fiction. False claims must be challenged and seen for what they are—vain imaginations. Fanaticism is a human problem, not a religion problem. Don't believe it? Just watch any sporting event, rock concert, or political rally. Atheist fanatics are just as unreasonable as their religious counterparts. Just as you don't dismiss politics because there are bad politicians or commerce because there are bad businesses, you certainly must know how to separate the precious from the worthless when it comes to God and faith.

Again, Jesus Christ stands apart from man-made philosophy and religion. He was the original critic of empty religious practices and shallow lives. With a little effort, you can have a faith that is "un-mahered," one that is free from defects or stains. This kind of faith begins with a rock-solid knowledge that God is indeed real. The false notions of the age must be examined like the one-hundred-dollar bill a cashier examines as potential counterfeit. We must not be misled by phony arguments or phony lives. Remember, it isn't enough simply to know God is real. Even the demons believe in God and tremble. We must be able to demonstrate and articulate God's truth in a way the people around us can clearly understand.

WHAT 9/11 TAUGHT US

Just days after the attacks I drove with some friends to New York to see how we could serve that great city in its unprecedented time of crisis. It didn't take long to realize that we needed to plant a church in the heart of New York City to minister to the spiritual needs of as many as possible on a consistent basis. Within a month we were flying every Sunday night from Nashville to New York and holding Sunday night services. Today that church, Morning Star New York, consists of three congregations.

After we had been flying in for a few weeks for the Sunday night meetings, the owner of one of my favorite restaurants was thanking us for our commitment to help his city. I recounted an incident that occurred in his restaurant in my book *Finding Faith at Ground Zero*. Sandy, the owner of Carnegie Deli, called me over to a table of TV-network executives for an introduction. He said, "Reverend [I really don't like it when people call me that!], these men are having to burn their furniture because of anthrax-poisoned letters they have been receiving. They need answers about what's going on."

I sat down at the table with these very important media leaders and paused to consider what I could say that might make an impact for Christ in a wise and believable way. I said, "Well, if there's anything 9/11 taught us, it's that all religions are not the same. The god that told those men to get in airplanes and come to this city and hurt people is not the same God that inspired us to get into airplanes each week and come here and help people."[20]

There is no way you can group every religious belief and practice together and then smugly denounce religion as a whole. All beliefs are not equal. Some are true, and others are false. History has proven that ideas—religious, philosophical, or scientific—have consequences.

BREAKING NEWS

The greatest idea in history, the one that has produced the most significant and enduring benefit to humanity, is Jesus Christ. God's idea to come to earth as a human, undeniably demonstrating the power of truth, has given us the ultimate message of hope, called the *gospel* or *good news*. God's good news is as current as any breaking news you'll see or hear today on any news channel.

It is so encouraging I will refer to it as often as I can so its message is not missed or misunderstood. The good news announces that God became man in Jesus Christ, He lived the life we should have lived, and in our place He died the death we should have died. Three days later He came back to life to verify His identity as the Son of God, and now He offers full pardon and forgiveness to all who will believe and turn from the darkness of sin and the futility of trying to save themselves. Those who turn and put their trust in Him will never be ashamed.

This message of hope, this good news, is true no matter what country or culture you're from. Christ came to deal with the legal consequences of humanity breaking God's law once and for all. Far from wanting us to be religious, He calls us simply to love Him and love others. The gospel changes us from the inside out. That is why many are quick to say that Christ didn't call us into religion but into relationship, relationship with Him and with one another.

WHY GOD'S EXISTENCE MATTERS

Once in Argentina at the University of Buenos Aires, I spent time talking to five young students who identified themselves as atheists. I spent a lot of time asking questions about the reasons for their atheism. Thanks to a good translator, Phillip Steele, I was able to understand the details of their disbelief. As I listened intently, a young man carrying a guitar with him asked me, "Why should we even be concerned with the question, 'Does God exist?' Does it really matter?"

I asked him, "Have you ever written a song?"

His facial expression changed instantly as it seemed I was changing the subject from God and to something he really wanted to talk about. He said yes, then I asked, "Why did you want to write a song?"

He raised his hand to emphasize his passion. "I wanted to share my feelings with others, to create something they could enjoy as well as express my heart and my thoughts."

"What would you do if you wrote a song for those noble reasons and someone either denied you wrote the song or mistakenly gave credit to someone else for writing it instead of you? Would that bother you?"

Looking like he knew I was going to make a bigger point, he agreed, "Yes, I would be upset if I didn't get recognized as the author of the song I wrote."

I paused for just a moment. "What if you created a planet?"

You could see the evidence of the connection between the two thoughts on his face.

God deserves the recognition for all He has created. Knowing that a Creator exists changes everything in our outlook and worldview. It should inspire us to honor Him more than we would honor any woman or man for any human achievement. It should also cause us to seek Him, to earnestly desire a relationship with Him.

The reality of God as Creator compels us to investigate the world He created with greater confidence and to understand His nature and character. All the beauty, grandeur, and provision on the planet should produce a gratitude that overwhelms us. This is the spirit of evangelism that sends us out with a message of love, hope, and reconciliation, not hate and division.

Summary

When you hear "God is back," that obviously doesn't mean He actually went anywhere. Faith in God is back. Not a blind, unreasonable faith, but one that is well grounded in evidence. The grounded evidence is the basis to communicate that faith in a straightforward, clear manner. If nothing else, the writings of the new atheists have succeeded in awakening millions of Christians from their dogmatic slumbers.

This book is one of the many works that have been inspired by the audacity and arrogance of some of these skeptical writers who have decided to take their personal battle and hatred of religion public. When I was doing my doctoral work at Fuller Theological Seminary, my mentor Dan Shaw would constantly advise me to keep my writing from sounding "preachy." The goal was to produce a doctoral thesis based on empirical data and research with personal opinions and preachments at a minimum. While I still endeavor to present sound, rational arguments for the existence of God based on the best explanation of the evidence, I also want to offer the encouragement and hope that real faith in God produces. Let's now turn to the reasons to believe in the existence of God—starting with *reason* itself.

2

REAL FAITH ISN'T BLIND

Faith is not a leap in the dark; it's the exact opposite.
It's a commitment based on evidence. . . . It is irrational
to reduce all faith to blind faith and then subject it to
ridicule.

—JOHN LENNOX[1]

Reason is a tool to help us better understand and
defend our faith; as Anselm put it, ours is a faith that
seeks understanding.

—WILLIAM LANE CRAIG, *REASONABLE FAITH*[2]

IT'S SAFE TO SAY THAT THE MOST UNUSUAL CONFERENCE
I've ever attended was the 2012 Global Atheist Convention in
Melbourne, Australia, promoted as "A Celebration of Reason."
More than 3,500 delegates came to hear speakers such as evo-
lutionary biologist Richard Dawkins, Daniel Dennett, and Sam
Harris. Very few if any Christians appeared to be in attendance.

My goal in attending was simply to listen. I thought that if atheists were gathering from around the world, then something earth-shaking would be said that I would want to hear first-hand—maybe some new discovery in science that demonstrated (in their minds) that God does not exist. Instead of the intellectual onslaught I was bracing for, the opening-night speakers were four professional comedians. Their profanity-laced rants were perhaps an attempt to demonstrate their disdain for any hint of morality that might be lingering from their admitted religious upbringings.

The next day, rather than offer scientific or philosophical reasons for the nonexistence of God, speaker after speaker railed against religion and continued the tone set by the comedians on opening night. Again, mockery and ridicule were the primary themes. Ironically, there was very little "reason" present at their Celebration of Reason. The emotionalism they claim religion relies on permeated every presentation.

I left the conference convinced that the primary strategy of these new atheists is to lay claim to the word *reason*, as a business owner might try to secure a domain name before the competition gets it. By doing this they can label anyone who opposes them as "anti-reason" or irrational. With the zeal of a political party, their hope is that science would eliminate any faith or religion as well as philosophy. This was stated clearly by Dawkins in a discussion with John Lennox at Oxford University, sponsored by the Fixed Point Foundation:

> What worries me is if you don't have, if you don't allow in a rational basis for what you believe then it is possible for people to say, I'm sorry I just believe that Allah told me to go kill all those people. And it's no good arguing with me

because arguing is not what it's about. Faith is what it is about, and that is the danger.[3]

John Lennox, an Oxford mathematician who has debated Dawkins on several occasions, responded to this remark in one of their encounters:

I understand it from my own perception of the New Testament that that is not what the Christian faith is, that's dangerous, that blind faith. But all faith is not blind faith and just as you say you have faith in the scientific method and so have I, I have faith in God and believe that it is evidence based.[4]

Reason serves as a type of immune system helping us sort out helpful beliefs from harmful ones. When humans look at any set of events, we use our reason to draw conclusions about what has happened. Whether it is an incident that just took place before our eyes or one that happened thousands of years ago, reason processes the events and decides whether the explanation being offered is plausible. Irrationality is not a religious thing; it's a human thing. Ever heard of a *mad scientist*? Making the point that real faith isn't blind includes not blindly believing everything said in the name of "science." The evidence that God exists is all around us and inside of us. You have been given the ability to observe the phenomena around you and reason whether it is the product of blind forces or an intelligent Creator.

The twenty-first century is the most astounding time in history to be alive: knowledge and innovation are expanding at almost exponential rates. Consider the discovery of the Higgs boson particle at the Large Hadron Collider near Geneva, Switzerland, in July 2012. This particle, nicknamed by nonscientists the "God Particle," is unlocking physicists' understanding of the mysterious subatomic world and producing the belief that humanity may soon understand the smallest detail of how the universe works. However, just because we know how a mechanism works doesn't eliminate the existence of the agent or designer of the mechanism. The way these facts are interpreted comes down to the beliefs you hold or the lens through which you look.

Atheists believe a fantastic story that the universe just happened, by chance, and that all of this life and complexity came from nothing. "The universe just is," asserts the naturalist. Yet is that really true? Is that the only option a rational person has to consider? The late Christopher Hitchens, one of the most outspoken atheists of this generation and considered their most eloquent voice, seemed quite taken aback when he encountered Christians in his debates who actually had reasons for their faith. He thought that all we had was our appeal to our subjective experience.

Reason demands that we examine claims made in the name of faith or science in the same way we would examine the ingredients on a pill bottle or food item on a store shelf. Not all claims are equal. Many skeptics assert that the only reliable tests for truth reside in the realm of science. As will be shown, science points to God. Inductive methods exist to test the reasonableness of and credibility not just for belief in God, generally, but Christianity, specifically.

I hope to demonstrate that faith and reason are vital partners and complementary components for the discovery of truth. Tim Keller, a best-selling author and pastor in New York City, made this challenge to skeptics: "I urge skeptics to wrestle with the unexamined 'blind faith' on which skepticism is based, and to see how hard it is to justify those beliefs to those who do not share them. I also urge believers to wrestle with their personal and culture's objections to the faith."[5]

GOD OR SCIENCE?

Time magazine's November 13, 2006, cover story was titled "God vs. Science." The title alone suggested that one must choose between the two. The tagline to the online edition of the article stated, "We revere faith and scientific progress, hunger for miracles and for MRI's. But are the worldviews compatible? *Time* convenes a debate."[6] The debate was between Francis Collins, a geneticist and a Christian who wrote about the fantastic evidence for intelligence found in DNA in the book *The Language of God: A Scientist Presents Evidence for Belief,* and Richard Dawkins, a biologist and an atheist. Collins breaks the stereotype of a closed-minded religious person that Dawkins characterizes as people of faith. In fact, *Time* noted before it presented the debate between the two men that a growing number of scientists were becoming more vocal in their support of an alternative to the harsh battle lines Dawkins and his cohorts were drawing: "And to balance formidable standard bearers [of atheism] like Dawkins, we seek those who possess religious conviction but also scientific achievements to credibly argue the widespread hope that science and God are in harmony—that, indeed, science is of God."[7]

The article went on to mention scientists like Collins who find no conflict between science and faith and are pointing out the common ground that allows for constructive dialogue. Similarly, physicist and Anglican priest John Polkinghorne has referred to the vital connection between faith and science as "binocular vision." He explained, "Seeing the world with two eyes—having binocular vision—enables me to understand more than I could with either eye on its own."[8] Remember, the notion being sold to the public is that science deals in fact and religion deals in faith. Yet science has its own tenets of faith, and real faith is based on facts.

SCIENCE AND FAITH

Science is indeed "of God" as *Time* stated. Because the Christian worldview pointed to the fact that the universe was designed, it could be rationally understood. As C. S. Lewis put it, "Men became scientific because they expected law in nature and they expected law in nature because they believed in a lawgiver."[9] Albert Einstein would concur, "The most incomprehensible thing about the universe is that it is comprehensible."[10] They believed the universe was crafted by a purposeful God who created humanity in His image, creatures who could (to borrow Johannes Kepler's famous phrase) "think God's thoughts after Him." To Kepler, "The chief aim of all investigations of the external world should be to discover the rational order which has been imposed on it by God, and which he revealed to us in the language of mathematics."[11]

When atheists reference the church's brutal treatment of Galileo as a result of his scientific discoveries, they are overstating the real story. It is not typical for faith to so oppose science. First, Galileo, as well as most scientists of that time, were people of faith. Second, he challenged not only the religious views of his day but the scientific and philosophical ones as well. In the end Galileo's observation that the earth was indeed rotating around the sun had no bearing on any tenet of faith but merely on an interpretation of Scripture that would eventually change. Some interpretations of scientific data seemed, at first, to contradict Scripture but later had to be adjusted and ended up confirming Scripture (such as the universe having a beginning), so the door swings both ways.

Insults Aren't Arguments

The tactic of insulting the opposition has never worked in this debate. Ridicule and mockery are, in fact, evidence that there is a reluctance to engage theism on rational and theological grounds. Just a few months before the 2012 Global Atheist Convention in Melbourne was the United States' gathering in Washington, DC. Keynote speaker Richard Dawkins called for this bitter tone and tactic from all present. "Mock them, ridicule them in public, don't fall for the convention that we're far too polite to talk about religion. Religion is not off the table. Religion is not off limits."[12]

He isn't alone in his emotional grandstanding. The legions of the unbelieving have learned to cry "reason" while they consistently hit below the belt with one emotional appeal after another. Any mistake made by someone with religious faith is gathered and collected as evidence that because of the mistakes of those who are believers, God isn't there. It's a little like saying that because my children make mistakes, I don't exist.

Peter Hitchens, the brother of Christopher Hitchens, one of the most outspoken atheists of our times, witnessed this firsthand and wrote about this tendency is his book *The Rage Against God*:

> The difficulties of the anti-theists begin when they try to engage with anyone who does not agree with them, when their reaction is often a frustrated rage that the rest of us are so stupid. But what if that is not the problem? Their refusal to accept that others might be as intelligent as they, yet disagree, leads them into many snares.
>
> I tend to sympathize with them. I too have been angry with opponents who required me to re-examine opinions I had embraced more through passion than through reason.[13]

In a *New York Times* review of atheist Lawrence Krauss's book *A Universe from Nothing*, David Albert identified the unreasonable anger that is exhibited against religion.

> . . . it seems like a pity, and more than a pity, and worse than a pity, with all that in the back of one's head, to think that all that gets offered to us now, by guys like [Krauss], in books like this, is the pale, small, silly, nerdy accusation that religion is, I don't know, *dumb*.[14]

Faith and Reason Aren't Enemies

Somehow the perception is that believers are afraid to deal with the hard questions that faith can give rise to. The picture is painted that believers must be sheltered from any opposing view and just "quit asking questions."

Joe Marlin, an MD and PhD student at NYU as well as an atheist, had read *The God Delusion* by Dawkins and many other works that attempted to dispel faith in God. He told me in an interview that at times he was "militant" in his atheism. "Especially when someone would 'thank God' for something. I felt they were giving God the credit for something a person had actually done." He described the process of beginning to doubt his doubts about his atheism and meeting consistently with a person of faith and openly, objectively dealing with his questions. He said, "Reason actually led me to God not away from Him."[15]

When something happens that we don't understand, suggesting the occurrence is simply "God's mysterious ways" is not abandoning reason and blindly accepting everything in the name of faith. If a drunk driver kills an innocent family, we ask, why did this happen? The reasonable answer is that it happened because someone was careless and illegally drove a car while impaired, and the death of an innocent family was the result. But the real question is, why did God let that happen? Couldn't He have stopped it? We hear of stories of divine intervention, so why didn't it happen in this case? When we appeal to mystery, we are simply acknowledging that there are many things we don't know. That certainly doesn't mean we live our lives with a fatalistic resignation. We should continue to seek for answers to these great questions. Many times the real mystery is in grasping the motivations of people who do the things they do.

In the next chapter, we will talk in more detail about evil and suffering and attempt to address the perplexing question of why bad things happen in our world.

Faith Is the Product of Thinking

Faith involves reasoning, remembering, and researching or study. Faith is hard work. We have to do our part to understand what God is promising, grasp the conditions of those promises, review the evidence of His faithfulness in the past, and hold on to our convictions about this regardless of our mercurial feelings, as C. S. Lewis suggestsed:

> When I was an atheist I had moods in which Christianity looked terribly probable. This rebellion of your moods against your real self is going to come anyway. That is why Faith is such a necessary virtue: unless you teach your moods "where they get off", you can never be either a sound Christian or even a sound atheist, but just a creature dithering to and fro, with its beliefs really dependent on the weather and the state of its digestion.[16]

Lewis was saying that faith is actually holding on to what your reason has led you to conclude despite your changing moods. This is almost completely opposite of how it is represented by skeptics. We are called to love God with all our hearts and minds. It is when we apply ourselves to understand, seek wisdom, examine everything, and hold fast to what is true that we discern the right path and make the wise decisions about our lives and our world.

Faith Involves Three Key Ingredients

Faith is the basis of all our relationships with one another and with God. In a marriage, we pledge faithfulness—our fidelity—to one person. Committing adultery is therefore called *infidelity*. Business is based on trust. Two parties make an agreement and pledge through a contract to each meet various obligations. In cases of both marriage and business, there are three key ingredients to faith:

1. *Knowledge:* the specific details of the agreement
   God chose to communicate with us through words. "In the beginning was the Word," begins the gospel of John. The knowledge of the Lord is the information He allowed to come into the earth. That knowledge is the bedrock of our faith. When my father told me he had purchased me a car after I graduated from university, I believed him without seeing the car. The basis of my faith was his promise. This knowledge is found not only in the Scriptures (see chapter 8) but also throughout nature:

   The heavens declare the glory of God;
      the skies proclaim the work of his hands.
   Day after day they pour forth speech;
      night after night they display knowledge.
   There is no speech or language
      where their voice is not heard.
   Their voice goes out into all the earth,
      their words to the ends of the world. (Psalm 19:1–4 NIV)

   God wants you to have knowledge of Him. This knowledge comes not only through Scripture but also through the evidence exhibited in the world He created. That which is known about God is evident through that which has been made (Romans 1:20).

2. *Assent*: willingness to enter into a contract

This assent is the product of reason. Having considered the promises and weighed the reality of the evidence to substantiate the specific claim, then we are to agree as a result of thinking and considering a matter. The aspect of assent is critical in that God has given man the right to choose freely, therefore this choice must be sincere and uncoerced. God doesn't want you to do something against your will. You, therefore, must desire to know Him and have a relationship with Him. "This day I call heaven and earth as witnesses against you that I have set before you life and death, blessings and curses. Now choose life, so that you and your children may live" (Deuteronomy 30:19 NIV).

3. *Trust*: belief that both parties will do what they say they'll do

This trust is not blind. It is based on knowledge and evidence that demonstrate the person making the promise is trustworthy.

How important is this to God? It is the ultimate sign of real faith in Him. Jesus said, "Do not let your hearts be troubled. Trust in God; trust also in me" (John 14:1 NIV). The Scripture is filled with praises to God for His faithfulness and trustworthiness. "Those who know your name will trust in you, / for you, LORD, have never forsaken those who seek you" (Psalm 9:10). Trust is possibly the most important ingredient in building a relationship. This is true not only between people but in a relationship with God as well.

Unbelief Is the Product of Not Thinking

The Scripture explains the tendency of the human heart to gravitate toward unbelief by suppressing the evidence for God. Like a lawyer who doesn't want certain incriminating evidence to come forth in a trial that could discredit his client, the skeptic is threatened by the believer who makes a case for God based on reason. Paul wrote, "The wrath of God is revealed from heaven against all ungodliness and unrighteousness of men, who suppress the truth in unrighteousness, because what may be known of God is manifest in them, for God has shown it to them" (Romans 1:18–19).

This is why there is such frustration and anger on the part of atheists when God is mentioned. All their hard work of suppressing the truth gets sabotaged. The tendency of the human mind is to suppress or ignore intentionally something it doesn't want to hear. Fear operates in a similar way. It is when we stop thinking and reasoning soundly that fear comes barging into our lives. For instance, I know that flying is much safer than driving and have flown several million miles in my travels over the last thirty years of ministry. Even though I know flying is safe, there are times when turbulence can cause me to needlessly worry about crashing. By using reason, I can calm my fears and restore my confidence that the turbulence isn't going to cause the plane to crash any more than a bumpy dirt road would cause my car to crash. Sound reasoning can restore my faith in flying.

Unbelief can result from failing to remember. Jesus performed many miracles, such as feeding thousands of people from a handful of bread loaves and a few fish. Time and time again, although His disciples had experienced miracle after miracle, they would forget Jesus' power as soon as they faced another challenge. The unbelief of the disciples was the result of not thinking clearly and not remembering. Sound reasoning can restore your faith in God.

IS SCIENCE THE ANSWER TO EVERYTHING?

While reason is obviously vital for our existence, it must not be applied in an unreasonable fashion. This tendency is seen when reason is used in a reductionist fashion and attempts to limit truth to only that which is scientifically and empirically verifiable, even eliminating logical and philosophical means of attaining knowledge. Atheists tend to do this when they portray science as the savior of humanity. This philosophy is called *scientism* and is the belief that science is the only source of knowledge; not even philosophy or theology may weigh in on the ultimate questions that face our world. "Indeed, it is the ideology of a great part of the scientific world. Its adherents see science as having a mission that goes beyond the mere investigation of nature or the discovery of physical laws. That mission is to free mankind from superstition in all its forms, and especially in the form of religious belief."[17]

Scientism is a philosophical position that all of life's challenges and riddles can and should be handled scientifically. Science is certainly important, but it is not able to answer the ultimate questions. In a review of Daniel Dennett's book *Breaking the Spell* in the *New York Times*, literary critic Leon Wieseltier wrote, "Scientism, the view that science can explain all human conditions and expressions, mental as well as physical, is a superstition, one of the dominant superstitions of our day; and it is not an insult to science to say so."[18] Linguist Noam Chomsky, by no means an advocate for religion, nonetheless pointed out the limits of science:

> Science talks about very simple things, and asks hard questions about them. As soon as things become too complex, science can't deal with them. . . . But it's a complicated matter: Science studies what's at the edge of understanding, and what's at the edge of understanding is usually fairly simple. And it rarely reaches human affairs. Human affairs are way too complicated.[19]

Therefore, we must look for something beyond science to guide us through this complexity with justice, fairness, and mercy. Yet finding such a source of ethics that originates in humanity is not easy.

LIMITS OF SCIENCE

Science is certainly important. It explains how the physical world works. It is the process that is used to investigate how to grow crops, cure disease, and develop inventions that make our world safer and more interconnected through technology. But science cannot explain some of the most important elements of human existence. Christian philosopher William Lane Craig, in a debate with atheist Peter Atkins, pointed out these things that demonstrate the limits of science. In a rather humorous exchange, Atkins shockingly asserted that "science is omnipotent,"[20] to which Craig retorted quickly that there were several things not provable by the scientific method. These include the following.

ETHICS AND MORALITY

Science can't tell us how we should live our lives—what is right and wrong, good and evil. Scientists can certainly be ethical and moral people, but they didn't derive character from scientific experimentation. In other words, a scientist didn't hold an experiment and conclude scientifically that murder was wrong. Science can't answer the deepest ethical issues of our day. Science doesn't determine ethics; ethics should be a guide to science.

It can explain what happens, but it can never determine how one ought to live. For instance, scientists can study the consequences of certain actions, such as charity or abuse. However, they can never justify why one action is morally superior to another.

MATHEMATICS

The mathematical order in the universe was discovered, not invented. Even more basic than the order are the numbers themselves; they must be accepted as simply true. It's because of this mathematical order that we can explore the world around us with such confidence. Mathematics allows us to send probes into outer space as well as into our own bodies. "The miracle of the appropriateness of the language of mathematics for the formulation of the laws of physics is a wonderful gift which we neither understand nor deserve. We should be grateful for it and hope that it will remain valid in future research."[21]

Mathematics is an abstract creation of rules and relationships by the human mind. Why should it explain so elegantly the mechanics of our universe with relatively few equations? Most significantly, mathematics is the language and foundation of science, so science can never justify its existence. In other words, if math is the basis of science, then science can't be math's source of verification. It would be like a house holding up a foundation rather than a foundation holding up a house. This is a glimpse of how difficult it is to have science be the ultimate judge of whether God exists, since God is the Creator and ground of all being.

REASON

Reason is like the central processing unit in a computer hard drive. When you buy a computer like the one I'm working on, the creator of the computer has placed within it a processor that is able to run the programs and the software that are loaded on the hard drive. Similarly God has created us to be rational creatures. We can think abstractly, learn languages at an amazing speed, and know the difference between right and wrong. In contrast, natural selection would only have developed in us the basic abilities to survive: acquire food, avoid danger, and find a mate. Nature would not have generated the capacity for higher reason. "The notion that the only rational beliefs are those that can be confirmed by scientific observation, experiment and measurement is yet another self-refuting proposition, since it is a statement that itself cannot be confirmed by scientific observation, experiment and measurement."[22]

God must necessarily exist in order for atheists not to believe in Him. There is no other explanation for the capacity to reason (even poorly). Atheism and naturalism can't account for reason. To say that reason came into being for no reason is unreasonable. The logical processes of reason and deduction in the scientific method must be assumed in order for scientific inquiry to take place; therefore, science can't verify itself in the strict sense.

WHY?

The biggest limitation of science is that it can't tell us why we are here. Why was the universe made? Why are we here? Why is there something rather than nothing? Dawkins now bristles at the *why* question and calls it silly, possibly because he knows that science will never really answer it. "'Why?' is a silly . . . 'Why?' is a silly question. 'Why?' is a silly question. You can ask, 'What are the factors that led to something coming into existence?' That's a sensible question. But 'What is the purpose of the universe?' is a silly question. It has no meaning."[23]

Curiously, just a couple of years earlier in a debate with John Lennox in Birmingham, Alabama, Dawkins's opening statement said that his motivation for getting into science was the why question. "My interest in Biology started with the fundamental questions of our existence. Why we are all here."[24] The question of why we're here is far from silly; it is fundamental to our existence, ground zero for our identity as humans, and part of our future.

RELIGION AND SCIENCE ARE ANSWERING DIFFERENT QUESTIONS

The late Stephen Jay Gould of Harvard spoke about faith and science being "non-overlapping magisteria."[25] This means they are two distinct, equally valid spheres of existence. While his work and contributions are celebrated by most skeptics, many skeptics are critical of Gould for not dismissing religion and faith as delusional and for conceding the contributions that people of faith have made to the world. "Science and religion are not mutually exclusive, [John] Polkinghorne argues. In fact, both are necessary to our understanding of the world. 'Science asks how things happen. But there are questions of meaning and value and purpose which science does not address. Religion asks why. And it is my belief that we can and should ask both questions about the same event.'"[26]

Science basically tells us how things work. Religion and faith tell us why things are here and how we should live ethically and morally. Neither of these questions can be answered by science.

> "Science tells us that burning gas heats the water and makes the kettle boil," [Polkinghorne] says. But science doesn't explain the "why" question. "The kettle is boiling because I want to make a cup of tea; would you like some? I don't have to choose between the answers to those questions," declares Polkinghorne. "In fact, in order to understand the mysterious event of the boiling kettle, I need both those kinds of answers to tell me what's going on. So I need the insights of science and the insights of religion if I'm to understand the rich and many-layered world in which we live."[27]

There is no real conflict between science and God, but there is a conflict between naturalism and faith. Naturalism is the belief that all that exists is nature. This excludes by definition anything supernatural or beyond nature. In a 1941 lecture called

"Science, Philosophy and Religion: a Symposium," prepared for a conference at the Jewish Theological Institute in New York, Albert Einstein gave insight into his view that both realms of religion and science are valid:

> Science can only be created by those who are thoroughly imbued with the aspiration towards truth and understanding. This source of feeling, however, springs from the sphere of religion. To this there also belongs the faith in the possibility that the regulations valid for the world of existence are rational, that is, comprehensible to reason. I cannot conceive of a genuine scientist without that profound faith. The situation may be expressed by an image: Science without religion is lame, religion without science is blind.[28]

While Einstein did not believe in a traditional understanding of God, he did express the understanding of many scientists then and today that science is as much dependent on faith as any major religion.

SUMMARY

Real faith is not blind. It is evidence-based and requires all our efforts in pursuit of the truth. God requires that we not bury our heads in the sand but open our eyes to behold the evidence of Him all around us. He calls us to use our reason and intellect (Isaiah 1:18; Matthew 22:37) as we develop a faith that is credible. The challenge for skeptics is to follow the evidence wherever it leads, regardless of preconceived ideas, not closing their eyes to the obvious when it contradicts their worldview. Ironically, it is the nature of skeptics to be unaware that they are blind to the truths evidencing a supernatural Creator. In this case their reasoning can become darkened and unreliable (Romans 1:21).

All faith should contain reason just as reason itself contains faith. I have heard it said that no one has absolute certainty except God and certain madmen. Tragically, when skeptics try to assert the nonexistence of God, they lose touch with reality and sound reason and unwittingly head down the long, dark road to insanity.

3

GOOD AND EVIL ARE
NO ILLUSIONS

I mean, in a way, I feel that one of the reasons for
learning about Darwinian evolution is as an object
lesson in how not to set up our values and social lives.

—RICHARD DAWKINS[1]

There must be an absolute if there are to be *morals,*
and there must be an absolute if there are to be real
values. If there is no absolute beyond man's ideas, then
there is no final appeal to judge between individuals
and groups whose moral judgments conflict.

—FRANCIS A. SCHAEFFER, *HOW
SHOULD WE THEN LIVE?*[2]

IT WAS ONE OF THE MOST ANTICIPATED MOVIE OPENINGS IN
history: *The Dark Knight Rises.* Literally millions of people around
the world counted the days until the premier of Christopher Nolan's
final film in his Batman trilogy. In Colorado, a real dark night was
rising. Bursting into Theater 9 was a twenty-four-year-old man,

dressed as the Joker, the central villain of the second Nolan film. Wearing a gas mask and a bulletproof vest, he began firing a gun randomly into the panicked crowd, killing twelve and wounding fifty-eight. Terrorized children and their parents huddled in horror and prayed to be spared from this madman's attack. I recall a survivor saying in one televised report, "I'll never look at life the same again."

Once evil has touched our lives, we never look at life the same either. These tragedies are like birth pangs that seem to be coming more frequently. The outcry in the aftermath of the tragedy was voiced in questions such as, "How could something like this happen?" and "What is wrong with our world?"

There are real answers to these questions. The short answer? Evil exists. So many used the adjective *surreal* to describe the shooting in Colorado. Why describe it this way? Maybe it's an attempt to say that this happens in movies all the time, but it's not supposed to jump off the screen into the real world. Sadly, these kinds of acts are gradually becoming more common because of the decreasing presence of the knowledge of God in society. This knowledge is an immune system in our souls. The less of that knowledge in people's minds, the more evil rises in any culture. The apostle Paul knew this: "Furthermore, since they did not think it worthwhile to retain the knowledge of God, he gave them over to a depraved mind, to do what ought not to be done. They have become filled with every kind of wickedness, evil, greed and depravity. They are full of envy, murder, strife, deceit and malice" (Romans 1:28–29 NIV). This is an apt description of the daily headlines of depravity, hate, and cruelty carried out by those who have learned to shut down their consciences.

When people dismiss belief in God as illusory, they tend to view the concepts of good and evil as illusory as well. Larry Taunton, a Christian author and debater, recounted a conversation with Richard Dawkins at his home in Oxford, England, and asked him whether humans were intrinsically good or bad. Taunton recounted his response: "Predictably, Dawkins deemed notions of good and evil to be mere artificial human constructs, opting instead to speak of 'genetic predispositions.'"[3]

Most of the world is not so naïve. If nothing else, the record of human history gives testimony to humanity's proclivity toward evil. The real mystery is in understanding what is good. Taunton summed it up: "God also blesses mankind by restraining our evil nature."[4] Although evil exists, there is also a force of good that keeps evil at bay. As astronomer Hugh Ross explained, "Evidently, God designed the laws of physics so that the more depraved people become, the worse consequences they suffer."[5] In the case of the shooting rampage, police arrived and kept the crazed person from destroying everyone present. In reality, the existence of good is actually a bigger question to answer than the problem of evil.

No God—No Evil

Once I sat next to a distinguished gentleman on a flight and struck up a pleasant conversation. He taught philosophy at a major university in England, so I had many questions about his favorite writers, although I was a little nervous about not confusing the philosophers and their philosophies. Finally I asked him if he had any religious faith, to which he replied with a smile, "I'm a militant atheist." I also smiled and shook his hand and thanked him for being so straightforward about it.

My next question was easy: "So why are you a militant atheist?"

He replied, "Two reasons. First, I believe in evolution." We talked about fossils and genetics and Darwin for several minutes, and I even pulled out the motion sickness bag and drew pictures on it to illustrate the geological layers of the earth. It wasn't long until I realized that he wasn't really comfortable with the details of evolution. Just because someone has a PhD doesn't mean he is an expert in every area of life; he may be a microspecialist in only one or two subjects. The reality was, this professor of philosophy had not done his homework on the one thing on which he was basing his entire worldview and belief system. The professor changed his course, announcing that evolution was not his main reason for rejecting God.

I paused for just a moment in anticipation of what his real reason for rejecting God might be. I actually braced myself for some incredible philosophical challenge I had never heard before, as if I were about to take a punch from Mike Tyson himself. When he finally told me his real reason for not believing, I was completely surprised.

"If there is a God," he said, "why is there so much evil in the world?"

I didn't say it, but I sure thought very loudly in my mind, *That's it? Is this the real reason for you being a militant atheist?* I was ready for this one. I turned over the motion sickness bag and wrote the words "No God—No Evil." Borrowing the logic of theologian Cornelius van Til, I explained to him, "If there is no God, there is no such thing as evil."[6] You see, without God evil doesn't really exist. The unbeliever can't describe the world we live in without borrowing the biblical concepts of good and evil.

In the end this thoughtful atheist said I raised an excellent point, a concession that happens rarely from the ranks of the militant atheists.

ALL MORALS ARE NOT CREATED EQUAL

The American Declaration of Independence declares that it is "self-evident, that all men are created equal," yet it is also self-evident that the morals they live by are not equal. To say that everyone's beliefs are equally valid is self-refuting. Not everyone can be right. But without God, the absurd notion that everyone's morals are true becomes a living nightmare. Someone who says it is permissible to hurt children or neglect the disabled and infirmed does not have the same moral status as someone who protects children or the disabled, elderly, and infirmed.

But if there is no God, there couldn't possibly be a transcendent morality that everyone should obey. *Good and evil would simply be illusions*, man-made and arbitrary. Certainly without a transcendent God or source of moral authority, it comes down to whatever are the opinions of the majority. So from where does this universal sense of right and wrong come?

C. S. Lewis said, "My argument against God was that the universe seemed so cruel and unjust. But how had I got this idea of just and unjust? A man does not call a line crooked unless he has some idea of a straight line. What was I comparing this universe with when I called it unjust?"[7] Because there are things that are wrong, regardless of the country or context, there is a real moral law that we did not invent and from which we cannot escape. We no more invented morality than we invented numbers or even reason itself. These are things that are written on our hearts by our Creator.

The problem of evil has plagued the minds of men and women since the beginning of time. Yet God intends for us to understand its source, not just be aware of its existence. The real challenge is this: whether you are a believer or an unbeliever, atheist or theist, evil is not just around us—it is in us. That is why it is safe to say the existence of evil is not evidence of God's absence in the universe but evidence of His absence from our lives. Rejecting God won't necessarily make you some horrible criminal, just like saying you believe in God won't automatically make you a saint. The Bible says, "You believe that there is one God. You do well. Even the demons believe—and tremble!" (James 2:19). Just because you believe the highway patrol exists doesn't necessarily mean you obey the posted speed limit. People who merely believe God exists and don't follow His commands receive the highest condemnation from Jesus Himself. "Why do you call Me 'Lord, Lord,' and do not do the things which I say?" (Luke 6:46).

9/11/2001

If evil has an anniversary, this might be the date. It was on this day that our world changed forever. Lives were lost because of the acts of terror; our vulnerability was exposed. Everyone alive knows those images of planes crashing into the World Trade Center, people fleeing in terror, and New York's Finest searching for survivors. The scenes of hundreds of people holding posters of their missing loved ones and friends are still etched in my mind. Time and time again we all wondered, *How could something like this happen?*

That moment sparked a new mission in my heart, a mission to help the people of New York in the best way I knew how: starting a church in Manhattan that would minister to the city on a daily basis. Week after week we watched people grow stronger in their faith in God and in their battles over fear. That was really the big issue—fear. After all, the goal of terrorists is to inflict terror that lingers beyond their acts of violence.

For atheist writer Sam Harris, 9/11 was the moment that convinced him to launch his own attack—against religion. In his book *The End of Faith*, he calls for the recognition of the evil of religion and the reality that faith is a bad thing, picking up Lennon's theme in "Imagine." Harris wrote, "The men who committed the atrocities of September 11 were certainly not 'cowards,' as they were repeatedly described in the Western media, nor were they lunatics in any ordinary sense. They were men of faith—*perfect* faith, as it turns out—and this, it must finally be acknowledged, is a terrible thing to be."[8]

Harris takes the reader through a discourse on the difference between rational thought and what he calls "blind faith" (as we discussed in chapter 2), gathering the worst aspects of various expressions of faith into one big picture of what he calls "religion." Indeed many cries against religious extremism came after the 9/11 attacks in New York and rightly so. However, people such as Harris and Maher used the events of that tragic day to call for the end of all religion, demonstrating their own form of irrationality and extremism. Somehow these people can't tell the difference between a suicide bomber and a Sunday school teacher.

In Search of a Moral Foundation

Knowing that morality must be grounded in some authority, the skeptics' desperate struggle is to find any alternative other than God. The real issue becomes identifying the basis for morality.

> So if God does not exist, why think that we have any moral obligations to do anything? Who or what imposes these obligations upon us? Where do they come from? It's very hard to see why they would be anything more than a subjective impression ingrained into us by societal and parental conditioning.[9]

While the New Age movement, characterized by a belief in the spiritual world where all beliefs are equal, offers *God without morals*, the new atheists attempt to offer a world with no spiritual dimension and give us *morals without God*. This creates an extreme dilemma. If you try to build a world without God, something else will take His place.

When humans play God they usually act in their own self-interests, not the interests of others. Harris proposes that science be the source and arbiter of ethics. Others in the atheist camp think that science can tell us what is good and evil. Most academics would admit that ethics is in the arena of philosophy, not science. However, when you hold to a worldview that only science can give you truth, you're forced to look to it for all your answers. This again is the philosophy of scientism. As Melanie Phillips said, "Take those scientists who promote not science but scientism—the belief that science can deal with every aspect of existence. The scorn and vituperation they heap upon religious believers is fathomless. And yet their materialism leads them to say things which are just . . . well, nutty."[10]

CAN HUMANITY BE GOOD WITHOUT GOD?

The short answer to this question is yes, but not because humanity doesn't need God to be good. God made us and put the moral law within us. That this moral law points to the existence of God was a central claim in the writings of C. S. Lewis. However, there is also the reality that though people know right and wrong, they many times don't do what they should do. This is true whether they claim to be religious or not. Lewis would make this clear in his classic work *Mere Christianity*.

> These, then, are the two points I wanted to make. First, that human beings, all over the earth, have this curious idea that they ought to behave in a certain way, and cannot really get rid of it. Secondly, that they do not in fact behave in that way. They know the Law of Nature; they break it. These two facts are the foundation of all clear thinking about ourselves and the universe we live in.[11]

The moral law is written on the heart of every person. If there are things that are wrong, regardless of the country, culture, or context they are committed in, then there is an ultimate law and therefore lawgiver. Lewis spoke about the existence of a transcendent moral law that is pressed upon the hearts of every person.

Harris, on the other hand, attempts to establish a "moral landscape" without God: "Science can, in principle, help us understand what we *should* do and *should* want . . . to live the best lives possible."[12] But science has its limits. Even British agnostic David Hume, famous for his writings against belief in miracles, argued that no description of the way the world is scientifically can tell us how we ought to live morally.[13] But Harris attempts the impossible in trying to do just this. He states his own version of a universal moral truth very succinctly: "I am arguing that, in the moral sphere, it is safe to begin with the premise that it is good to avoid behaving in such a way as to produce the worst possible misery for everyone."[14]

So according to Harris, morality comes down to this: judge your actions by whether they hurt everyone. Does this mean that if my actions hurt only a few, I'm okay? That's like someone who committed a murder standing before the judge and saying, "I know I killed that man, but think of all the people in this town that I didn't kill."

THE CATEGORICAL IMPERATIVE

In direct contrast to Harris is Immanuel Kant, an eighteenth-century philosopher who spoke of the evidence of God coming from the "starry sky above me and the moral law within me."[15] In other words, the natural order of the cosmos spoke of the existence of God, and the moral order within us does as well. Kant explained morality in terms of this axiom, possibly giving a hint of the type of language Harris attempts to employ: "Act only according to that maxim whereby you can at the same time will that it should become a universal law."[16] This was what Kant called the *categorical imperative*.[17] In other words, judge the rightness of your actions by asking this question: What if everyone acted this way? This truth is synonymous with what Jesus taught in the golden rule: "Do to others as you would have them do to you" (Luke 6:31 NIV).

It's almost humorous how atheists both affirm this moral law taught by Jesus and simultaneously downplay its importance, referring to it as common sense. That's because they are projecting the cultural backdrop of the twenty-first century on previous generations. Historically the golden rule is a complete reversal of the survival-of-the-fittest mind-set of the past. Can you imagine Alexander the Great or Napoleon agreeing to live by that rule?

Friedrich Nietzsche, who heralded the phrase "God is dead," also asserted that with the death of God came the death of morality. By saying God is dead, he did not mean he believed in a God who existed then literally died. He saw it as the death of the idea of the Christian God. He understood the implications of eliminating this ideal in terms of its impact on morality. "When one gives up the Christian faith, one pulls the right to Christian morality out from under one's feet. This morality is by no means self-evident. . . . By breaking one main concept out of [Christianity], the faith in God, one breaks the whole: nothing necessary remains in one's hands."[18]

When the restraining force of God and His knowledge are removed, evil is free to fully express itself.

DARWINIAN ETHICS?

Let's for a moment look at the primary scientific story of our existence and major alternative to believing in a divine Creator, Darwinian evolution. It claims all of the species that exist today have come through the process of natural selection, or as Herbert Spencer called it, "survival of the fittest."[19] Weaker organisms are eliminated as natural selection picks the stronger genes to pass to the next generation. Elements of this theory are unquestioned and verified from a scientific standpoint, yet the real question remains: Is that the whole story; is there no other law or influence at work in our midst?

Let's return to the question of why humans possess this universal sense of right and wrong. Good and evil exist, and we know it. How could a blind process such as natural selection, which came into existence by chance, produce this universal sense of right and wrong? If life arose spontaneously from random chemical processes, we would have no more moral obligation than a bowl of soup. Amazingly, evolutionists tend to distance themselves from the ethical and philosophical implications of Darwinian evolution. Thomas Huxley, known as "Darwin's bulldog," tried to say that this instinct of survival of the fittest should be resisted. "The ethical progress of society depends, not on imitating the cosmic process, still less in running away from it, but in combating it."[20] Combating it? That would mean denying our evolutionary instincts programmed into our DNA. As Richard Dawkins insisted, "DNA neither cares nor knows. DNA just is. And we dance to its music."[21] If DNA neither knows nor cares, then how do you explain the fact that we can know and care? Why would we care if our genetic wiring were just the opposite?

Why do we know that we should fight these instincts? In a debate with the archbishop of Sydney, Dawkins flatly stated that living by Darwinian ethics wouldn't be pleasant, demonstrating the inconsistency and contradictory nature of those who claim there is no God and we are the product of blind forces:

> I very much hope that we don't revert to the idea of sur-
> vival of the fittest in planning our politics and our values
> and our way of life. I have often said that I am a passionate
> Darwinian when it comes to explaining why we exist. It's
> undoubtedly the reason why we're here and why all living
> things are here. But to live our lives in a Darwinian way, to
> make a society a Darwinian society, that would be a very
> unpleasant sort of society in which to live.[22]

This attitude seems to be in direct contrast to the emphatic statements that our purpose is simply to propagate our DNA, and our DNA doesn't care, and the universe doesn't care.

Why do we still care? Aldous Huxley, grandson of Thomas, would see the evolutionary worldview as liberation from that struggle. Far from an object lesson on how not to live life, Darwinian evolution was freedom to live as one pleases. He said, "For myself, no doubt, as for many of my contemporaries, the philosophy of meaninglessness was essentially liberation from a certain political and economic system and liberation from a certain system of morality. We objected to the morality because it interfered with our sexual freedom."[23]

Without God, All Things Are Permissible

During the nineteenth century, Russia was experiencing the birth pangs of its future upheaval. In the face of a rising tide of atheism and nihilism, Fyodor Dostoevsky's books such as *Crime and Punishment* and *The Brothers Karamazov* spoke to the sluggish conscience of a nation. The warning rang out through his writing: "without God all things are permissible." Jean-Paul Sartre, himself an atheist, connected the absence of God with the absence of real moral foundations.

> Existentialists . . . find it extremely distressing that God no longer exists, for along with his disappearance goes the possibility of finding values in an intelligible heaven. . . . Nowhere is it written that good exists, that we must be honest or must not lie, since we are on a plane shared only by men. Dostoyevsky once wrote: "If God does not exist, everything is permissible."[24]

Dostoyevsky's own suffering led him to a religious awakening that gave him relief for the rampant despair of the age. While in prison he read the New Testament and discovered the difference between a dead religion and a relationship with Christ. "It is the belief that there is nothing finer, profounder, more attractive, more reasonable, more courageous and more perfect than Christ, and not only is there not, but I tell myself with jealous love that there cannot be."[25] The rationale that if you eliminate God, you've taken away the foundation of morality still must be addressed. In an almost blind leap of faith, by denying God, atheists simply assert that they are moral and have a basis for morality without God. The problem is, they never identify it. It's simply asserted and assumed. Dawkins made this assertion in a public debate in Birmingham against John Lennox: "I cannot conceive of a logical path that says because I am an atheist therefore it is rational for me to kill or murder or be cruel."[26] It was precisely this fact of the logical movement of atheism toward violence and cruelty that made the twentieth century the bloodiest in history. The godless regimes of Stalin, Hitler, Mao Zedong, and Pol Pot eclipsed the horrors of previous centuries primarily because the moral restraint was removed when God was eliminated from their thinking. Without God, moral commands are met by the schoolyard cry of, "Says who?" Why should we obey any moral commands if they are simply one group's opinion?

Moral Law Exists to Protect Us

Skeptics claim that if God is a loving Father, then He should be held responsible for not doing something about evil and suffering. Let me offer an analogy from my own life. As a father of five children, I prepare my children to face the challenges of evil in the world. The most important lesson I try to teach them is to first keep evil subdued in their own hearts. They are taught to walk wisely in their relationships with others. They are also taught to care for their physical health and protect themselves from being exposed to harmful influences. I do everything to prepare them to face people who would intentionally hurt them or circumstances that could be dangerous. Using wisdom and common sense, they can avoid an enormous amount of pain, at least the part that is self-inflicted. The other pain that comes from the evil actions of others can be either avoided or understood in a clearer way.

In the same way, God gives us instructions on how to live our lives so as to avoid the maximum amount of pain. His commandments are like signs in the road warning us of coming danger. If these signs are heeded, we have a better chance to experience greater joy and peace in the long run. God is not just a Father. He is the Creator who designed a planet with a multitude of interconnected parts, systems, and processes. Imagine stepping into a complex factory where the activity is necessary for the successful operation of the systems but hazardous to the humans if they come in contact with it without taking the necessary precautions. Understanding your environment would be crucial for your survival. God created a world where humans are exposed to factors that are necessary to their ecosystem and the proper functioning of the planet at large but are also harmful to people if they come in contact with these elements in a wrong way. Science, medicine, and reason are helping us become aware of ways to avoid these things and find cures when we are afflicted. Technology that can help humanity can also be harmful if abused. God gives us wisdom to improve our lives and rid our world of disease, poverty, and abuse. To be angry with God for allowing evil is to be angry with Him for allowing you to be born and live.

He gives us not only understanding to harness the physical world around us and the dangers that are present but also insight into the unseen spiritual world. There are not only evil humans but evil spirits. Far from a premodern view that all disease and mishaps are due to spirits that must be pleased and appeased, there are evil entities that we must be aware of. Jesus dealt first with these evil entities at the beginning of His earthly ministry (Mark 1:21–27). Later Peter would tell the Gentiles, "God anointed Jesus of Nazareth with the Holy Spirit and with power, who went about doing good and healing all who were oppressed by the devil" (Acts 10:38). God's mercy is demonstrated by His becoming a man in Jesus Christ and dealing with our ultimate enemy who lives in the unseen world.

The skeptical mind scoffs loudly at this, but there is evidence of this unseen evil entity that inspires and energizes evil in humans. This evil may be ignored by Western culture and its naturalistic worldview, but evil is understood very well by the non-Western developing world, which constitutes two-thirds of the planet.

THE ORIGINS OF EVIL

So where did evil come from? Did God create it? How could a loving, all-powerful God subject us to this kind of a world? The answer is straightforward: God created beings who had the capacity to fail. Failing meant making the choice *not* to do good. From the beings we call *angels* to the humans made in His image, God's creations have real power to make real choices. If God created us without that right and ability, we wouldn't be having this discussion.

In countries where dictators rule, fundamental freedoms such as freedom of speech and freedom of expression are missing. We live in a world where God allows the atheist, skeptic, and believer to express themselves. Christopher Hitchens used to say that he refused to believe in God as a Supreme ruler because a world ruled by God he envisioned as "a celestial North Korea."[27] The irony is that the world he lived in was made by God and was the furthest thing from the cruel dictatorship he wrongly compared it to. In North Korea Hitchens never would have been able to voice such an opposing view of the leader. He never would have been heard from. In God's world Hitchens had a real choice. God gave us this right to choose, realizing that we would make the wrong choice. This started with angels and spread to men. The fact that God didn't create a species of robots that had to obey Him blindly underscores the awesome privilege and responsibility we have for making choices.

God created a world that runs by laws, and He allows real decisions to be made by men and angels. The ability to make good choices and to perform heroic acts also gives the opportunity to do the opposite, which is evil. God gave us His moral laws to reveal His character and nature, which are pure and spotless. "God is light and in Him is no darkness at all" (1 John 1:5). He also gave us His laws so that we would function properly as people and could minimize the damage to our lives that breaking those laws results in. "In reality, moral rules are directions for running the human machine. Every moral rule is there to prevent a breakdown, or a strain, or a friction, in the running of that machine. That is why these rules at first seem to be constantly interfering with our natural inclinations."[28]

The Best Possible World?

When we see evil and suffering in the world, we are compelled to ask, with mathematician and philosopher Gottfried Leibniz, "Is this the best possible world?" He believed that in light of all the contingent factors, this was the best possible world.[29] This is not to say by any means that it is a perfect world.

Christopher Hitchens would strongly disagree, citing a world with disease and collapsing stars as evidence of poor engineering.[30] He and others feel that the imperfections in the universe point to the absence of an intelligent Designer. However, anything created that is finite is subject to death and deterioration. God did create us as humans with an eternal spiritual dimension. At our core we are spiritual beings who live in physical bodies. Though these bodies decay, the spiritual parts will live forever.

As the apostle Paul said in the first century, "Even though our outward man is perishing, yet the inward man is being renewed day by day" (2 Corinthians 4:16). The short lives we live on this planet don't even register in significance, if this life is all there is. In light of the vast eons of time and the ominous backdrop of eternity, we are less than a drop in a bucket. This existential crisis has gripped people for centuries. There are primarily three worlds God could have created:

1. Control
   God could have created us without the capacity or option to do evil. No choices, just programmed goodness. As I just mentioned, if this were the case, we wouldn't be having this discussion. We as humans would be nothing more than the animatronic characters at Chuck E. Cheese. We tend to demand our freedom and then curse the fact that we have such a thing. Though God is in control of history, He has allowed us real choices that have real consequences.

2. Chaos

   God could have created a world with absolutely no intervention on His part. He creates everything and lets it take
   its own course. An individual can do whatever he or she
   wants without consequence. Without any intervention at
   any time, it is truly the survival of the fittest. I don't think
   anyone really would want to live in a world where there is
   no hope for any help beyond human effort.

3. Cooperation

   God could have created a world in which He gives us real
   choices to make. He works among us and acts according to His purposes and promises. By making a covenant
   with humanity, He enters our lives as we invite Him to
   come in. That's the reason we pray and ask Him for help
   as well as choose to follow His commandments.

Option 3 seems to be the world God has created. There are
real choices with real consequences for our actions. At the same
time, God is able to interact in His creation. He is not just the
playwright who sits and watches, but is an actor in His own story.
As the great writer C. S. Lewis pointed out,

> God created things which had free will. That means crea-
> tures which can go wrong or right. Some people think they
> can imagine a creature which was free but had no possibil-
> ity of going wrong, but I can't. If a thing is free to be good
> it is also free to be bad. And free will is what has made evil
> possible. Why, then, did God give them free will? Because
> free will, though it makes evil possible, is also the only
> thing that makes possible any love or goodness or joy worth

having. A world of automata—of creatures that worked like machines—would hardly be worth creating.[31]

WHY DOESN'T GOD REMOVE EVIL FROM THE WORLD?

There could be no knowledge of what good is without the contrast of evil. How could you know what light is without the existence of darkness? Hot without the existence of cold? God allows us to comprehend reality through His use of contrasts.

By creating beings that were spiritual and not physical and giving them the right to choose as well, God gave the possibility for unseen evil beings to exist. Somehow these beings have the capacity to inflict harm as well as inject disease into the human condition. By allowing free will into the universe, God knew He would give these creatures the option to commit evil, but He prepared us with spiritual weapons, insight, and prayer to combat the evil.

God *defines* evil. He tells us what it is. His commandments aren't burdensome but are there to protect us. Like warning signs on the highway or warning labels on chemicals, God's laws are acts of mercy not anger.

God *denounces* evil. He commands us to avoid and abstain from evil. No one is against evil more than God. His very nature is the opposite of evil. He calls us to turn away from evil, yet He allows us the choice and opportunity to disobey Him.

God *defeats* evil. By His life and death on the cross, Christ came to break evil's power over mankind. At His crucifixion, He absorbed the punishment for our evil and provided forgiveness for it and freedom from it.

God *destroys* evil. Just as evil had a beginning, it will have an end. Hugh Ross explained that God allowed the possibility of evil in space and time so that He could eliminate it for all eternity in a new creation that will replace the universe:

> As an expression of his love for humanity, God created the universe the way he did to protect us from a future touched by evil. He made this cosmos to serve as an arena in which evil and suffering can be rooted out, finally and eternally—while simultaneously maintaining the human capacity to exercise free will and, thus, to experience and express love.[32]

By allowing evil a momentary presence in human existence, He not only defeated it on the cross but also will ultimately remove it forever.[33] Because of this, in eternity, we will be able to exist with our free wills intact without the presence of evil.

A True Picture of Ourselves

People who are delusional think they are something they aren't. The question is, who decides what reality is? When you look in a mirror, you see an image that corresponds to what you know to be true. Seeing yourself as you really are is the beginning of improving your life. On the other hand, ignoring reality leads to futility. As Christian philosopher Ravi Zacharias noted, "That is why atheism is so bankrupt as a view of life, for it miserably fails to deal with the human condition as it really is."[34]

Sitting on an airplane at thirty-five thousand feet is one of the best places to have a discussion about God and spiritual things. Maybe it's the turbulence or just being a little closer to heaven. Regardless, when you are seated next to a stranger for a few hours on a plane, you can speak more honestly than in any other place on earth. I have had some remarkable, unforgettable moments on airplanes when it comes to sharing the gospel. These encounters have ranged from the ridiculous to the sublime.

One of those took place when I was next to a man in seat 14D. As soon as we started talking and he found out I am a minster, he loudly stated that there was no way God could exist because of "all the evil in the world." Whenever this issue is raised, I'm careful not to trivialize evil and suffering because bad things may have happened to the people I'm talking to or to the ones they love. It's important to ask discreetly about the other's pain.

In this case I felt the evil excuse was more of a smokescreen. I told the man in 14D, "God could get rid of all of the evil in the world in a moment. All He would have to do is kill everybody." Think about it. That's exactly what happened in the biblical account of Noah and the flood. God "saw that the wickedness of man was great in the earth, and that every intent of the thoughts of his heart was only evil continually. And the LORD was sorry that He had made man on the earth, and He was grieved in His heart" (Genesis 6:5–6). He eventually destroyed the majority of living things and saved one family of eight. The virus of evil was in them as well, though not fully manifested, and it has grown into the world we have today.

I continued, "God has a plan to get rid of all the evil in the world without having to destroy us." The man was now somewhat stunned that his reason for rejecting God was being critiqued.

"He wants to remove all the evil in your heart without having to destroy us for being a carrier of this virus. God wants to get rid of all the evil in the world, starting with seat 14D." The problem was the passenger wanted to get rid of others' evil, but he wasn't willing to give up his. The truth is, we want God to stop evil consequences but not our own evil actions. We want evil to stop happening to us, but not through us.

While in New Orleans a few years ago, taking my three boys to a basketball game, we passed the table of a palm reader promising to "read your palm and predict your future." Feeling a tug on my heart from the Lord, I asked my friend Troy to wait for a moment with my sons while I talked to this palm reader.

I introduced myself, sat down at his table, identified myself as a minster, and asked if I could ask him some questions. My first one was, "Why did you become a palm reader?"

His answer surprised me. "I was a Christian and spent a lot of time at a revival in Florida searching for the power of God. When I couldn't seem to find it, I started dabbling in the occult and even voodoo. All that scared me, and I decided to study palm reading because it seemed safer."

I continued asking him questions and genuinely listening to his answers. I purposely refrained from challenging him too quickly. After fifteen to twenty minutes, he looked at me and said, "Now tell me, why do you do what you do?"

"I preach the gospel for two primary reasons. First, the gospel is the only thing on this planet that can tell a person what is really wrong with him or her. A few years ago my wife was sick, and we couldn't figure out the source of her pain. While in Israel a sweet little doctor at Hadassah Hospital diagnosed her condition, and that knowledge brought us great hope that she could now be properly treated. You see, the gospel tells us that the source of our pain is our separation from God because of sin. As we have broken God's moral laws, it has resulted in our lives and our souls becoming broken."

John (let's call him) was genuinely listening as I explained the gospel. Like a doctor delivering tough news, I did my best to be kind while honestly telling him his real condition. I didn't soften the message in the name of some twisted version of being loving. I then concluded, "The second reason I preach the gospel is because it is the only thing on this planet that can tell us what to do to heal our condition." I then stated the gospel clearly and offered him God's answer for his life.

He thanked me and allowed me to pray for him. He then said, "I have a mother in Nashville who is praying for me every day. I bet you are sitting here because of her prayers."

SUMMARY

The moral law is written on every human heart. Good and evil are very real and only truly understood in light of the existence of a transcendent authority. This is because there are moral principles that are universally true, regardless of culture or context. The existence of evil is not evidence of God's absence in the universe but evidence of His absence from our lives.

Yes, the world is filled with evil and suffering, but humans are the only creatures to realize this and the only creatures capable of an intrinsically evil or good act. Man is moral, yet atheism cannot really explain why. Naturalism offers no help in answering the question of why evil exists, outside of the belief that man, unlike other animals, simply has this inborn proclivity.

As Dr. William Lane Craig said in his debate with Sam Harris at Notre Dame:

> Thus, Dr. Harris's naturalistic view fails to provide a sound foundation for objective moral values and duties. Hence, if God does not exist, we do not have a sound foundation for objective morality, which is my second contention. In conclusion then, we've seen that if God exists, we have a sound foundation for objective moral values and objective moral duties, but that if God does not exist, then we do not have a sound foundation for objective moral values and duties. Dr. Harris' atheism thus sits very ill with his ethical theory.
>
> What I'm offering Dr. Harris tonight is not a new set of moral values—I think by and large we share the same applied ethics—rather what I'm offering is a sound foundation for the objective moral values and duties that we both hold dear.[35]

This same offer for a solid moral and ethical foundation is available to every person. That is why believing God exists is so vital to *our* existence. As we have looked to the moral law within to see the evidence for this Creator, let's now turn our gaze to the starry skies above as Kant suggested.

4

THERE WAS A BEGINNING

A common sense interpretation of the facts suggests
that a superintellect has monkeyed with physics.

—FRED HOYLE, "THE UNIVERSE: PAST
AND PRESENT REFLECTIONS"[1]

The best data we have [concerning the Big Bang] are exactly
what I would have predicted had I nothing to go on but the
five books of Moses, the Psalms, and the Bible as a whole.

—ARNO PENZIAS, NOBEL LAUREATE IN PHYSICS[2]

IT SOUNDS LIKE A GOOD JOKE:

"What did Moses know about the universe that Einstein
didn't?"

"That it began."

But it's no joke. The opening statement in the Bible, recorded
over thirty-five hundred years ago, makes a scientifically accurate
claim that there was a beginning to everything. Cosmologists
(physicists who study the structure and origins of the universe)
came to agree that there was an initial moment where everything,
including space and time, came into being. As theoretical astro-
physicist Stephen Hawking commented, "Almost everyone now

believes that the universe, and time itself, had a beginning at the Big Bang."[3] The fact that the universe is now believed to have begun is a startling development in cosmology. The accepted view from Aristotle to Einstein was that it had always existed.

Closely related to this view was that nothing exists outside our universe. "The Cosmos is all that is or ever was or ever will be," is the opening declaration of Carl Sagan's best-selling book *Cosmos*.[4] This was turned into a television series as well and gave legitimacy to the notion that the material world is all that has ever existed, or as atheist philosopher Bertrand Russell argued, "the universe is just there, and that's all."[5]

To provide some historical perspective, this view was supported in the nineteenth century by Charles Darwin's release of *On the Origin of Species*, which proposed that all of life arose spontaneously through natural causes. This seemed to confirm the notion that there was no need to look beyond nature itself for the answer to how everything began.

As the twentieth century dawned, there were virtually simultaneous breakthroughs in the fields of physics and astronomy. Einstein gave the world the theory of relativity and started a revolution in the way we understand how the world works. The subatomic world was redefined by quantum mechanics that gave us a counterintuitive view of how particles at the smallest level really operated. But maybe the most earthshaking discovery came through the observations of astronomer Edwin Hubble in 1929. Like Galileo over three hundred years before him, he looked through his telescope and observed something that would change the world: he saw that the light measured from distant stars appeared to be redder as the distance of the stars from the earth increased. Light appears redder when a star is moving away from the earth and bluer when coming toward the earth. This is called the *red-shift effect*, and it demonstrated that all distant galaxies are moving away from Earth at velocities proportional to the distance from Earth. This discovery led to the big bang theory, the idea that if you put the observed expanding universe in reverse, everything would come back to a single starting point (single infinitesimally small volume).

"For this reason most cosmologists think of the initial singularity as the beginning of the universe. On this view the big bang represents the creation event; the creation not only of all the matter and energy in the universe, but also of space time itself."[6] Most significantly, this evidence about the beginning of the universe shows that its Creator must have existed outside of time and space, exactly as implied in Genesis.

The Implications of the Big Bang

Astronomer, agnostic, and former head of the Goddard Institute at NASA, Robert Jastrow, captured the tension of the big bang theory in his book *God and the Astronomers*.

> When a scientist writes about God, his colleagues assume he is either over the hill or going bonkers. In my case it should be understood from the start that I am agnostic in religious matters. . . . However, I am fascinated by the implications in some of the scientific developments of recent years. The essence of these developments is that the Universe had, in some sense, a beginning—that it began at a certain moment in time.[7]

Many in the skeptical community would try to downplay the notion of a definite beginning because of the religious implications. Sir Arthur Stanley Eddington would echo this same reluctance: "Philosophically, the notion of a beginning of the present order of Nature is repugnant to me . . . I should like to find a genuine loophole."[8] The idea of a beginning was uncomfortable for the naturalist who was committed to a worldview that excluded the existence of a supernatural realm. Stephen Hawking noted this discomfort in his bestseller *A Brief History of Time*: "Many people do not like the idea that time has a beginning, probably because it smacks of divine intervention."[9]

Astronomer Fred Hoyle came up with the term *big bang* out of ridicule. The thought of a beginning to him was tantamount to slipping in the concept of a Creator:

> At first sight one might think the strong anticlerical bias of modern science would be totally at odds with western religion. This is far from being so, however. The big bang theory requires a recent origin of the universe that openly invites the concept of creation, which so-called thermodynamic theories of the origin of life in the organic soup of biology are the contemporary equivalent of the voice in the burning bush and the tablets of Moses.[10]

Regardless of the implications, the entire universe along with all matter, energy, space, and time had a beginning. Trying to conceive of what could have existed before the beginning or caused the beginning is mind-bending. However, the logic of connecting the evidence for a beginning of the universe to a Creator is too challenging to ignore.

The Logic of Faith

When someone says, "Belief in God isn't logical," they are simply hurling an insult at people of faith much like candidates from rival political parties try to marginalize their opponents. Maybe a person can't articulate her or his faith logically, but that doesn't mean faith in God itself is illogical or irrational. This is illustrated by one of the oldest arguments for God's existence, known as the *cosmological argument*. William Lane Craig is a noted philosopher and theologian who has become a leading voice in the origins debate. He has written numerous books and published scores of peer-reviewed articles on these related issues. He and coauthor J. P. Moreland are also experts on the cosmological argument, the concept that there was a "first cause" or "uncaused cause" to the universe.

> The cosmological argument is a family of arguments that seek to demonstrate the existence of a Sufficient Reason or First Cause of the existence of the cosmos. The roll of the defenders of this argument reads like a *Who's Who* of western philosophy: Plato, Aristotle, ibn Sina, al-Ghazali, Maimonides, Anselm, Aquinas, Scotus, Descartes, Spinoza, Leibniz and Locke, to name but some.[11]

One form of the cosmological argument is stated in this way:

1. Whatever begins to exist has a cause.
2. The universe began to exist.
3. Therefore, the universe has a cause.[12]

Step one is undoubtedly true. The key phrase is "begins to exist." This obviously would not include a Being with no beginning. *Step two* is as close to a physical fact that there is:

> For not only all matter and energy but also space and time themselves came into being at the initial cosmological singularity. . . . On such a model the universe originates ex nihilo in the sense that it is false that something existed prior to the singularity.[13]

Step three is a cause that must itself be uncaused. The cause of the universe must exist outside of space and time, since space and time came into existence in this beginning. It must be therefore eternal, nonmaterial, and ultimately personal since the universe appears to have the purposeful intent of supporting human life.

> The uncaused First Cause must transcend both time and space and be the cause of their origination. Such a being must be, moreover, enormously powerful, since it brought the entirety of physical reality, including all matter and energy and space-time itself, into being without any material cause.
>
> Finally, and most remarkably, such a transcendent cause is plausibly taken to be personal.[14]

Some are content to give token assent to the fact that a divine force is behind the universe. The sheer magnitude of evidence for this so-called uncaused cause calls for consideration for the existence of God. Just so long as this entity remains anonymous and impersonal, everything's fine. But a caring, personal God, who answers prayer and judges sin is frightening to the imagination. If the Creator of the eye actually sees or if the Maker of the ear actually hears, then we are responsible and accountable for our words and actions.

WHY IS THERE SOMETHING RATHER THAN NOTHING?

The German mathematician and philosopher Gottfried Leibniz posed the question in the seventeenth century, "Why is there something rather than nothing?"[15] This question seems to capture the essence of the quandary the skeptical position is in. Why are we here? Why is anything here? The responses to this question have ranged from the absurd to the sublime.

Once at the University of New Orleans, I was conducting a meeting for students on campus and made this statement: "Either everything you see around you started itself, or it was started by something besides itself." I thought, *Surely this is just simple logic.*

Surprisingly a student in the back of the class raised his hand and said, "Well, there's a third choice."

"What is it?" I asked.

Trying to sound very philosophical he said, "Maybe we aren't really here at all." So much of contemporary dialogue is riddled with blatant assertions like this. People say anything they want, regardless of the evidence or logic, and expect the idea to be given equal consideration to other, far more reasonable voices.

My only comeback was, "If we aren't really here, then you wouldn't be here, so be quiet."

Though the class laughed, the fact remains: we are here!

The skeptical responses to the question of why we are here are divergent and at times as irrational as the one just described in that classroom. For instance, on the one hand, Dawkins says that the *why* question is silly. Silly? He tries to avoid the topic by pretending it isn't important. This is whistling in the dark at best. He frequently flip-flops like an inexperienced politician who hasn't quite realized that his previous comments have been recorded. In fact, in a debate with John Lennox, he stated that the why question was what lured him into his career in science.[16] It wasn't a silly question when he asked it.

Lawrence Krauss, a physicist from Arizona State, tried to answer the why question in his book *A Universe from Nothing*. As a devout materialist he attempted to give an answer to this question from a purely naturalistic, or at least an impersonal, point of view. Any notion of the impossibility of such an explanation would be disastrous.

His first trick was to redefine the word *nothing*. Nothing isn't really nothing in Krauss's view. "For surely 'nothing' is every bit as physical as 'something,' especially if it is to be defined as the 'absence of something.' It then behooves us to understand precisely the physical nature of both these quantities. And without science, any definition is just words."[17]

Much Ado About Nothing

This kind of science gives legitimacy to as many absurd ideas as skeptics claim religion does. Just think for a moment how much time and effort has to be spent to define *nothing*. The atheists tell a tale worthy of a Shakespearean play, truly *Much Ado About Nothing*. I must digress for a moment and acknowledge how obscure and pedantic this discussion may sound to many. In spite of this, it must be addressed because it is within this obscurity that the proof for God's *non-necessity* or *non-personality* is asserted.

The reality is that what Krauss means by *nothing* isn't really nothing. Throughout *A Universe from Nothing* Krauss continually changes his definition of nothing, and his definitions almost always are not *nothings* but actual *somethings*. Most nothings do not eliminate the need for something beyond the universe that explains how the "lacks" become filled. In a detailed review of Krauss's book, Hugh Ross explained that the nothings Krauss describes can do amazing things that, nonetheless, still require God.[18]

Similarly, atheist Victor Stenger attempts to explain the origin of the universe by simply stating, "Something is more natural than nothing,"[19] and his colleague Michael Shermer stated,

In both the Judeo-Christian tradition . . . and the scientific worldview, time began when the universe came into existence, either through divine creation or the Big Bang. God, therefore, would have to exist outside of space and time, which means that as natural beings delimited by living in a finite universe, we cannot possibly know anything about such a supernatural entity. The theist's answer is an untestable hypothesis.[20]

Ironically, Shermer goes on to propose multiple untestable hypotheses about why there is something rather than nothing. The critical mistake in logic Shermer makes is limiting how we can know something to be true by testing only. There is no way for us to repeat and experimentally test such a one-time event. However, the universe can be observed, its properties ascertained, and its theoretical implications, including the existence of a causal, personal Agent beyond space and time, be put to rigorous scientific testing. Therefore, the theory that provides the best explanation is believed to be true.

Another mistake Shermer makes is to assume that just because we as humans are limited by our finite existence, the Creator is not limited by space and time and can choose to make Himself known to His creation. The way the Creator does this is the subject of the remaining chapters. Allan Sandage, winner of the Crawford Prize in astronomy (equivalent to the Nobel Prize), remarked, "I find it quite improbable that such order came out of chaos. There has to be some organizing principle. God to me is a mystery, but is the explanation for the miracle of existence, why there is something instead of nothing."[21]

COULD THE UNIVERSE *POP* INTO EXISTENCE?

Now we come to a very critical point in deconstructing the skeptics' attempt to eliminate the need for God. If everything that exists came from nothing, then the first trace of anything would have had to appear suddenly. One of the most celebrated scientists of our day who espouses this is Stephen Hawking. Hawking has been an undeniable force in the arena of theoretical physics. However, in his latest work, ironically titled *The Grand Design*, Hawking emphatically stated that the universe could literally pop into existence without God, ultimately as a consequence of the laws of nature. "Because there is a law like gravity, the universe can and will create itself from nothing. . . . Spontaneous creation is the reason there is something rather than nothing, why the universe exists, why we exist. It is not necessary to invoke God to light the blue touch paper and set the universe going."[22] This belief derives from the quantum theory that describes how particles (such as quarks) appear and disappear without apparent cause. This is in contrast to Newton's laws of physics, which assert that objects are set in motion when they are influenced by other objects. The central claim of some in physics is that the quantum theory eliminates the need for a cause. The first episode of the Discovery Channel program *Curiosity* was titled "Did God Create the Universe?" It dramatically illustrated Hawking's assertions about the possibility of spontaneous creation of the universe, without the need for God.

> What could cause the spontaneous appearance of a universe? At first it seems a baffling problem. After all, in our daily lives things don't simply materialize out of the blue. You can't just click your fingers and summon up a cup of coffee when you feel like one, can you? You have to make it out of other stuff, like coffee beans, water, perhaps some milk and sugar. But travel down into this coffee cup, through the milk particles, down to the atomic level, and right down to the subatomic level, and you enter a world where conjuring something out of nothing is possible, at least for a short while. That's because at this scale particles such as protons behave according to the laws of nature we call quantum mechanics. And they really can appear at random, stick around for a while and then vanish again, to reappear somewhere else. Since we know the universe

itself was once very small, smaller than a proton in fact, this means something quite remarkable. It means the universe itself in all of its mind-boggling vastness and complexity could simply have popped into existence without violating the known laws of nature.[23]

To the average observer, it seems as if the discussion is over. If science shows that everything could simply *pop* into existence without apparent cause, then God as a needed First Cause is rendered unnecessary. However, in their rush to eliminate the need for causality, atheist scientists fail to mention that without the laws of nature, nothing would take place at all. This reminds me of the scene in *The Wizard of Oz* where the curtain is pulled back and Dorothy and her three friends behold the Wizard himself. The veil of intended mystery is torn down. The Wizard frantically says, "Pay no attention to that man behind the curtain."[24] In the same way, the atheist wants you to ignore these laws behind the universe and simply accept they are there and quit asking about where they came from.

> The world consists of things, which obey rules. If you keep asking "why" questions about what happens in the universe, you ultimately reach the answer "because of the state of the universe and the laws of nature." . . .
>
> Theologians sometimes invoke "sustaining the world" as a function of God. But we know better; the world doesn't need to be sustained, it can simply be.[25]

So where did the laws of physics come from? They must be assumed in order for particles to pop into existence.

In any case, even in a universe with no miracles, when you are faced with a profoundly simple underlying order, you can draw two different conclusions. One, drawn by Newton himself, and earlier espoused by Galileo and a host of other scientists over the years, was that such order was created by a divine intelligence responsible not only for the universe, but also for our own existence, and that we human beings were created in his image (and apparently other complex and beautiful beings were not!). The other conclusion is that the laws themselves are all that exist. These laws themselves require our universe to come into existence, to develop and evolve, and we are an irrevocable by-product of these laws. The laws may be eternal, or they too may have come into existence, again by some yet unknown but possibly purely physical process.[26]

So there is either an eternal set of laws or an eternal lawgiver. Notice that Krauss is faithful to his dogma of naturalism and asserts that the laws of physics could "possibly" be the result of a "purely physical process." However, the laws themselves point in a different direction.

THE FINE-TUNING OF THE UNIVERSE

One of the most astonishing pieces of evidence for the existence of God is called the *fine-tuning* of the universe. This refers to the incredible calibration of a vast number of variables that had to have precise values to allow for a life-permitting universe such as our own. Only if a Designer had specifically created our universe with the intention of supporting life would we exist. This evidence is so compelling for the presence of an intelligent designer that atheists, such as Dawkins, admit it's a problem. "The physicist's problem is the problem of ultimate origins and ultimate natural laws. The biologist's problem is the problem of complexity."[27]

UNIVERSE STARTER KIT

When I was growing up, there were knobs on radios and TVs that helped you fine-tune the sound and picture. You can imagine the tuning of a piano or an instrument as another example of the necessity to calibrate something to a precise position for it to function properly. Astrophysicists tell us that there were dozens of physical constants (such as gravity) and quantities (such as entropy) that had to be carefully adjusted (fine-tuned) in order for there to have been a life-producing universe.

Imagine you have a universe starter kit, and it comes with dozens of knobs that must be precisely set. Maybe it looks like a sound board at the back of a concert. The ranges for many of these knobs are not between one and one hundred, but between one and one trillion. Each knob must be precisely set, or you don't have a life-permitting universe.

> One reaction to these apparent enormous coincidences is to see them as substantiating the theistic claim that the universe has been created by a personal God and as offering the material for a properly restrained theistic argument—hence the fine-tuning argument. It's as if there are a large number of dials that have to be tuned to within extremely narrow limits for life to be possible in our universe. It is extremely unlikely that this should happen by chance, but

much more likely that this should happen if there is such a person as God.[28]

These values include the strengths of the fundamental forces of gravity, the strong nuclear force (which holds the nucleus together), the weak nuclear force (which governs radiation), and the electromagnetic force (which governs the attraction of opposite charges to one another). Other quantities range from the charge of an electron to the expansion rate of the universe. Some values must be set within modestly tight ranges. For instance, if the neutron mass were 0.1 percent more massive, the universe would not have sufficient heavy elements essential for life, or if it were 0.1 percent less massive, all of the stars would have collapsed into black holes.[29] Likewise, if the strong nuclear force were just 2 percent weaker or 0.3 percent stronger, the universe would lack sufficient quantities of essential elements.[30]

Other values are far more precisely set. Hugh Ross described in *The Creator and the Cosmos* the example of the ratio of the number of electrons to the number of protons in the universe: "Unless the number of electrons is equivalent to the number of protons to an accuracy of one part in 10^{37} or better, electromagnetic forces in the universe would have so overcome gravitational forces that galaxies, stars, and planets never would have formed."[31] In total, Dr. Ross has identified hundreds of details that required fine-tuning in relation to the laws of physics, our galaxy, the sun, the moon, and planet Earth.[32] The point cannot be stressed enough: from the beginning the universe was engineered by a fantastic intellect that is beyond human comparison. And the formation of our world was also shaped by that Designer to meet equally exacting criteria.

Great minds like Sir Isaac Newton understood the mathematical order the universe displayed. However, no mind has conceived the level of precision that existed from the very start. Oxford mathematician John Lennox would say that we are using "realms of precision far beyond anything achievable by instrumentation designed by humans."[33] These facts are often glibly dismissed by naturalists in favor of wild speculation on unproven theories devoid of experimental support. For intelligent people to dismiss such overwhelming odds proves no amount of evidence can overturn their predetermined stance that there is no God.

As a clear example, Victor Stenger wrote in an encyclopedia entry about the anthropic principle, "In short, much of the so-called fine-tuning of the parameters of microphysics is in the eye of the beholder, not always sufficiently versed in physics, who plays with the numbers until they seem to support a prior belief that was based on something other than objective scientific analysis."[34] Regardless of the evidence pointing overwhelmingly to an Intelligence that fine-tuned nature, Stenger's worldview blinds him from seeing that evidence.

Anthropic Principle

The name *anthropic principle* stems from the Greek word for human beings, male or female: *anthropos*. The term was introduced on the five-hundredth anniversary of Copernicus's discovery that the earth was not the center of the solar system but orbited the sun instead. The principle in essence states the universe was designed for conscious life to emerge.

To better understand the implications of the concept, let me use a popular analogy. Imagine you arrive at a hotel room and all your favorite things are there already: your clothes, your favorite foods, pictures of your family. It would be safe to say that someone knew you were coming to that room and prepared it for you. That's what the anthropic principle suggests. The universe was made with humans in mind. "The universe in some sense must have known we were coming."[35] Sir Fred Hoyle noted the amazing unlikely appearance of life in its most basic elements, such as carbon.

> Would you not say to yourself, "Some super-calculating intellect must have designed the properties of the carbon atom, otherwise the chance of my finding such an atom through the blind forces of nature would be utterly minuscule."? Of course you would. . . . A common sense interpretation of the facts suggests that a super-intellect has monkeyed with physics, as well as with chemistry and biology, and that there are no blind forces worth speaking about in nature. The numbers one calculates from the facts seem to me so overwhelming as to put this conclusion almost beyond question.[36]

Paul Davies, a physicist as well as an agnostic, echoed the sentiments of Hoyle:

> Scientists are slowly waking up to an inconvenient truth— the universe looks suspiciously like a fix. The issue concerns the very laws of nature themselves. For 40 years, physicists and cosmologists have been quietly collecting examples of all too convenient "coincidences" and special features in the underlying laws of the universe that seem to be necessary in order for life, and hence conscious beings, to exist.

Change any one of them and the consequences would be lethal. Fred Hoyle, the distinguished cosmologist, once said it was as if "a super-intellect has monkeyed with physics."[37]

Atheists have recognized the clear implications of acknowledging that a universe had a beginning and that it was fine-tuned for life. Therefore, they have attempted to rationalize this dire threat to their worldview by developing various theories, which deny both of these conclusions.

Dawkins also challenged the faith of physicist John Barrow, an Anglican. Like several other speakers, Barrow emphasized how extraordinarily "fine-tuned" the universe is for our existence. Why not just accept that fine-tuning as a fact of nature? Dawkins asked. Why do you want to explain it with God? "For the same reason you don't want to," Barrow responded drily. Everyone laughed except Dawkins, who protested, "That's not an answer!"[38]

ATHEISTS' RESPONSE? THE MULTIVERSE

In order to dismiss the evidence for fine-tuning, a large number of atheists appeal to the concept of a multiverse. The multiverse is the hypothesis that our universe is one of a virtually infinite number of universes. Atheists argue that in such a multiverse it is mathematically possible, by chance alone, that one of the universes would exhibit all the just-right features for life, including humans. This idea shows how desperate many are to embrace any alternative to the overwhelming implications of the fine-tuned universe. The multiverse theory is not testable or observable; it must simply be assumed without any evidence of it.

As an example, Stephen Hawking attempts to ignore the universe's beginning by appealing to the notion of imaginary time. He then appeals to string theory, which supposedly allows for the possibility of an infinite number of universes. Likewise, Krauss asserts that cosmic inflation could generate an infinite progression of universes with different physical properties. However, neither of them has developed a detailed theory that makes testable predictions. As such, their claims reside more in the realm of science fiction, not science. Cosmologist Edward Harrison has made this deduction:

> The fine-tuning of the universe provides prima facie evidence of deistic design. Take your choice: blind chance that requires multitudes of universes or design that requires only one. . . .
>
> Many scientists, when they admit their views, incline toward the teleological or design argument. . . .
>
> Here is the cosmological proof of the existence of God—the design argument of Paley—updated and refurbished.[39]

Even if one granted the fantastic, unprovable hypothesis for the existence of numerous other universes with slightly varying laws, any mechanism that could produce the required universe-generating machine would itself need to be fine-tuned and therefore designed.[40] Therfore, any attempt to create a theory of the universe from nothing inevitably leads to the reality of a universe *from nothing visible* (Hebrews 11:3).

Mind Before Matter

A simple way to think about all of this was presented by the legendary writer and philosopher C. S. Lewis. He would say that the ultimate power behind the universe had to be mind and not matter. How could something like a rock communicate to humans what they ought to do?[41] Lennox told Dawkins at their Oxford discussion that the primary essence of the universe is a mind, not matter. Mind comes first, then matter—not mind emerging from matter.

> Then the fact of the creator, remember the claim I'm making is, is perhaps even bigger than you realize. What I am claiming is this; there are two worldviews. There is your worldview which is as I understand it is an essentially a materialist or naturalist worldview. The universe is self-explanatory in terms of matter and energy and the laws of nature and so on. So that matter energy is essentially primary in the universe. And mind is a development, a development after a long process wherever. Whereas my claim is that it is the exact opposite way round. Mind is primary in the universe. God is the ultimate reality.[42]

As the gospel of John opens, "In the beginning was the Word." The Greek word *logos* is translated here as "word," but logos can also mean "reason" or "logic." Therefore, before matter there was reason, logic, and intelligence. This conclusion is what the scientific evidence suggests. Robert Jastrow, formerly of NASA, was willing to follow the evidence, even if it led to God:

and under circumstances that seem to make it impossible—not just now, but ever—to find out what force or forces brought the world into being at that moment. Was it as the Bible says, "Thou, Lord, in the beginning hast laid the foundations of the earth, and the heavens are the work of thine hands"? No scientist can answer that question.[43]

Lennox would boldly bring this truth into the discussion with Dawkins in their Oxford discussion. After he explained the two options of either matter or mind coming first, he made the logical case that mind must have preceded matter. But he did not stop there; he went on to show that we can know more about that mind.

> Whereas my claim is that it is the exact opposite way round. Mind is primary in the universe. God is the ultimate reality. Everything else, including you and me is derivative, so that means that here's the claim, let me set it out. In the beginning was the Word, the word was with God, the word was God. All things were made by him. So I'm claiming that whatever mechanisms that were used, that we can tease those out scientifically, and so that's the fascination of science.[44]

Ultimately it's the mind of God, the Word of God that is responsible for them.

Summary

The fact that the universe began is a recent realization in the disciplines of astrophysics and cosmology. In one moment, all space and time itself came into being. This notion of a beginning of everything was resisted due to the fact that it pointed people toward a Creator. What's more, the incredible fine-tuning of the fundamental laws of physics is evidence as well of a personal superintellect responsible for a universe that is life-permitting. The naturalist asserts that the universe came into being from nothing, by nothing, for nothing. The theist believes the universe came from nothing, by Someone, for something.

Clearly the naturalistic theories of an infinite number of potential impersonal, mindless universes or an eternal set of equally impersonal, mindless laws of physics are not as reasonable as an eternal, uncreated, personal Creator. Therefore, when someone asks for evidence of the existence of God, you stand on solid ground by referencing the fact that the universe itself demonstrates the reality of our God.

5

LIFE IS NO ACCIDENT

If it could be demonstrated that any complex organ
existed which could not possibly have formed by
numerous, successive, slight modifications, my theory
would absolutely break down.

—CHARLES DARWIN, *ON THE ORIGIN OF SPECIES*[1]

The illusion of design is so successful that to this
day most Americans (including, significantly, many
influential and rich Americans) stubbornly refuse to
believe it *is* an illusion.

—RICHARD DAWKINS, "THE ILLUSION OF DESIGN"[2]

*THERE IS A GOD: HOW THE WORLD'S MOST NOTORIOUS
Atheist Changed His Mind* was the title of a book published in
2004. The writer was Anthony Flew, the most outspoken atheist
of his generation. While at Oxford in the 1940s, he presented a
paper on atheism to the Socratic Club, chaired by C. S. Lewis.
Flew was a prolific writer, publishing over thirty books. His
conversion from atheism to theism at age eighty was a source of
tremendous controversy. Regardless of the debate over the extent
of his "conversion" from atheism, the fact is that he did convert.

In a symposium in New York in May 2004, Flew was asked if his recent work on the origins of life pointed to intelligence behind creation. He declared that it did and retold the story in his book.

> Yes, I now think it does . . . almost entirely because of the DNA investigations. What I think the DNA material has done is that it has shown, by the almost unbelievable complexity of the arrangements which are needed to produce (life), that intelligence must have been involved in getting these extraordinarily diverse elements to work together. . . . It is all a matter of the enormous complexity by which the results were achieved, which looked to me like the work of intelligence.[3]

Flew goes on to reveal that his conversion was a result of the commitment he had made to follow the evidence wherever it leads. "This statement represented a major change of course for me, but it was nevertheless consistent with the principle I have embraced since the beginning of my philosophical life—of following the argument no matter where it leads."[4]

Flew is not alone in recognizing the window into the world of the cell that has given us a glimpse of the fantastic complexity of life. Specifically, the developments over the last forty years in biochemistry and biology have shown us the micro universe of the cell and have led to the logical conclusion that life is no accident.

In the last chapter we looked at the incredible fine-tuning of the universe from the very beginning of creation. The evidence shows that the universe was designed with life in mind. However, the actual emergence of life itself brings into focus equally fascinating fine-tuning evidence that points to the reality that life itself was intentionally engineered. When life walked onto the stage of history, it was no inconsequential event.

DNA: The Language of Life

Let's look at the very thing that changed Flew and is giving the objective mind overwhelming evidence for God . . . DNA.

Discovered in 1953 by James Watson and Francis Crick, deoxyribonucleic acid (DNA) is an instruction manual for operating any living thing. As Bill Gates said, "Human DNA is like a computer program but far, far more advanced than any software ever created."[5] Watson and Crick may have discovered the book of life (DNA), but Francis Collins opened it up and taught us how to read it. Collins is a theist and a Christian, who mapped the human genome. He has been featured in *Time* magazine[6] and is a vital voice for the evidence in the magnificent order and information that makes up this indispensable component of life.

Bacteria have DNA. Yeast have DNA. So do porcupines, peaches, and people. It is the universal language of all things. We are in a truly historic era, when this language from many different species is being revealed for the first time. All of the DNA of an organism is called its *genome*, and the size of the genome is commonly expressed as the number of *base pairs* it contains. Think of the twisted helix of DNA as a ladder. The rungs of the ladder consist of pairs of four chemicals, called bases, abbreviated *A, C, T, G*.[7]

Our human genome stacks up as 3.1 billion rungs of the DNA ladder. Again, the probability it could have happened by chance is staggering. Have you ever received a pocket text? You receive a few letters strung together that make no sense. Such texts usually happen when people randomly touch their keypads without realizing they are hitting the keys. If you received a text that had an understandable message like, "Don't tell anyone, but I won the lottery," the chances the writer could claim the text was typed randomly would be astronomically improbable. Few would disagree with that straightforward conclusion. What if it was an ordered sentence of a billion letters? That amount is comparable to the intelligent information in the human genome, our DNA. Chances of pocket texting that? The most accurate statement about us as humans is, we are "fearfully and wonderfully made" (Psalm 139:14).

CHANCE OR DESIGN

Was life engineered by intelligence, or did it arise spontaneously from random processes? The answer to this question has a bearing on whether you are a theist or an atheist, if you are using logic to determine your beliefs.

For the last two thousand years, scientists and philosophers for the most part have agreed that life was designed. When Charles Darwin published *On the Origin of Species* in 1859, he sparked a revolution in how the scientific community would view life. "Darwinism removed the whole idea of God as the creator from rational discussion."[8] Dawkins explained how this theory caused him to leave the Christian faith and embrace atheism:

"At about fifteen I recognized that there was no good reason to believe in any kind of supernatural Creator. My last vestige of religious faith disappeared when I finally understood the Darwinian explanation for life."[9]

Einstein, on the other hand, who was fully aware of evolutionary theory, said the scientist's "religious feeling takes the form of a rapturous amazement at the harmony of natural law, which reveals an intelligence of such superiority that, compared with it, all the systematic thinking and acting of human beings is an utterly insignificant reflection."[10] Likewise, many other scientists over the past several decades are recognizing to greater degrees how design is revealed throughout science.

BACK IN DARWIN'S DAY

Trying to go back to the nineteenth century and recapture the cultural mind-set that existed when Darwin's work was first published is not difficult. It's safe to say that Darwin threw the proverbial match into the powder keg. His ideas exploded onto the scene with the force of an earthquake and set off a subsequent firestorm much like the wildfires seen in the western part of the United States after a long period of drought.

Darwin's explanation that all things have a natural cause made the belief in a creatively superior mind quite unnecessary. He created a secular world, more so than anyone before him. Certainly many forces were verging in that same direction, but Darwin's work was the crashing arrival of this idea and from that point on, the secular viewpoint of the world became virtually universal.[11]

The scientific community was looking for an explanation for life other than God. Darwin gave them their God substitute: *natural selection.*

Natural selection is the blind process that slowly selects small differences between individuals in species to outsurvive others. Over time the beneficial differences, such as larger size, become more dominant in a population. These small changes are believed to accumulate over time and eventually cause a species to dramatically transform. Natural selection combined with mutations is seen as the explanation for all of the variety of life as well as the emergence of every species. For this to happen, life would have emerged gradually over millions of years. "Life on Earth evolved gradually beginning with one primitive species—perhaps a self-replicating molecule—that lived more than 3.5 billion years ago; it then branched out over time, throwing off many new and diverse species; and the mechanism for most (but not all) of evolutionary change is natural selection."[12]

In Dawkins's work called *The Blind Watchmaker*, he goes into great detail to laud the complexity of living things only to assert that their complexities arise from natural selection rather than as the result of an intelligent Creator.

Natural selection is the blind watchmaker, blind because it does not see ahead, does not plan consequences, has no purpose in view. Yet the living results of natural selection overwhelmingly impress us with the appearance of design as if by a master watchmaker, impress us with the illusion of design and planning.[13]

Evolution is certainly observable within a species or genus. Even a single type of bird, like the finches Darwin observed, have massive amounts of variety, which can allow for such changes as larger size and harder beaks. This type of evolution is called *microevolution*. However, this process can only drive very limited changes. As Hugh Ross has explained,

> This microevolution is not linear as Darwin presumed. It behaves like a sine curve (it oscillates). During the few years Darwin spent on the Galapagos Islands he observed the beaks of some finch species getting wider and others getting longer. However, now that biologists have been observing those finch species for over 150 years they note that the beaks get wider then narrower and longer then shorter in response to varying available food. That is, each beak characteristic is seen to vary about a mean. Rather than microevolution arguing for dramatic changes it appears instead to argue for stasis.[14]

The theory that this process could eventually cause one species to evolve into another significantly different one (like a fish becoming an amphibian) is *macroevolution*. The former has been clearly observed; however, the latter has no experimental or observational support.

Darwin's Vision

Darwin envisioned all of the history of life resembling a giant tree. The base of the tree would represent the first living organisms.

The branches of the tree would represent the growth and development of various species from one kind to another. As life progressed, natural selection would cause viable organisms to survive and ultimately form completely new species. Therefore, all of life was interconnected, every living thing ultimately a product of common descent.

Darwin's ideas about evolution congealed after his three-year voyage on the *Beagle* as a young naturalist in 1834. He eventually arrived in a chain of islands off the coast of South America called the Galapagos Islands, where the bulk of his study focused on the finch species on the island chain. He noticed traits that caused certain finches to thrive in that environment. Once he returned to England, it would be twenty-five years before he would fully develop these observations and publish *On the Origin of Species by Means of Natural Selection, or the Preservation of Favored Races in the Struggle for Life.*

Darwin knew his theory would be controversial. He fully understood the religious implication, that natural selection would eliminate the need for divine guidance in nature. But he also understood that his theory had many unanswered questions. Ultimately he knew that if natural selection couldn't explain the emergence of all of life, it could, in fact, explain nothing beyond trivial changes in species.

Contrary to the current tenets of evolutionary dogma that pervade modern science, no conclusive evidence has been presented that all of life arose from a common ancestor by an unguided natural process.

Yes, there are noteworthy connections between humans and chimpanzees, who share a significant percentage of the same DNA. In addition, human embryos look a lot like other types of embryos in the animal world. But the real issue is how these observations are interpreted. These similarities between species could just as easily result from a common Designer rather than a common ancestor.

Origin of Life

When Darwin wrote *On the Origin of Species*, the title mistakenly implied that the theory of evolution offered evidence of how life arose from natural processes. Nothing could be further from the truth. His theory was the origin of species, not the origin of life. As Darwin wrote, "Science as yet throws no light on the far higher problem of the essence or origin of life."[15]

Think about it. According to Darwin's theory, every living thing from algae in the ocean to elephants in the desert was derived from one single-celled ancestor. Natural selection used the extremely rare occurrence of positive mutations and accumulated those variations to produce all the species of everything that is alive. But where did that original cell come from? How could something this fantastic just happen? Natural selection tells you only what happens after you get life. If there is no life or no cell to begin with, then there is nothing to select. This is exactly what Oxford mathematician John Lennox pointed out to Richard Dawkins in the God Delusion Debate in Birmingham, Alabama, in 2008: "Richard, evolution only tells you what happens once you get life; it can't explain where the mechanism of the replicating mutator came from."[16]

Several Christians in Darwin's time and today feel that the theory of evolution poses no threat to a belief in the existence of God. They simply see evolution as the tool God used to shape life throughout history. Although it is not a position I hold, I can respect their interpretation. However, all thoughtful Christians would agree that a *blind* evolutionary process could not produce the wondrous forms of life we see today, particularly humanity. The idea defies abundant scientific discoveries as well as common sense. Even if the mechanism that accounts for all the changes in life from one species to another were natural selection, it would have taken a supernatural Designer to have constructed such an astounding process. The evidence from the microscope points as clearly to a Creator as does the evidence from the telescope.

MYTH BUSTERS

Skeptics delight in calling all religion a myth and comparing belief in God to belief in the tooth fairy or one of the multitudes of fictitious deities of the ancient world. But which belief is the myth? One of my son's favorite shows is *MythBusters*. Each episode takes on a popular legend or myth and tries to validate it. Things like, is it safer to drive a car with an airbag or without one? Or one of the more controversial topics: Are men better drivers than women? I'm waiting for them to take on the most important myth of all: Could life arise from nonlife?

The rumor that life has been created in a test tube is a myth that was busted years ago. In the 1950s Stanley Miller and Harold Urey attempted to reconstruct the *primordial soup* they postulated would have been the conditions of the early earth where life could have arisen spontaneously from nonlife. Although there is no evidence that these were the initial conditions on earth when life began, their experiment gained attention because it was just that: an experiment. Electricity was sent through a concoction of methane, ammonia, and hydrogen; and the result was very simple nonliving amino acids. However, Dr. Frankenstein was closer to creating life than these men were.

The relevance of this experiment was eventually discredited because the experimental conditions did not match those of the early earth. In more realistic conditions such experiments do not yield significant quantities of the building blocks of life. As Hugh Ross explained,

> Earth never had a prebiotic soup nor any kind of prebiotic mineral substrate. Physicists now know why earth never could have possessed any prebiotics. It is due to the oxygen-ultraviolet paradox. If the environment of earth at the time of life's origin contained any oxygen, that oxygen would immediately and catastrophically shut down prebiotic chemistry. On the other hand, if earth's environment at the time of life's origin contained no oxygen, ultraviolet radiation from the sun would penetrate earth's environment to a sufficient degree as to similarly, immediately, and catastrophically shut down prebiotic chemistry. Either way, earth never could have naturalistically possessed any prebiotics.[17]

LIFE: WHAT ARE THE CHANCES?

The design argument has been one of the great roadblocks to atheistic dogma because any hint of design logically indicates an intelligent mind behind it. This argument leads smart men like Dawkins to say absurd things like, "Biology is the study of complicated things that give the appearance of being designed for a purpose."[18] The presence of design is so overwhelming that biologists decide the design they witness everywhere isn't real. Nobel Laureate Francis Crick, who initially discovered DNA, would say, "Biologists must constantly keep in mind that what they see was not designed, but evolved."[19] However, as more and more is learned about just how complex life really is, these kinds of disclaimers are becoming increasingly difficult to justify intellectually.

Life is beyond amazing. It's way beyond explanation. As biologists understand more and more about the processes of life, they have to make greater and greater intellectual leaps to assume that its origins could ever be explained through any unguided natural process. The stunning miracle of how reproductive life emerged—male and female—is so impossible to imagine that it sounds like a fairy tale. And how could a genetic code or all the essential parts of the eye appear at once?

As mentioned, even if the earth were filled with all of the building blocks of life, those pieces would never have assembled into a cell. In their book *Evolution from Space*, Fred Hoyle and Chandra Wickramasinghe argue that the probability of life arising on earth on its own is on the order of one chance in 10^{40000}.[20] (I hear Jim Carrey's voice right now from *Dumb and Dumber*: "So you're saying there's a chance.") They said it was the same probability that a tornado could blow through a scrapyard and piece together a Boeing 747 airplane, full of gas, ready to fly.[21] (Their point was that since life couldn't have arisen on its own, it must have come from outer space.[22])

Their conclusions point to the fact that naturalists are willing to postulate anything imaginable to account for the evidence for design in life. We have already discussed the great lengths naturalists will go to in order to avoid the possibility of an intelligent Creator, such as arguing for an eternal universe or an infinite number of universes called the multiverse. In order to account for the complexity of life and the impossibility of life starting itself, one of the most unusual explanations of all is the conjecture that life on earth is simply an alien experiment, or we were somehow planted here by extraterrestrials. So is this science or science fiction?

WHO DESIGNED THE DESIGNER?

The evidence for design is so overwhelming that skeptics such as Dawkins have to try and dismiss or deflect this in order to avoid the obvious implications. In fact, the central claim in his international bestseller *The God Delusion* is that though the universe "appears to be designed," we must reject this conclusion because we can't answer the question "Who designed the Designer?"[23]

Dr. Daniel Came of Oxford, who is an atheist as well, responded sharply to Dawkins on this central tenet of his book:

> Dawkins maintains that we're not justified in inferring a
> designer as the best explanation of the appearance of design
> in the universe because then a new problem surfaces: who
> designed the designer? This argument is as old as the hills
> and as any reasonably competent first-year undergraduate
> could point out is patently invalid. For an explanation to be
> successful we do not need an explanation of the explanation.
> One might as well say that evolution by natural selection
> explains nothing because it does nothing to explain why

there were living organisms on earth in the first place; or that the big bang fails to explain the cosmic background radiation because the big bang is itself inexplicable.[24]

As Dr. Came pointed out, it is a logical fallacy to say you have to have an explanation for an explanation because it sets up an infinite regress. Philosophers such as Alvin Plantinga have dealt brilliantly with the utter nonsense of this claim.

Suppose we land on an alien planet orbiting a distant star and discover some machine-like objects that look and work just like a 1941 Allis Chalmers tractor; our leader says "there must be intelligent beings on this planet—look at those tractors." A sophomore philosophy student on the expedition objects: "Hey, hold on a minute! You have explained nothing at all! Any intelligent life that designed those tractors would have to be at least as complex as they are!" No doubt we'd tell him a little learning is a dangerous thing and advise him to take the next rocket ship home and enroll in another philosophy course or two.[25]

The rebuttals given for the argument for complexity are almost humorous in their absurdity. Dawkins spelled out one such argument at a TED.com talk:

The standard creationist argument is . . . living creatures are too complex to have come about by chance. Therefore, they must have had a designer. This argument of course shoots itself in the foot. Any designer capable of designing anything, something really complex has to be even more complex himself. Complexity is a problem that any theory of biology has to solve. And you cannot solve it by postulating an agent even more complex. Thereby simply compounding the problem.[26]

This is a rather astonishing attempt at using a logical device called Occam's razor. It is a principle attributed to the fourteenth-century Franciscan friar William of Occam in England. "The most useful statement of the principle for scientists is, when you have two competing theories that make exactly the same predictions, the one that is simpler is better."[27] So atheists seize on this concept of simplicity (forgetting it was proposed by a theist) and rule out God as a possible explanation because the idea of God would be too complex to be the answer to why things appear designed. That's like saying that a painting couldn't be produced by an artist because an intelligent human with a complex brain being the artist would be more complex than the painting. These kinds of arguments are more like word games that serve as a red herring to divert the dialogue away from a truly simple conclusion: design points to a designer.

CAN EVOLUTION EXPLAIN EVERYTHING?

As was mentioned, the probability for a cell, an organ, or any of the millions of complex species coming into existence naturally is so fantastically small that biologists have to give natural selection godlike qualities. They justify their claim by arguing that all changes can be broken down into small steps. That's because the probability is so vanishingly small for random chance to explain the origin of life as well as the fantastic development of millions of complex species. Dawkins tried to explain:

> It is grindingly, creakingly, crashingly obvious that, if Darwinism were really a theory of chance, it couldn't work. You don't need to be a mathematician or physicist to calculate that an eye or a haemoglobin molecule would take from here to infinity to self-assemble by sheer higgledy-piggledy luck. Far from being a difficulty peculiar to Darwinism, the astronomic improbability of eyes and knees, enzymes and elbow joints and all the other living wonders is precisely the problem that *any* theory of life must solve, and that Darwinism uniquely *does* solve. It solves it by breaking the improbability up into small, manageable parts, smearing out the luck needed, going round the back of Mount Improbable and crawling up the gentle slopes, inch by million-year inch. Only God would essay the mad task of leaping up the precipice in a single bound.[28]

But without an intelligence behind the universe, could chance alone so easily find the step-by-step paths envisioned by Darwin? Such a claim is based almost exclusively on a massive leap of faith. Even more problematic, evidence from molecular biology over the past several years has all but disproven in many cases the possibility of such scenarios.

IRREDUCIBLE COMPLEXITY

I opened this chapter with a quote from Darwin: "Is there any complex organ or aspect of life for that matter that couldn't have evolved or been produced by natural selection?" Here's a term that the naturalists love to hate: *irreducible complexity*. This concept refers to the observation that most organs, biological processes, and cellular machines contain multiple parts that are all needed simultaneously, or they do not function.

Therefore, they cannot develop through a step-by-step process of adding or modifying one piece at a time. As such, Dawkins's scenario of life climbing Mount Improbable completely breaks down when applied to real living systems.

BACTERIAL FLAGELLUM

The most common example is the bacterial flagellum, a molecular machine in bacteria, which acts like an outboard motor. It includes dozens of essential pieces, such as the filament (propeller), bearings, drive shaft, hook, and motor. If even one of numerous essential pieces is missing, the flagellum cannot be built. Only an intelligent Designer could arrange so many pieces so precisely for the specific purpose of locomotion.[29]

In response, biologists again deny the obvious by appealing to several implausible scenarios. They typically claim that irreducibly complex machines could have come about through a process called co-option. Namely, similar pieces from other parts of the cell could have been borrowed and then brought together to form a new structure. As an analogy, one could imagine constructing a mousetrap by borrowing wood from a doorstop, a spring from a clock, and a piece of wire from a clothes hanger. Such claims are understandable from biologists who have no experience in engineering. However, anyone who has been involved in any sort of design process will immediately reject such a claim.

Imagine receiving a self-assembly bookcase. Even if all the

pieces are present, randomly arranging them will not magically cause a functional bookcase to come together. Tools and assembly instructions are needed to put the pieces together in the correct order in the proper manner. Similarly, the construction of the flagellum is directed by an assembly program that builds the pieces in the correct order. In addition, several other molecular machines are required to construct the different pieces and connect them together properly.[30] Therefore, a cell cannot borrow new pieces from someplace else without simultaneously creating the assembly program and finding the needed assembly tools. Such coordinated events are fantastically improbable.

The flagellum is easiest to discuss since its pieces are identifiable, and we are quite familiar with the design of outboard motors. However, the difficulty of the flagellum evolving pales in comparison to the evolution of the eye.

THE EYE

Ming Wang, a world-renowned eye surgeon, received his MD from Harvard and his PhD in laser physics from MIT. He has performed over fifty-five thousand eye surgeries and holds ten patents in this field. He came to America from China and was led to Christ by a professor at Harvard. He flatly stated, "As a medical doctor and a scientist I can firmly attest to the fact that it is impossible for natural selection to explain the amazing intricacies of the eye."[31] The eye contains countless components that focus images, adjust for brightness, and process information to create a picture in the mind. In addition, the visual system is coordinated with locomotion and balance. Such a system clearly requires numerous parts to function together properly to be of any use.

Darwinists have responded to this challenge by presenting a vague story of how the eye could have developed through a series of stages. However, their description resembles the description of Calvin from the *Calvin and Hobbes* comic strip imagining a box turning into an airplane.[32] Calvin could imagine such a scenario, since a six-year-old boy has no knowledge of engineering or aerodynamics. Similarly, evolutionists can present such stories only by ignoring virtually all relevant details.

GOD OF THE GAPS

Such fantastic theories are justified by the claim that any theory is better than looking to God as an explanation. The skeptics claim that such an appeal is giving up on science and appealing to a "God of the Gaps" in areas where we may be ignorant of certain details, which could be explained at a future date. Using such language is a part of the diversionary tactics of people who are desperate to find any possible alternative to God. The argument goes as follows: "Yes, there are many things we don't know as scientists, but it is lazy and cowardly to simply attribute something that we don't understand to the 'work of God.'" Hugh Ross explained it this way:

> Typically, whenever Christians present this degree of scientific evidence for God and the Bible, non-theists will attempt to dismiss the evidence by claiming that such Christians are committing the God-of-the-gaps fallacy. Gaps in our understanding of the record of nature, these

non-theists will point out, are continually being filled in by advancing discoveries in science. The filling in of such gaps, they assert, establish that God is not necessary to explain the record of nature.

From a Christian perspective the record of nature bears testimony of both natural processes and the miraculous handiwork of God. Our understanding of both should increase as we learn more about the record of nature. The real difference between non-theists and Christian theists is that non-theists predict that *all* phenomena manifested in nature's record can be attributed to strictly natural causes whereas Christian theists hold that there will be *some* phenomena that only can be attributed to divine intervention.[33]

First, what is overlooked by the naturalists are the enormous and ever-increasing gaps in the naturalistic worldview. For instance, as science advances cosmologists have increasingly difficult times explaining why so many features of nature were designed with us in mind. In addition, as the intricacies of the cell are better understood, a naturalistic origin seems increasingly implausible.

Even more important, the identification of design is based not on what we do not know about science but on what we do know about signs of intelligence. Mathematician Bill Dembski has developed a system for detecting design, which has proven reliable in diverse fields such as forensics and the search for extraterrestrial life.[34] The detection process involves identifying patterns that meet three criteria:

1. They could not have been produced by natural causes (such as ice crystals).
2. They are highly improbable.
3. They contain specified complexity.

When these criteria are applied to the cell, particularly the information contained in DNA, the conclusion of design becomes apparent. The term *specified complexity* simply refers to patterns that demonstrate purpose, intentionality, or meaning, such as the faces on Mount Rushmore. Applying these criteria to life, such as the information in the cell, clearly shows that life must be the product of intelligence. This evidence has been described in detail in Stephen Meyer's book *Signature in the Cell*.[35]

Moreover, it's not lazy to attribute a work of art to a painter we've never met or the ingenuity in some technological gadget we have purchased to the work of an inventor. In addition, just because we see the marks of design in something doesn't mean we cease to attempt to understand how it works. A very simple example is that every device in our home was designed by someone we never met. When we purchased these items and brought them home, it was our passion to read and understand how they worked. To this day we strive to grasp all the potential the designer or inventor put in them.

Believing God designed life causes us to seek to understand how He did it, not lazily turn off our minds. Likewise, recognizing a Creator behind our universe does not prevent us from understanding how the creation unfolded. When the evidence for an intelligent Creator is overwhelming, we should listen to the advice of everyone from Plato to Lawrence Krauss and follow the evidence wherever it leads. Acknowledging our Creator would not hamper science but free it from the shackles of naturalistic dogma. Scientists could then ask new questions and design new studies that would only enrich our understanding of nature.

Argument from Imperfection

A last assault on design is the argument from imperfection. Skeptics often point to apparent examples of poor design in nature. A classic example is "junk DNA," which are regions of DNA without any seeming purpose. However, the argument from imperfection has grown increasingly weak over time. As science advances, most examples of what originally appeared to be poor design or even useless remnants from some ancestor (e.g. appendix) were later shown to be very well crafted and to have clear purposes. For instance, increasing numbers of examples of junk DNA have been shown to likely perform useful functions. When skeptics appeal to imperfection, they are making an "imperfection of the gaps" argument based on ignorance, not evidence.

The great irony is that natural selection is given all the credit for producing the amazing structures of life with all its varieties, but any breakdown or misfiring of a system is seen as evidence for the absence of a Designer. However, such examples, even if genuine, do not challenge the notion of design any more than rust on a car indicates that the entire car was the product of the blind forces of nature. A car can be designed and built by intelligence, but a multitude of factors can lead to its breakdown or malfunctioning. This breakdown due to human error or environmental impact does not prove it was not a product of intelligence.

Speaking of Gaps: What Do the Fossils Say?

The notion that fossils record the history of evolutionary development is grossly overstated. The lack of transitional forms, that is, one species changing into another, is so glaring that it prompted Stephen Jay Gould, a Harvard paleontologist, to propose the theory of *punctuated equilibrium*. This theory states that a species remains basically the same throughout time and then transforms so quickly that no evidence is left in the fossil record. However, this pattern in the fossils of no change and then sudden appearance of new, radically different creatures is exactly what one would expect from a design standpoint.

For instance, one of the oldest types of rocks is from the Cambrian era. According to evolutionary theory, the oldest rocks should contain simple organisms. Then as life develops, the younger rocks should record life branching out and becoming more complex. In stark contrast to this pattern is an event called the *Cambrian explosion*, during which complex life appears suddenly without clear ancestors.

Time's cover story heralded, "Evolution's Big Bang: New discoveries show that life as we know it began in an amazing biological frenzy that changed the planet almost overnight." The story that life evolves slowly from simple to complex organisms doesn't seem to be verified by the fossil record. The cover article explained, "In a burst of creativity like nothing before or since, nature appears to have sketched out the blueprints for virtually the whole of the animal kingdom. This explosion of biological diversity is described by scientists as biology's Big Bang."[36] *Time* went on to describe the fact that the development of life does not follow the Darwinian script. The evidence that the Cambrian explosion points to design is described in detail in another book by Stephen Meyer, *Darwin's Doubt*.[37]

> Indeed, while most people cling to the notion that evolution works its magic over millions of years, scientists are realizing that biological change often occurs in sudden fits and starts. . . . All around the world . . . scientists have found the mineralized remains of organisms that represent the emergence of nearly every major branch in the zoological tree.[38]

Darwin himself was stumped by the reality of the Cambrian explosion. He simply assumed the missing transitional forms, or missing links, would be found. "These difficulties and objections may be classed under the following heads: First, why, if species have descended from other species by fine gradations, do we not everywhere see innumerable transitional forms? Why is not all nature in confusion, instead of the species being, as we see them, well defined?"[39]

The Cambrian explosion is not unique. New life forms typically appear suddenly in the fossil record and then don't significantly change. However, the Cambrian period is the most dramatic. What it indicates is that life changed dramatically in a geological instant. This provides additional evidence for God intervening in the development of life throughout earth's history. Recall that Darwin's explanation was that changes happened so gradually that we should see series of fossils that vary only slightly from each other. He thought that there had not been enough digging yet, that more time was needed. After more than 150 years of excavation, transitional links remain elusive, except in the theoretical artists' renditions in biology textbooks. "'What Darwin described in the *Origin of Species*,' observes Queen's University paleontologist G. M. Narbonne, 'was the steady background kind of evolution. But there also seems to be a non-Darwinian kind of evolution that functions over extremely short time periods—and that's where all the action is.'"[40]

When confronted with the implications of such evidence, evolutionists often respond by claiming that some "transitional" species have been identified. However, what they call transitions are not actually species that lie on a direct line of descent between two other identified species. They are simply fossils that share features of two groups, much like a toaster oven shares the features of a toaster and an oven. However, dramatic similarities between unrelated species are extremely common, such as the similarities between the eyes of octopuses and humans. Therefore, simply identifying similarities between fossils does not prove those similarities are the result of common ancestry. In fact, evolutionists typically argue for evolution where the fossil record is most ambiguous. Where it is most complete, the pattern of sudden appearance and then no change is overwhelming.[41]

SUMMARY

The overwhelming evidence for design is seen in the complexity of life at the smallest level. Furthermore, Darwinian evolution fails to account for all of the diversity and complexity of life. Though evolution is observed to drive small changes, it cannot drive the major changes of life. In particular, the fact that certain functions of life are irreducibly complex, meaning that they can't function without all the parts present at once, points to the presence of an intelligent Designer. Moreover, naturalistic models for the origin of life have been shown implausible by the facts that the early earth would likely not have contained life's basic building blocks, and the information in the cell could have come about only through intelligence.

Finally, life appears in the fossil record suddenly (the Cambrian explosion) and then changes only slightly. The evolutionary narrative simply isn't present. These gaps point to the fact that life in its major forms was designed with the genetic capacity to adjust and adapt to a changing environment but has limits as far as its capacity to change to a completely different genus. This leads to the definitive truth that life is no accident. Because life is no accident, human life can have real meaning and purpose.

6

LIFE HAS MEANING
AND PURPOSE

We now know that we are more insignificant than
we ever imagined. If you get rid of everything we see,
the universe is essentially the same. We constitute
a 1 percent bit of pollution in a universe . . . we are
completely irrelevant.

—LAWRENCE KRAUSS[1]

Consequently Atheism turns out to be too simple. If
the whole universe has no meaning, we should never
have found out that it has no meaning.

—C. S. LEWIS, *MERE CHRISTIANITY*[2]

ASTRONOMER CARL SAGAN WAS A PROLIFIC WRITER AND
trustee of the SETI Institute (Search for Extraterrestrial Intelligence) founded in 1984 to scan the universe for any signs of life
beyond earth. Sagan's best-selling work *Cosmos* also became an
award-winning television series explaining the wonders of the

universe and exporting the belief not in an intelligent Creator but in potential intelligent aliens. He believed somehow that by knowing who they are, we would discover who we as humans really are. "The very thought of there being other beings different from all of us can have a very useful cohering role for the human species."[3] Sagan's reasoning? If aliens could have contacted us, knowing how impossible it is for us to reach them, they would be far more advanced than us as a species. Therefore, they would have the answers we seek to our ultimate questions. This thought process shows the desperate need we have as humans for answers to the great questions of our existence. Does life have any ultimate meaning and purpose? Do we as humans have any more value than the other animals? Is there a purpose to the universe, or more specifically, to our individual lives? These are the questions that grip our minds and potentially vex our souls.

The order of creation that we have studied in earlier chapters screams that everything was planned by an intelligent Designer. That's true not just for stars, galaxies, and tiny organisms but for humans especially. Because God exists we can know we were made on purpose for a purpose. However, when that reality is obscured, the consequences are devastating.

William Lane Craig, an American philosopher and theologian who has had a profound impact on millions of people through his vigorous public defense of the Christian faith, has summed up man's condition apart from God: "My claim is that if there is no God then meaning, value, and purpose are ultimately human illusions. They're just in our heads. If atheism is true, then life is really objectively meaningless, valueless, and purposeless, despite our subjective beliefs to the contrary."[4]

Man's Search for Meaning

Viktor Frankl was imprisoned in a Nazi concentration camp during World War II. There he experienced the horrors of the death camps and the accompanying emotional despair of watching friends, family, and completely innocent people executed because of their ethnicity. He witnessed firsthand what happens when a human is stripped of every dignity and freedom and subjected to torment and torture from which there is no foreseeable relief. In the midst of these unspeakable evils, Frankl began to realize man's ultimate need is for meaning in his life. "Terrible as it was, his experience in Auschwitz reinforced what was already one of his key ideas: Life is not primarily a quest for pleasure, as Freud believed, or a quest for power, as Alfred Adler taught, but a quest for meaning. The greatest task for any person is to find meaning in his or her life."[5]

In his book *Man's Search for Meaning*, Frankl described how those in captivity who clung to some sense of meaning in the midst of the madness were able to survive. Those who lost that meaning would inevitably die. He quoted Nietzsche: "He who has a why to live for can bear with almost any how."[6]

The Western world is suffering from the backlash of the meaninglessness of atheism and unbelief. Suicide is increasing. Drug abuse, especially the respectable version of the abuse of prescription drugs, is choking the life out of a generation desperately self-medicating in hopes of not drowning in a sea of emotional pain. This isn't surprising. When you tell people there is no God, that they are just animals that have evolved from lower life forms and are the product of random chance, you offer them little hope for deriving any sort of ultimate meaning out of that philosophy.

The atheist quickly denies that atheism leads to meaninglessness, but it can lead to no other place. Nietzsche would agree: "So to live that life no longer has any meaning: this is now the 'meaning' of life. . . ."[7] This despair gripped the communist world for decades. The attempt to eradicate God from the mind and soul of nations only produced a greater void and a greater hunger for spiritual truth.

In communist China, Western missionaries were expelled in the 1950s, and Chairman Mao replaced the Bible with *The Little Red Book*. Instead of Christianity disappearing as he had intended, it exploded. Millions of people worshiped in secret and spread the Word to others, risking imprisonment and even death. Today, the Chinese church is stronger than ever. Because following Christ is still very challenging in this environment, believers are more resolved to be faithful to the Lord. I have worked in China and have seen the happiness and peace that these believers possess. Think about it: if happiness came from material things, Americans and other Westerners should be the happiest people on earth. Instead, our souls long for something beyond merely material existence. We are desperate for relationships, for significance, and for a real reason to live.

In *The God Test*, a small booklet of questions that serve to promote dialogue between believers and unbelievers, the question is asked of atheists or agnostics, Does life have any ultimate meaning or purpose?[8] The answers to this question are revealing. Average people claiming to be an atheist or agnostic will be quick to say yes. They will cite their concern for education and for human rights as well as the pursuit of knowledge about the world we live in. But such answers are not what ultimate meaning and purpose truly are. They are citing their own subjective pursuits without having justification for those goals having objective, transcendent significance. The ultimate questions are easy to ignore by just staying busy and distracting your mind, but sooner or later they cannot be avoided by a thoughtful person. Is there any ultimate plan or design to the world, or are we simply "lucky mud"? If there is a plan, then where did that purpose come from?

THE DESPAIR OF ATHEISM

As we mentioned in chapter 3, translating Darwinian evolution into a philosophy of life would be dangerous, according to Darwin himself. However, Richard Dawkins is the first to say that we should accept the truth of our situation regardless of how good or bad it is: "Nature is not cruel, only pitilessly indifferent. This is one of the hardest lessons for humans to learn. We cannot admit that things might be neither good nor evil, neither cruel nor kind, but simply callous—indifferent to all suffering, lacking all purpose."[9] Likewise, Bertrand Russell said we have no choice but to build our lives "on the firm foundation of unyielding despair."[10] They believe we are supposed to live in a world of cold, hard facts and ruthless truth, for the universe doesn't care.

Without God ultimate meaning is an illusion. French existentialist Jean-Paul Sartre summed up the philosophical implications of reality without God, saying it is only a "vague dream of the possible . . . bursting like a bubble."[11] He believed that if life has no real meaning then we should face the sheer barrenness of our existence and realize that all this talk of meaning and purpose is absurd. It is the cruelest of cosmic jokes that we should feel compelled to continue this masquerade as if anything we as humans did really mattered.

Man's search for meaning takes a tragic wrong turn without belief in God, leaving man with an existential philosophy of despair. In other words, how could meaningless, random processes produce conscious, rational creatures who are aware of meaning and purpose?

PURPOSE-DRIVEN EXISTENCE

It's no wonder that the best-selling book of our time, next to the Bible, is *The Purpose Driven Life* by Rick Warren. With 60 million sold and counting, it also has been translated into more than 130 languages, which makes it one of the most translated books.[12] Regardless of the culture or nation, humans long for a solid sense of purpose and meaning in their lives. There is something deep in the human psyche, a yearning for significance, a desire to believe that there is more to life than simply physical survival. Yet all that naturalists offer is the bleak news of a pointless universe with no real ultimate purpose. This posture is voiced clearly by Lawrence Krauss: "The universe is the way it is, whether we like it or not. The existence or nonexistence of a creator is independent of our desires. A world without God or purpose may seem harsh or pointless, but that alone doesn't require God to actually exist."[13]

Krauss and his comrades bristle at the notion that atheists do not believe there is such a thing as meaning and purpose. They regale their audiences with the overwhelming passion for the pursuit of knowledge and truth that comes from a life devoted to science, while asserting that they don't need God to believe in purpose or meaning. But honestly, they can only say that natural selection has given us this trait in our genetics to help us survive. So something so wonderful, so indispensable to life, so vital to our mental and emotional health, was only the product of a pointless, meaningless, purposeless past. I doubt any of these guys are asked to give the pregame motivational speech at the Super Bowl or World Cup Final.

But how could those same blind, impersonal forces produce creatures who are deeply curious about the meaning of life? Remember, science itself rose out of the Christian worldview that the world was rationally understandable and could be investigated and understood because God existed.

Remember the fairy tales where the wicked witch would have a boiling pot of some magic brew that could produce any desired effect imaginable? Even people or monsters could come out of that simmering pot. The naturalist believes that given enough time, everything living can come out of a similar boiling pot of chemicals, but it's absurd to think that love, beauty, morality, and meaning could develop in such a way (unless you are Billy Crystal in *The Princess Bride*). But that's exactly what the atheist has to believe. As David Robertson pointed out in his letters to Richard Dawkins about *The God Delusion*:

> First of all its presupposition and assertion/assumption that everything is chemical or the result of chemical reaction is itself an unprovable assertion. Secondly it is not an assertion that fits with the observable facts around us. Indeed it requires a great deal of special pleading before one can honestly come to the position that religion is just a chemical reaction, beauty is just a chemical reaction, evil likewise and

the sense of God also. Furthermore the logical consequences of such a belief are disastrous. We end up with the absurdity of man as God—the most highly evolved chemical reaction.[14]

Is man simply a highly evolved chemical reaction? Are the feelings of love, loyalty, and devotion the same? Atheism reduces all of life down to a natural process.

THE TWO-STORIED HOUSE

But this leaves us in a tragic place as humanity when we desperately try to assert meaning where there isn't any. Francis Schaeffer explained this predicament by describing a two-storied house that modern man lives in. In the downstairs he lives in a world solely driven by human reason and natural forces where no God exists. But he can't live there consistently so he makes a leap of faith into the second story where there is meaning and purpose, but he has no rational basis for this jump. Existentialism, as Schaeffer would say, is like a peg "hung in midair."[15]

This is the crisis that unbelief brings you to. Life is absurd without any meaning, so the atheist simply asserts that it is indeed meaningful. But what is the basis? Greg Graffin of the band Bad Religion articulates this faulty position: "However, people make a big mistake if they conclude from the anarchy of the physical world that life has no meaning. I draw just the opposite conclusion. The purposelessness of the natural world emphasizes the tremendous meaning inherent in the human world."[16] So in the atheistic worldview:

- Life came from no-life.
- Meaning came from non-meaning.

This ultimate leap of faith is a prime example of the Nietzschean *will to power* phenomenon. Nietzsche taught that though life was meaningless, the *superman* simply asserts his own meaning by exerting his own will to push against the darkness of despair. This superman represented the next level of human evolution. Tragically, this is the philosophy of the Nazis who acted out this wrong idea to its fullest extent. Ideas do have consequences.

The critical point here is that humans cannot live without meaning and purpose. Though we may assert that God does not exist, we can't do the same where values, meaning, and purpose are concerned. In essence, God is the foundation, and the meaning, purpose, and values are the building blocks set on that foundation. And no house stands without a foundation.

Because God exists life has meaning and purpose. The logical reasoning would be the following:

1. If God does not exist, life has no ultimate purpose or meaning.
2. Life has ultimate meaning and purpose.
3. Therefore God exists.

Our inherent recognition of the existence of meaning and purpose is one of the many ways to clearly see that God exists. Yet you can know God exists and lose sight of the reality that He has created you for a purpose and end up in despair as well. This is why it's so important to have a relationship with your Creator and not just an acknowledgment that He is real.

This past year I presided over the funeral of a wealthy man who took his own life. His house was one of the most spectacular ones I've ever seen. The man had everything—except peace and real purpose. His family testified to dizzying lives of worldwide tours and experiences that should have brought happiness but didn't. Though he believed in God, he lost sight of the light of His hope, and he panicked in the darkness and took his own life.

When we attach our own meaning and purpose to life, it works until those things we are trusting in and leaning on give way and collapse. The reason that we are to have no other gods before the real God is because anything we lean on other than God will let us down. His desire is for our good, not for destruction. As John Lennox said to Richard Dawkins, "Man-made gods are a delusion."[17]

God made you for a purpose. It is imbedded deep within your genetics as well as in every living molecule. As God told the prophet Jeremiah,

"Before I formed you in the womb I knew you;
Before you were born I sanctified you;
I ordained you a prophet to the nations." (Jeremiah 1:5)

The infinite God who knows the stars by name (Psalm 147:4) knows you and desires a relationship with you. The crushing feeling of insignificance can be lifted as you look to God for the answers to the questions that science can only hint at. When you really believe God exists, your view of yourself should change dramatically. Life has real purpose and meaning—especially yours. Because purpose and meaning are throughout the universe, it is *not* a blind leap of faith to believe you were made for a purpose as well. You could say that both the atheist and the theist are making inductive leaps. However, the evidence is overwhelming that you should take that step toward God instead of toward the darkness of skepticism. We were designed to receive perfect love from our Creator, worship His beauty and wonder, and serve as His agents eternally to steward creation. Only perfect love and an eternal purpose will fill the longings of our hearts.

MAN IS NOT JUST ANOTHER ANIMAL

Beyond the philosophical and ethical implications surrounding the existence of God is the belief on the part of the naturalists that man is simply another animal, merely a product of natural selection. This picture has been marketed and promoted from the halls of the Smithsonian to the textbooks in high schools. This campaign has been so thorough that the belief that man is just a highly evolved primate has become a societal fact. "People today are trying to hang on to the dignity of man, and they do not know how to because they have lost the truth that man is made in the image of God."[18]

But is human macroevolution the truth? If man was not created separately from the animals and is just an evolutionary freak of nature, then how can we consider ourselves special? Would there be any real transcendent meaning to our human condition other than mere biological oddities? "It is because man is made in God's image, as Schaeffer constantly emphasised, that explained his longing for significance, and this is basic to the human condition, including the post-modern condition."[19] This is the center of the debate. Skeptics will concede that believers may have an intellectual argument for the existence of God based on evidence

such as the fine-tuning of the universe or the inexplicable existence of sequenced information in DNA, but this is where they
take their stand: human evolution.

The psalmist asked, "What is man?" (8:4). Is there anything
special about us? Is man just another animal? In the search
for significance we come to the very essence of discovering if
there is a transcendent meaning to our lives. At the urging of
my wife, Jody, I sent off my saliva sample to 23 and Me to have
my DNA analyzed and mapped. The results revealed over eight
hundred others had similar genetic profiles and actually were
distant cousins I never knew I had. More interesting, however,
was a category that showed whether I was descended from
Neanderthal lineage or not. There was a little artistic depiction of
a Neanderthal man (with no clothes on, of course) matching the
images I have seen countless times in biology books and Geico
Insurance commercials. There was a small connection in my
DNA to the Neanderthals. Thinking back over my family tree, I
tried to imagine the relatives whom I might have suspected were
a little odd, but this was no real help. Neanderthals were said
to have become extinct over thirty-five thousand years ago, yet
their DNA still lives in many of us?

We discussed this evidence in the last chapter when pointing
out the miracle of the origin of life as well as the origin of species. As mentioned, the Cambrian explosion refers to the sudden
appearance of complex life in the fossil record, followed after-
ward by minimal change within each species. When presenting
human evolution, however, great effort is made on the part of
the naturalists to connect humans and chimpanzees with a common ancestor through a blind, undirected process that "did not
have us in mind." They will be quick to correct you if you say

that humans descended directly from apes and you fail to mention the hypothesized common ancestor, but the notion of man emerging from lower life forms, yes primates, is still their belief. *Humans did not evolve from lower life forms.* I can't say it any plainer or be any clearer. There are many brilliant people, much smarter than me, who believe God used the grand scheme of Darwinian evolution to produce all of life, including humanity. These people are sincere, and I would not question their faith in God. I do believe, however, the evidence from the fossil record (as well as the other distinctions we have discussed) indicate that humanity was created both male and female, and though humans have developed and adapted, we've always been human. The fossils that are linked to man are conjectured by the naturalist to be our ancestors, not because of direct observable evidence. Any similarity in those fossils or in the genetic codes of chimpanzees and humans can be attributed to a common Designer, not common descent.

I am lingering on this issue because at the heart of Darwinian evolution is the tenet that man is simply another animal, no more intrinsically valuable than any other life form. The only real distinction is our advanced evolutionary place, due merely to the vagaries of natural selection. If there is no God and, therefore, no ultimate plan, then at best we are simply freaks of nature. As legendary Harvard paleontologist Stephen Jay Gould affirmed, "Moreover and more important, the pathways that have led to our evolution are quirky, improbable, unrepeatable and utterly unpredictable. Human evolution is not random, it makes sense and can be explained after the fact. But wind life's tape to the dawn of time and let it play again—and you will never get humans a second time."[20]

Christopher Hitchens addressed his audiences as "my fellow primates."[21] Richard Dawkins claims he is "an African ape"[22] and that we are all African apes as well. If that's what we really are, then we should simply get over it and admit it. Remember, if Darwinian evolution is really the true story of our origins and we were not designed or intended as anything special, then we must also jettison any notion of having any special place in the universe. Our sense of importance or distinction is just an illusion. Furthermore our death is no more tragic than that of any other animal. How arrogant of us to think our fate is any different after death than that of a cow or a pig.

Human Evolution: A Matter of Interpretation

The main reason many believe humans are indistinct from other animals is that the theory of evolution claims we evolved from a common ancestor of modern primates millions of years in the past. This claim has historically been supported by pictures showing several stages of a monkey gradually evolving into a human. However, these pictures are quite misleading. Paleontologists have found various fossils that share different characteristics with humans. But interpretations of these specimens rely more on evolutionists' imaginations than on hard evidence. As biologist Jonathan Wells noted,

> According to paleoanthropologist Misia Landau, theories of human origins "far exceed what can be inferred from the study of fossils alone and in fact place a heavy burden

of interpretation on the fossil record—a burden which is relieved by placing fossils into pre-existing narrative structures." In 1996, American Museum of Natural History Curator Ian Tattersall acknowledged that "in paleoanthropology, the patterns we perceive are as likely to result from our unconscious mindsets as from the evidence itself."[23]

As mentioned in chapter 5, new species typically appear suddenly in the fossil record with massive gaps separating them from their closest theoretical ancestors. The fossils connected with human evolution follow this same pattern. They are either fairly apelike or fairly humanlike, and the transition between the two groups took place suddenly without a clear progression of intermediate forms. "It appears that our own species, in particular, is the product of a remarkable event of quantum [massive changes taking place quickly] speciation."[24] This fact is also stated objectively by Stephen Gould: "Moreover, we still have no firm evidence for any progressive change within the hominid species."[25]

Given the problems with the fossil record, evolutionists often attempt to bolster their case with evidence from DNA. For instance, they often cite the fact that human and chimpanzee DNA share pseudogenes, which are genes with the same genetic errors. Several committed Christians, such as Francis Collins, claim that this evidence seems very compelling, so they have argued that evolution is compatible with Christianity.[26] However, even if God used an evolutionary process in the development of life, that process would still need to have been directed intelligently. For instance, the reprogramming required to create the human brain and the many other distinctly human characteristics would not have been possible in a geologically short time span by any undirected process. Moreover, pseudogenes and similar junk DNA shared by humans and other species have been shown to have actual functions, so common design then provides an equally valid explanation for the similarities.[27] Therefore, the cumulative evidence does not convincingly support the claim that humans gradually evolved from some apelike creature by the blind forces of nature.

THE VIOLENCE IN THE ANIMAL WORLD

The survival-of-the-fittest programming in the animal world is replete with aggression and death. Of all the species that have ever lived, most are now extinct. Just watch any show that highlights the traits of animals in the wild. The predators stalk their prey and attack in order to eat and survive. We watch these shows with fascination, but with no sense of moral outrage, when a lion runs down an antelope and eats it for dinner. We may cringe at the gory sight of a shark eating a tuna, but we don't call 911. A lion shouldn't feel sorry for its animal nature, so should we as humans resist or seek to modify our nature? How could we if we are only animals?

Atheists are committed to the belief that we are simply another form of animal. Our instincts and behaviors should, therefore, be treated as simply programmed and determined by our DNA. It's ironic that there is protest from the ranks of skeptics when the implications of evolution on philosophy and ethics are pointed out. If it's true, then why pretend it's not? If God is dead, then we are simply another species subject to the laws of natural selection. Men like Hitler couldn't be ultimately evil because they were merely acting out their innate evolution-ary instincts. How could you judge anyone harshly for acting on their instincts and impulses when that's just who they are? Skeptics are quick to use adjectives such as *cowardly* when they spot people denying the implications of their own beliefs, yet Dawkins and others fail again and again to own up to their own. As Ravi Zacharias said, "One of the great blind spots of a philosophy that attempts to disavow God is it's unwillingness to look into the fact of the monster it has begotten and own up to being its creator."[28] This philosophy had a monstrous impact on the twentieth century and proved once again that man's problems are solved not by trying to eliminate God but by believing and obeying Him.

SPECIESISM

Humanism was the attempt to make humanity the "measure of all things." In short, we don't need God but could establish truth on the basis of reason alone. This phiosophy has led to extraor-dinary claim that people should avoid *speciesism*, which is the elevation of one species over another: "'Speciesism' is the idea that being human is a good enough reason for human animals to have greater moral rights than non-human animals."[29] This is taking animal rights to a whole new high while bringing humans down to a new low. Shockingly, this kind of logic seems to get a free pass. One of the chief proponents of this is Peter Singer, an avowed atheist. He has certainly made the logical connection that if man is simply another animal, then we shouldn't assume we are better than any other animals. His book *Animal Liberation* is the foundational work of the animal rights movement. "So out of concern for both fish and human beings we should avoid eating fish. Certainly those who continue to eat fish while refusing to eat other animals have taken a major step away from speciesism; but those who eat neither have gone one step further."[30]

Jesus loved the animals He created; but according to this logic, by feeding thousands of people fish, He was a speciesist. Certainly animals should be treated humanely; this is a command of Scripture:

> A righteous man cares for the needs of his animal,
> but the kindest acts of the wicked are cruel.
>
> —PROVERBS 12:10 NIV

This thinking leads to unbelievable comparisons between the slaughterhouses where animals are processed and the gas chambers of Auschwitz, a leap into absurdity. Theoretically we shouldn't feel outrage when humans act like animals or are treated like animals, but we do. Why? Because deep down we know there is a difference. It's the same reason why the accidental death of an animal on a highway isn't treated as a crime scene. In the same way, the breakfast bar at Shoney's isn't treated as a grotesque celebration of the mass murder of swine.

DIFFERENCES BETWEEN HUMANS AND ANIMALS

We are different from other animals, and we know it. The problem is evolution and atheism have no compelling evidence for their explanations for these differences.

1. Thinking About Thinking

Transcendent thought means that we as humans are able to think about thinking. It is called *metacognition*. It was eighteenth-century philosopher René Descartes who said, "*Cogito, ergo sum*," which means "I think; therefore, I am." As a result, we can ponder our condition from an almost-objective position, to think about ourselves in comparison to others, to be self-conscious of our weaknesses and our strengths. This capacity allows us to be philosophical. It also allows us to think generationally, to demonstrate concern for our family lineage. This ability is beyond the animal instinct to care for their offspring.

2. Aesthetic Recognition

We appreciate the aesthetic values of beauty, art, and other concepts such as nobility and honor. Dawkins admits this as well: "We are hugely different from other animals in that we have language, we have art, we have mathematics, philosophy. We have all sorts of emotions that other animals probably don't have."[31] Today we don't find even crude drawings on the dwellings of animal caves that are made by the animals themselves. Though they can be trained to imitate human behavior in some respects, it is a far cry from the human ability we see in art museums and libraries.

3. Language

"Human language appears to be a unique phenomenon, without significant analogue in the animal world."[32] Parrots may be able to mimic human sounds, but they aren't communicating their own thoughts and ideas about their own existence. If that were the case, you might hear them complaining about the food or debating the justice of cages for their fellow parrots. Animals can respond to human voice commands, but these are simply adaptive traits that are conditioned through the reward of food for the performance of an act or response to a command.

Celebrated linguist Noam Chomsky points out that humans have a language acquisition device (LAD) that animals lack.[33] Not only do we have the mental capacity for advanced thought, but we also have unique centers in the brain designed specifically for both language production and language processing. Moreover, our larynx is uniquely designed to create complex sound patterns required for advanced speech. This ability is not found in the animal world, only in humans.

4. CREATIVITY AND SCIENTIFIC EXPLORATION

Humans have not only the mental capacity for creating tools but also an advanced visual system to learn about the outside world. We have hands uniquely designed for complex, intricate motor tasks. We have the ability to take the world around us and make new things, such as iPhones. As Michael Denton wrote in *Nature's Destiny*, "In addition to our brain, our linguistic ability, and our highly developed visual ability, we possess another wonderful adaptation, the ideal manipulative tool—the human hand. No other animal possesses an organ so superbly adapted for intelligent exploration and manipulation of its physical surroundings and environment."[34]

An additional advantage is our bipedal (using only two limbs) posture and the ability to walk upright. These features allow us to manipulate tools while moving. This unique combination of multiple features allows us to explore the world and to develop technologically. "It is only because our brain can sense and experience the world and translate our thoughts into actions that we are able to explore, manipulate, and ultimately understand the world."[35]

5. MORALITY

As humans we are able to act beyond our instincts. There are certainly herd instincts and tribal taboos within the animal world, but nothing that compares with human morality. The best way to illustrate this wide gap is through a pet hamster we owned. It was an exciting event when that hamster had babies. My kids were so excited and gave each of them a name. A few weeks later tragedy struck. We woke up one morning to find one of the baby hamsters missing. For a moment we searched frantically to try and locate the missing hamster. But then the unthinkable became apparent. The mother had eaten one of her babies. I was outraged. Needless to say, that was the last hamster we ever owned.

A moral framework can be seen in virtually every culture. For instance, nearly all people groups recognize the importance of honesty, honoring property, and respecting the marriage covenant. These values do not correspond well with the Darwinian drive to outsurvive one's neighbors. However, they are consistent with the view that all people are the result of a loving God, who wishes for people to live in harmony.

6. HIGHER INTELLIGENCE

Remember the famous illustration of how improbable it would be for a room full of monkeys to produce the works of Shakespeare? Former atheist Anthony Flew said that they actually put the monkeys in a room for months, and they weren't able to produce one word. "There is an enormous difference between life and intelligent life. I don't mean clever crows or dolphins, but minds capable of self-awareness and of developing advanced technologies—that is, not just using what's at hand but transforming materials into devices that can perform a multitude of tasks."[36] Logic and reasoning are hallmarks of this ability in humans and cannot be accounted for as arising spontaneously from natural processes.

7. PERSONHOOD

You are a unique entity, a human being with a unique set of fingerprints and DNA. You are able to think objectively about your existence and uniqueness. Animals can be owned without any moral implications, but persons cannot be ethically owned. In addition, we have the unique abilities to refer to ourselves as *self* and to make free decisions.

> Besides wanting and choosing and being moved *to do* this or that, [humans] may also want to have (or not to have) certain desires and motives. They are capable of wanting to be different, in their preferences and purposes, from what they are. Many animals appear to have the capacity for what I shall call "first-order desires" or "desires of the first order," which are simply desires to do or not to do one thing or another. No animal other than man, however, appears to have the capacity for reflective self-evaluation that is manifested in the formation of second-order desires.[37]

When societies deny personhood as an intrinsic quality of humans, they commonly digress into injustice and dehumanize portions of their populations.

8. CULTURE

Only humans have the capacity to develop complex cultures that advance over time. Michael Tomasello, codirector of the Max Planck Institute for Evolutionary Anthropology, asked "How Are Humans Unique?" in a piece for the *New York Times*.

When you look at apes and children in situations requiring them to put their heads together, a subtle but significant difference emerges. We have observed that children, but not chimpanzees, expect and even demand that others who have committed themselves to a joint activity stay involved and not shirk their duties. When children want to opt out of an activity, they recognize the existence of an obligation to help the group—they know that they must, in their own way, "take leave" to make amends. Humans structure their collaborative actions with joint goals and shared commitments.[38]

This is a point that philosopher Merlin Donald also made very well in his work *A Mind So Rare: The Evolution of Human Consciousness*. As Donald wrote in the prologue, "This book proposes that the human mind is unlike any other on this planet, not because of its biology, which is not qualitatively unique, but because of its ability to generate and assimilate culture. The human mind is thus a 'hybrid' product of biology and culture."[39]

9. BEYOND THE PHYSICAL

Naturalists reduce consciousness to merely the firing of neurons within the brain. We are not, however, merely brains, but we have brains. There is an eternal dimension we possess that lasts beyond physical life. The mystery of this immaterial dimension in humans gives a glimpse of the immaterial personhood and existence of the God in whose image we are made. Evidence for the soul comes from several different sources.[40]

In addition the brain operates in ways that seem to defy the limitations of computational machines. Most notably, we seem to have the capacity for free will.[41]

10. SPIRITUAL HUNGER

The existence of the soul, which is a spiritual or nonmaterial component of our existence, explains the phenomenon of "spiritual hunger." Longing for the eternal is evidence that God has made humanity in His image and has set "eternity in their hearts" (Ecclesiastes 3:11). The fact that over 90 percent of human beings believe there is a God and a life after death points to this reality. This spiritual hunger is just as real as physical hunger, and the experience of hunger always points to something that can truly fulfill that longing. As Saint Augustine wrote, "You have made us for yourself and our hearts find no peace until they rest in you."[42]

SUMMARY

A pointless beginning points to a pointless existence. A purposeful beginning proves life has real purpose and meaning. Humanity's universal need for purpose and meaning in life points to the existence of God. If there were no God, then there would be no such thing as ultimate meaning and purpose. But we inherently know these things do exist. We are created in the image of God, on purpose and for a purpose. When this meaning and purpose is denied, the results can be catastrophic on the human soul. It's as necessary to our survival as the air we breathe.

Man is not just another animal. There is a wide chasm of distinction including the ability to think about our thinking, as well as the existence of an immaterial soul that is beyond the physical brain. This eternal dimension in mankind gives us another glimpse into the reality of an immaterial, eternal God. In essence, Sagan was partially right. There is intelligent life beyond human life that, when discovered, will bring an extraordinary sense of cohesion to us as the people of the earth. That life has indeed reached us in Christ and offers a real and enduring hope.

7

JESUS AND THE RESURRECTION

That a few simple men should in one generation have
invented so powerful and appealing a personality,
so lofty an ethic, and so inspiring a vision of human
brotherhood, would be a miracle far more incredible
than any recorded in the Gospels.

—JOSH MCDOWELL, *MORE THAN A CARPENTER*[1]

Jesus existed, and those vocal persons who deny it do
so not because they have considered the evidence with
the dispassionate eye of the historian, but because they
have some other agenda that this denial serves.

—BART EHRMAN, *DID JESUS EXIST?*[2]

IT WAS A GREAT PRIVILEGE TO LIVE IN JERUSALEM. EVEN
though it was only for a few months, it was a life-altering experience. Unlike the many short trips I've taken to Israel with my
family, friends, and coworkers, this visit allowed me to experience

the profound impact of living in the land of the Bible. Israel is indeed a historic place where the Bible can serve as a map for the many tours and excursions you can take. Even a few days in this amazing country will convince you that the stories told in the Book are far from fairy tales and legends.

During our extended stay a few years ago, I met a young man from Nigeria in one of the local parks who asked me, "Can you tell me where Jesus was crucified?" After a few moments, I was able to point him to the place where this event would have happened. He related to me that he was actually a Buddhist and was visiting Israel in hopes of marrying a Jewish girl.

After asking him several questions about his stay in the city and some of the challenges he had faced, I took the step to ask him, "Do you know why Jesus was crucified?" He paused to think for a moment and then responded that he wasn't quite sure. I was able to explain that Christ had actually died for the sins of the world—including his sins and mine. I gave him directions to the place where Jesus died, but also told him the meaning of that event and prayed for him to receive Christ as his savior.

Christianity started in the city of Jerusalem three days after Jesus' death when His body was reported missing from the tomb where He had been buried. Even more mysterious were immediate reports of men and women seeing Him alive again. It is the story that has divided history and divides hearts to this day. There is no doubt that the land of Israel is the perfect backdrop to the stories of God in history. I love to take people there and witness the profound impact that environment has on them.

The Upset of the Century

The debate between Richard Dawkins and John Lennox in Birmingham, Alabama, in 2007 on the subject "Is God a Delusion?" was called a revelation by the *Wall Street Journal*.[3] Throughout the evening Lennox was on the offensive, pointing out the numerous fallacies in Dawkins's book *The God Delusion*, as well as making a compelling case for an intelligent Creator. If this had been a heavyweight fight, it could have been called the upset of the century because of Lennox's success in the face of the overwhelmingly critical mind-set fostered by a large segment of the academic community.

The clear, compelling evidence for God presented by Lennox was astonishing to those who seriously underestimated the case for a Creator. It is rumored that Dawkins is normally so overconfident he barely reads the opponent's writings prior to such events. After the opening statements at the debate from this gracious, intelligent mathematician, Dawkins undoubtedly realized that this was a worthy opponent.

In his closing remarks, Lennox said something that almost brought Dawkins out of his chair. He boldly declared that he, as a scientist, believed that Jesus Christ was indeed God's Son and was raised from the dead. Dawkins appeared stunned by this admission. "Well there you have it. Just when you think Professor Lennox is making a case for an intelligent designer, he brings up the resurrection of Jesus. It's so petty; it's so parochial; it's so beneath the universe."[4]

Lennox would later meet with Dawkins at Oxford for a discussion moderated by Larry Taunton. Dawkins seemed shocked that

Lennox, a brilliant scientist, could actually believe in something as incredible as the resurrection of Christ. Lennox responded that it is not a mismatch to hold to the scientific evidence for the existence of God and to the ability of that Creator to feed a new event into the system, whether it be the virgin birth of Christ or His resurrection from the dead.[5] By the end of the debate, the fact that he was a brilliant scientist who also possessed faith in a miraculous God dispelled the myth that those two positions were mutually exclusive.

JESUS: NOT A MYTH

We have come to the heart of the multifaceted case that proves God is not dead: the life, death, and resurrection of Jesus Christ. The evidence we have presented so far points overwhelmingly to the existence of God. There is no better explanation for the beginning of space and time, the fine-tuning of the universe from its very beginning and our planetary system, the complexity of life that could not have arisen from natural processes, the reality of objective moral laws, the inborn need in every man and woman for meaning and purpose, and the distinctions between humans and the animals. "God is not dead" is certainly a logical, rational, provable statement both scientifically and philosophically.

Now we turn our attention to the evidence for God in a historical sense. God gave the ultimate evidence for His existence by entering His own creation as a human. In this chapter we don't just offer another proof for God's existence, but we behold this God as He stepped into space and time through Jesus Christ.

This is the anchor of our hope and faith. The life, death, and resurrection of Jesus Christ demonstrated that God exists and give a vivid picture of His nature and character. Jesus said, "He who has seen Me has seen the Father" (John 14:9).

JESUS: MAN OF HISTORY

It is important to start with the simple fact that Jesus Christ actually lived. The evidence of the historical Jesus is beyond dispute, though critics have written works such as *The Quest of the Historical Jesus* attempting to disprove it. Others have argued that even if Jesus did live, we could never know what He was really like or what He really said. The importance of His life cannot be overstated. It was the fact of His resurrection that launched the Christian faith three days after Jesus had died a cruel death on a Roman cross.

Bart Ehrman is arguably the most influential Bible critic of our day. He frequently debates Christian scholars about the reliability of the New Testament gospels from a historical standpoint. While he is a skeptic in terms of the overall truth of the Christian faith, he is not skeptical about the existence of a real Jesus. To Ehrman and countless other scholars, such a denial is not founded on the evidence. Ehrman has emphasized that the fact of Jesus being a man of history is incontrovertible. I quote him because he is not a Christian. As more or less a hostile witness against the Christian faith, he finds himself actually helping the cause of Christ by underscoring the truth of His earthly existence. Once that existence is accepted, it becomes a rather straightforward investigation about His impact.

I am not a Christian, and I have no interest in promoting a Christian cause or a Christian agenda. I am an agnostic with atheist leanings, and my life and views of the world would be approximately the same whether or not Jesus existed. . . . But as a historian I think evidence matters. And the past matters. And for anyone to whom both evidence and the past matter, a dispassionate consideration of the case makes it quite plain: Jesus did exist.[6]

Nonbiblical Sources

Contrary to the claims of some skeptics, the life of Jesus is attested to by a variety of non-Christian historical sources. Here are a few examples:

The Roman historian Tacitus in AD 115 wrote about the persecution of the Christians under Nero and referenced Jesus' crucifixion:

Consequently, to get rid of the report, Nero fastened the guilt and inflicted the most exquisite tortures on a class hated for their abominations, called 'Christians' by the populace. Christus, from whom the name had its origin, suffered the extreme penalty during the reign of Tiberius at the hands of one of our procurators, Pontius Pilatus, and a most mischievous superstition, thus checked for the moment, again broke out not only in Judaea, the first source of the evil, but even in Rome, where all things hideous and shameful from every part of the world find their centre and become popular. Accordingly, an arrest was first made of all who pleaded guilty; then, upon their information, an immense multitude was convicted, not so much of the crime of firing the city, as of hatred against mankind. Mockery of every sort was added to their deaths. Covered with the skins of beasts, they were torn by dogs and perished, or were nailed to crosses, or were doomed to the flames and burnt, to serve as a nightly illumination, when daylight had expired.[7]

Pliny the Younger, a Roman governor of Bithynia, not only referred to Jesus but also alluded to belief in His deity in a letter to the emperor Trajan in AD 112:

They were in the habit of meeting on a certain fixed day before it was light, when they sang in alternate verses a hymn to Christ, as to a god, and bound themselves by a solemn oath, not to any wicked deeds, but never to commit any fraud, theft, or adultery, never to falsify their word, nor deny a trust when they should be called upon to deliver it up; after which it was their custom to separate, and then reassemble to partake of food—but food of an ordinary and innocent kind.[8]

As a particularly interesting secondary source, the third-century historian Julius Africanus cited the first-century historian Thallus, who wrote about the darkness that occurred at the time of the crucifixion:

On the whole world there pressed a most fearful darkness; and the rocks were rent by an earthquake, and many places

in Judea and other districts were thrown down. This darkness Thallus, in the 263 book of his *History*, calls, as appears
to me without reason, an eclipse of the sun. For the Hebrews
celebrate the passover on the 14th day according to the
moon, and the passion of our Savior fails on the day before
the passover [see *Phlegon*]; but an eclipse of the sun takes
place only when the moon comes under the sun. And it cannot happen at any other time but in the interval between
the first day of the new moon and the last of the old, that is,
at their junction: how then should an eclipse be supposed
to happen when the moon is almost diametrically opposite
the sun?[9]

References to Jesus even appear in unsympathetic Jewish
sources. For instance, near the end of the first century, the Jewish
historian Flavius Josephus mentioned Jesus, John the Baptist,
and the death of Jesus' brother James.[10] The details of the most
detailed quotation about Jesus are more controversial due to
their positive portrayal of Him, but the reference is most likely
original. In addition, several Jewish rabbinic traditions allude to
various details of Jesus' life and ministry.[11]

THE GOSPELS AS HISTORICAL RECORDS

The Bible is not one book. It is actually a collection of sixty-six
ancient books that have been gathered together and established
by a multitude of scholars as reliable. The notion that the Bible's
claims about Christ is somehow circular reasoning is absurd.
More than forty different authors wrote down their witnesses

to the working of God in history. The fact that these diverse writings were gathered into one larger book should in no way disqualify the things that are said, any more than a history book of the United States should be dismissed because it combines the numerous historical documents of that country.

The life of Jesus was recorded in four distinct accounts in the books of the Bible known as the Gospels. Each provides detailed descriptions of Jesus' life, ministry, and teaching. The similarities with each other and with outside historical sources are so numerous and striking that no competent historian could deny their general reliability. "I claim to be an historian. My approach to Classics is historical. And I tell you that the evidence for the life, the death, and the resurrection of Christ is better authenticated than most of the facts of ancient history . . ."[12]

MAN, MYTH, MESSIAH?

Critics have tried to marginalize Jesus by asserting that even if He indeed lived, what we can know about Him is more myth and legend than reality. Some go to the extreme of trying to compare the life of Jesus to ancient pagan deities such as Horus of Egypt and Mithras of Persia, or the more contemporary idols such as Marilyn Monroe, John Kennedy, or Elvis. Legend and myth can indeed grow up quickly around a visible public figure. In fact, Jesus addressed this with His disciples when He asked them,

> "Who do men say that I, the Son of Man, am?"
> So they said, "Some say, John the Baptist, some Elijah, and others Jeremiah or one of the prophets."

He said to them, "But who do you say that I am?"
(Matthew 16:13–15)

This is the question not only for them, but for us today. We must cut through the opinions of others and answer this question about Christ: man, myth, or Messiah?

The story of Jesus is nothing like the writings in ancient mythology. Comparing the writings of the New Testament to the stories written about the gods of the Egyptians, Greeks, and Romans is the equivalent of comparing a German history book to a copy of Grimm's Fairy Tales.

Movies such as *Zeitgeist* and *Religulous* claim the Egyptian god Horus and many other mythological characters like him had similar traits to Jesus—born of a virgin on December 25, had twelve disciples, performed miracles, was crucified, and was resurrected. No significant Egyptologists vouch for these claims. These myths of Horus can be traced back to the writings of men such as Gerald Massey in the early 1900s. Other would-be parallels, such as the Persian god Mithras, have literally no surviving ancient texts recording anything specific about this pagan god. Mithraic scholar Richard Gordon said unequivocally that there is "no death, burial, and resurrection of Mithras. None."[13] Even skeptics such as Richard Carrier acknowledge that alleged parallels typically are either fabricated or from documents that postdate the writing of the New Testament by centuries.[14]

The most popular and relevant claims of borrowing relate to Jesus' resurrection. For instance, the mystery cults worshiped dying-and-rising Gods, which are often compared to Christian teaching on the resurrection. However, relevant parallels appear well after Christianity became established, and the Mysteries themselves borrowed Christian concepts to compete with the ever expanding church.[15]

So the enormous impact of the Christian faith gave rise to a rash of works that retold ancient myths in the likeness of the gospel story. The same happens today when a great story generates a host of copycats.

> The larger issue is the question of who influenced whom. With Christianity exploding onto the scene of the Roman Empire, it is evident that other religions adopted certain teachings and practices from Christianity in order to stem the tide of departing adherents or, perhaps, to attract Christians to their side.[16]

Some alleged parallels do predate Jesus, such as the Egyptian god Osiris, who was said to have been resuscitated. However, upon close examination, these similarities are superficial at best. Osiris was not truly resurrected in a transformed new body, but he was simply awakened in the underworld.[17] Craig Keener summarized the evidence in his seminal work *The Historical Jesus of the Gospels*:

> Supposed parallels to the resurrection stories prove weak; Aune even declares that "no parallel to them is found in

Graeco-Roman biography" . . . plainly none of the alleged parallels involves a historical person (or anyone) resurrected in the strict sense. This is probably in part because resurrection in its strict (bodily and permanent) sense was an almost exclusively Jewish belief, and among Jewish people was reserved for the future.[18]

Likewise, Old Testament scholar Tryggve N. D. Mettinger described the case in similar terms: "There is now what amounts to a scholarly consensus against the appropriateness of the concept [of dying and rising gods]. Those who still think differently are looked upon as residual members of an almost extinct species."[19] *So the real myth is that the story of Christ was borrowed from other ancient myths.* Christ's story is unique and rooted in history, not mythology.

Another significant factor must be mentioned that came out of my interview with William Lane Craig. He spoke of the anti-Semitic motives of many of these false stories that attempted to dismiss the Jewishness of Jesus. If critics could link the gospel to Egyptian or Persian myths, then the fact that Jesus was Jewish could be obscured and history revised.

On the streets of Jerusalem today, no one doubts that Jesus was Jewish. The history of His life and death are all over the city. It has been one of my great joys to have many Jewish friends in Israel who share so much in common with me as a Christian. The primary thing that separates us is not the life and death of Jesus, but the resurrection. It is the resurrection of Christ that gives the historical witness and proof that anchors our faith.

JESUS: MORE THAN A MAN

. . . his Son, who . . . through the Spirit of holiness was declared with power to be the Son of God by his resurrection from the dead: Jesus Christ our Lord. (Romans 1:3–4 NIV)

Dave Sterrett, a Christian evangelist and apologist, summarized these thoughts of Gary Habermas:

Virtually all scholars agree that the following statements about Jesus and His followers are historically true:

- Jesus died by Roman crucifixion.
- He was buried, most likely in a private tomb.
- Soon afterwards the disciples were discouraged, bereaved, and despondent, having lost hope.
- Jesus' tomb was found empty very soon after His interment.
- The disciples had encounters with what they believed was the risen Jesus.
- Due to these experiences, the disciples' lives were thoroughly transformed. They were even willing to die for their belief.
- The proclamation of Christ's resurrection took place very early, from the beginning of church history.
- The disciples' public testimony and preaching of the resurrection took place in the city of Jerusalem, where Jesus had been crucified and buried shortly before.[20]

The only plausible explanation for these facts is that Jesus actually died and rose from the dead. Therefore, the resurrection of Jesus Christ was a supernatural miracle that demonstrated God exists and that Jesus is the Savior of the world promised throughout the Scriptures. How else could Christianity have started in the very place it would have been easiest to disprove, Jerusalem, three days after Jesus had been crucified? Because the resurrection is historical, it is subject to the tests of any historical event to determine in a reasonable way whether it actually happened. And, as shown, the facts clearly demonstrate its reality.

GOD REVEALS HIMSELF IN THE EXTRAORDINARY

The key objection to the resurrection is not from a historical standpoint but from a philosophical one. This is based on the argument from David Hume that we should accept as true the events that are the most likely explanation, that follow the most probabilistic pattern.

However, not all real-life events follow predictable patterns. The usual suspects are not always the real culprits. Piecing together the string of witnesses and clues allows us to follow the threads of evidence that can lead us to the answers we seek. In cases of criminal justice we are required to follow the evidence wherever it leads. How much more should we do this in looking for evidence of God?

An event like the resurrection was indeed colossal and unusual. The fact that dead people usually stay dead makes the resurrection of Christ a miraculous single event that defied the odds and shattered the expected course of nature. What else should we expect of God in revealing Himself to humanity? Jesus' miracles were signs as well that He was no ordinary man. They weren't magic tricks used by someone trying to exploit the masses for profit; they were signs that pointed to God and the fulfillment of His promised salvation.

Lee Strobel, a journalist formerly with the *Chicago Tribune*, set out to establish the case for the resurrection of Jesus from a historical standpoint, using the principles for verification that an attorney would use to try a case. He explains the evidence for the resurrection through the use of the five *E*s.[21] These represent the events that history points to as factual.

1. EXECUTION

Jesus died. The Romans were experts at Roman crucifixion, and Roman soldiers were charged under penalty of death to ensure the victim died on the cross. Under no circumstance would a crucified individual have survived the ordeal. The certainty of Jesus' death has been confirmed in an article by the *Journal of the American Medical Association*:

> Clearly the weight of historical and medical evidence indicates that Jesus was dead before the wound to His side was inflicted and supports the traditional view that the spear, thrust between His right ribs, probably perforated not only the right lung, but also the pericardium and heart and thereby ensured His death. Accordingly, interpretations based on the assumption that Jesus did not die on the cross appear to be at odds with modern medical knowledge.[22]

2. EMPTY TOMB

After Jesus' death He was buried in a tomb owned by Joseph of Arimathea, a leader of the Jewish people. The burial of Jesus was called by the late John A. T. Robinson of Cambridge University, "one of the best attested facts we have about the historical Jesus."[23]

Not only was He buried, but His tomb was empty after three days. The fact that there was a rumor that exists to this day that His disciples stole the body gives further evidence that the tomb was empty. "I think we need have no doubt that given Jesus' execution by Roman crucifixion he was truly dead and that his temporary place of burial was discovered to be empty shortly thereafter."[24] Since the disciples proclaimed the resurrection in the very city of the crucifixion and burial, the Romans easily could have produced the body *if* it had not vanished. The first witnesses to the empty tomb were women, something the disciples never would have fabricated since the testimony of women was not considered reliable.

3. EYEWITNESSES

The strongest historical evidence for the resurrection is the eyewitness testimonies of the disciples and more than five hundred other witnesses, which later would include the apostle Paul.

For what I received I passed on to you as of first importance: that Christ died for our sins according to the Scriptures, that he was buried, that he was raised on the third day according to the Scriptures, and that he appeared to Peter, and then to the Twelve. After that, he appeared to more than five hundred of the brothers at the same time, most of whom are still living, though some have fallen asleep. Then he appeared to James, then to all the apostles, and last of all he appeared to me also, as to one abnormally born. (1 Corinthians 15:3–8 NIV)

The transformation in these early disciples was so great that even skeptical New Testament scholars acknowledge that the disciples really believed they encountered the risen Christ. For instance, the famed New Testament scholars and skeptics E. P. Sanders and Bart Ehrman acknowledge this fact:

That Jesus' followers (and later Paul) had resurrection experiences is, in my judgment, a fact. What the reality was that gave rise to the experiences I do not know.[25]

It is a historical fact that some of Jesus' followers came to believe that he had been raised from the dead soon after his execution. We know some of these believers by name; one of them, the apostle Paul, claims quite plainly to have seen Jesus alive after his death. Thus, for the historian, Christianity begins after the death of Jesus, not with the resurrection itself, but with the belief in the resurrection.[26]

One of the most striking features of the eyewitness testimony, as stated previously, is that the first witnesses to Jesus' resurrection were women. The early church never would have made this up because, during that time, the testimony of women was not considered valid or admissible as evidence.

4. Early Records

The accounts of the resurrection originate from the time period immediately after the crucifixion event. John Dominic Crossan, New Testament scholar and skeptic, wrote with Jonathan Reed,

> Paul wrote to the Corinthians from Ephesus in the early 50s C.E. [Common Era, or another way to say AD]. But he says in 1 Corinthians 15:3 that "I handed on to you as of first importance which I in turn received." The most likely source and time for his reception of that tradition would have been Jerusalem in the early 30s when, according to Galatians 1:18, he "went up to Jerusalem to visit Cephas [Peter] and stayed with him fifteen days."[27]

5. Emergence of the Church

A final evidence for the resurrection is the formation of the early church. Before the resurrection, nearly all of Jesus' followers abandoned Him. Many fled in fear for their very lives. Then suddenly His followers came together and formed the Christian church. This group of believers not only boldly proclaimed that Jesus rose from the dead but centered their lives on celebrating this event and following His teaching. Eventually the church grew, despite great opposition, until it dominated the Roman Empire and spread throughout the known world.

> This scared, frightened band of the apostles, which was just about to throw away everything in order to flee in despair to Galilee; when these peasants, shepherds, and

fishermen, who betrayed and denied their master and then failed him miserably, suddenly could be changed overnight into a confident mission society, convinced of salvation and able to work with much more success after Easter than before Easter, then no vision or hallucination is sufficient to explain such a revolutionary transformation.[28]

This sudden emergence of the Christian community can be seen as the "third big bang" in history. The first was the beginning of the universe, the second was the Cambrian explosion, and the third was the explosion or sudden emergence of the Christian community.

What Does the Resurrection Mean?

The fact that Jesus of Nazareth was raised from the dead after three days would simply be a curiosity if it were not for the meaning ascribed the event in the Scriptures (1 Corinthians 15:1–3). Through God's Word we are able to grasp the significance of the resurrection.

1. Jesus Is the Son of God

The existence of multiple religions has led some to ask the question, how could there be such confusion if God is real? Three of the five major religions—Christianity, Judaism, and Islam—are connected by the common belief in figures such as Abraham, Moses, and Jesus, but even these faiths have significant distinctions. The only answer is that people were somehow separated from God, as taught by Scripture. Therefore, all views of God would be different and imperfect. The resurrection of Jesus, however, demonstrates that Jesus truly is the "Son of God," or perfect representation of God on earth. This fact sets Christianity apart from every other religion or philosophy and makes Jesus the only reliable source to fully know God.

2. HIS WORDS ARE TRUE

Because of the resurrection we can have confidence that Jesus' words are the words of God Himself. The resurrection of Jesus was the fulfillment of the promises made to Abraham and Moses and the prophets of Holy Scripture. Jesus said, "Heaven and earth will pass away, but My words will by no means pass away" (Matthew 24:35). When the Old Testament prophets spoke, they prefaced their remarks with the phrase, "Thus says the LORD," but when Jesus spoke He said, "Truly I say to you" (Luke 21:3). The difference? God Himself was speaking.

3. OUR SINS ARE FORGIVEN

The great quest of humanity is to be accepted by God and considered righteous. The question is asked, what does God expect of us? He expects that we keep the moral law. When that moral law is broken, the crime is called *sin*. Jesus Christ offers real forgiveness because the resurrection verified that His death for the payment of our sins was accepted. "He was delivered over to death for our sins and was raised to life for our justification" (Romans 4:25 NIV). Justification is a legal term that declares that we are not guilty.

4. GOD EXISTS

The miracle of the resurrection demonstrates that God is not dead! In the naturalistic worldview, miracles are impossible due to the philosophy that suggests we should not accept an improbable act as true. They forget that God created the laws of nature and can interject something from the outside into the system. Because there are laws that explain what ordinarily happens, we are able to know when something extraordinary has taken place. God has revealed His nature and character through both the ordinary laws and processes He established as well as through extraordinary miracles such as the resurrection of Jesus Christ.

5. CERTAINTY IS POSSIBLE

Because Christ has been raised from the dead, we have been given the gift of certainty. It's ironic that one of the key scientific principles is called the *uncertainty principle.* In short, we cannot know both the speed and location of subatomic particles. There are other ideas such as those offered by Immanuel Kant in the eighteenth century that contend we can't really know what's beyond the physical world. These ideas reveal the limitations of knowledge. There are limits to our finite understanding.

The miracle of the resurrection of Christ is that it demonstrated how God pierced the veil of the physical world by becoming a human in Jesus Christ. The resurrection verified the truth of this reality. Though we are still limited in what we can ultimately know, God gave us the ability to know that He is real, His word is true, and there is life after death. Just as my young children aren't able to comprehend certain things but can know enough to trust me as their father, we can know enough through the resurrection of Jesus to trust God in the things that we cannot understand on this side of eternity.

The Name Above Every Name

No other name produces such a reaction as the name of Jesus Christ. All the religious figures combined don't generate as much debate or controversy, "nor is there salvation in any other" (Acts 4:12). The reason that Christ is the only source of salvation is He did what no other person in history did by living a perfect life and then offering that life for the sins of the world.

The death and resurrection of Christ verified His identity as the Son of God and proved His words were the words of God Himself. Because God became a man in Jesus, we have been given the gift of certainty. As finite beings we can't be certain about everything, but we can be certain of enough to trust God in the things we cannot possibly know.

> Your attitude should be the same as that of Christ Jesus:
> Who, being in very nature God,
>> did not consider equality with God something to be grasped,
> but made himself nothing,
>> taking the very nature of a servant,
>> being made in human likeness.
> And being found in appearance as a man,
>> he humbled himself
>> and became obedient to death—even death on a cross!
> Therefore God exalted him to the highest place
>> and gave him the name that is above every name,
> that at the name of Jesus every knee should bow,
>> in heaven and on earth and under the earth,
> and every tongue confess that Jesus Christ is Lord,
>> to the glory of God the Father. (Philippians 2:5–11 NIV)

In short, the impact of the life of Christ has altered the course of human history.

Summary

Dr. James Allan Francis wrote *One Solitary Life* during the early 1900s. This description of the life and impact of Christ has become one of the most quoted and beloved pieces of Christian literature since that time.

He was born in an obscure village, the child of a peasant woman. Until He was thirty, He worked in a carpenter shop and then for three years He was an itinerant preacher. He wrote no books. He held no office. He never owned a home. He was never in a big city.

He never traveled two hundred miles from the place He was born. He never did any of the things that usually accompany greatness. The authorities condemned His teachings. His friends deserted Him. One betrayed Him to His enemies for a paltry sum. One denied Him. He went through the mockery of a trial.

He was nailed on a cross between two thieves. While He was dying, His executioners gambled for the only piece of property He owned on earth: His coat. When He was dead He was taken down and placed in a borrowed grave.

Nineteen centuries have come and gone, yet today He is the crowning glory of the human race, the adored leader of hundreds of millions of the earth's inhabitants. All the armies that ever marched and all the navies that were ever assembled and all the parliaments that ever sat and all the rulers that ever reigned—combined—have not affected the life of man upon this earth so profoundly as that One Solitary Life.[29]

8

THE WITNESS OF SCRIPTURE

The existence of the Bible, as a book for the people, is the greatest benefit which the human race has ever experienced. Every attempt to belittle it . . . is a crime against humanity.

—IMMANUEL KANT, *LOOSE LEAVES FROM KANT'S ESTATE*[1]

I believe the Bible is the best gift God has ever given to man. All the good of the Savior of the world is communicated to us through the Book. But for it, we could not know right from wrong.

—ABRAHAM LINCOLN[2]

THE KING DAVID HOTEL IN JERUSALEM IS ONE OF THE most picturesque and historically significant places in the world. So much drama has taken place there, from negotiations between heads of state to bombings during the ongoing Middle East crisis. It was there I met one of the most unusual men in the world, George Blumenthal. Besides being a pioneer in the cell phone industry, his passion is digitizing rare documents such as the Dead Sea Scrolls, which he did digitize for the Israel Museum.[3]

George is truly one of the most colorful characters I've ever met. He's even had many small parts in various movies, including brief cameos in *Wall Street* and *Wall Street: Money Never Sleeps* with his friend Michael Douglas. "I wish you could come with me tomorrow—I'm giving Jerry Bruckheimer [a movie producer] and some others a little tour of the city." His little tour would include some of the most fantastic archaeological digs uncovering the Israel of the last five thousand years.

My wife, Jody, and I were scheduled to leave the next day and regretfully declined his invitation. Over the next two years I ran into George on several occasions. When we first met in 2006, he was an agnostic about the existence of God, but his passion about the history and archaeology surrounding the Bible was making an impact on his skepticism. "The people and places that the Bible mentions are actually real," he would tell me.

Our paths crossed again on May 15, 2008, at the United Nations. We both attended a small event surrounding the sixtieth anniversary of the modern State of Israel. George was excited about yet another discovery that confirmed the Bible's historical accuracy. I felt the time had come to suggest that he connect the dots between the historical realities he was listing and the God of history who was behind it all. I paused to gather my nerves and said, "George, do you now believe?" The question seemed to hit him right between the eyes. He paused as if to say, "Let me think about that."

Almost a month later a special delivery shipment from

George arrived at our home. Inside that carefully packed box were ancient artifacts dated between 1000 BC (the time of King David) and AD 400. We were stunned at this incredible collection of antiquities and the certificates of authenticity that he had given us. Along with the artifacts was a handwritten letter from George, dated June 20, 2008:

Dear Rice and Jody,

In answer to your question "George, do you believe?" As Einstein believed I do believe in the Creator of the Universe. Moreover, I believe in the Creator who gave us Ethical Monotheism at Mt. Sinai to complement the gift of Free Will he had already given us. Now, it is in our hands to make the world a better place! I have been waiting for years to give someone—the right someone—this group of antiquities. Please enjoy them in your home and share them with others!

Best Regards,

George B.

He had been deeply grateful for his Jewish heritage but was agnostic. Looking at the facts of history and having a willingness to follow the evidence wherever it led, he found faith in God.

I recently asked him another question: "George, as a Christian, my faith is anchored in the resurrection of Christ as clear evidence for my faith. As a Jew, what anchors your faith?"

He didn't hesitate. "The Hebrew Bible." He went on to recount the integrity of the *Tanakh* (the Jewish name for the Old Testament), verified through such discoveries as the Dead Sea Scrolls.

It is that Bible that provides another compelling witness to the long list of evidence that points to the fact that God is not dead.

"The Books"

That's what *bible* literally means. It looks like one book, but it is an anthology, a collection of sixty-six books written by forty different authors over a period of sixteen hundred years. These books were copied by hand and faithfully passed down to us today. It wasn't until 1454 that Johannes Gutenberg's printing press rolled out the first typed Bible.

Scripture refers to what Christians call the Old and New Testaments. The Old Testament covers the period from the beginning of the universe and creation of life to the refounding of Israel after the Babylonian exile about 400 BC. Most prominently it is the record of God's dealings with the people of Israel. The New Testament begins with the life of Jesus in 4 BC, describes the early Christian church, and ends with an apocalyptic vision for the world in the book of Revelation.

The Old Testament books were written primarily in Hebrew. These were translated into Greek between the third and first centuries BC and became known as the Septuagint version or the LXX. "The name Septuagint comes from *septuaginta*, the Latin word for 'seventy.'"[4] (This refers to the seventy-two translators who were said to have worked on this project.) This version was used by the early church as it expanded into the larger non-Jewish world.

The New Testament books were written originally in Greek.

The earliest writings—the letter to the Galatians and the other epistles—appeared about twenty years after the resurrection of Christ.[5] They witness the fact that Christ had been raised in complete harmony with and fulfillment of the Old Testament scriptures. The first gospel account of Jesus' life, the book of Mark, first appeared between AD 50 and AD 70. All the New Testament books were written within the first century and were referenced in the writings of the early church fathers. That's a key difference in distinguishing the true writings from the false and spurious: the real Gospels were written in the first century while the other imposters (such as the Gospels of Thomas and Judas) were written well into the second century. Most importantly, the true Gospels were recognized throughout the known world as having originated from either the apostles or close associates.

What Happened to the Originals?

The original writings of the New Testament are called the *autographs*. These were written on perishable material, which we no longer have. Does that mean we cannot know what was originally written? Of course we can know. Remember, all ancient books were copied by hand and passed down. We study those copies through the science of textual criticism.

Imagine you are in a classroom of one hundred students on a university campus, and the instructor puts a letter from the president of the university on the overhead projector. The entire class is asked to copy the letter and keep the copy in their records. Now suppose the original letter was lost. Could we reconstruct the original letter from the one hundred copies the students made? Of course. What if there were mistakes in some of the copies, such as misspelled words or skipped sentences due to human error? The science of textual criticism would help you decide with a high degree of probability what was originally said. Each copy would be compared with the others, and you would assume the text found in the majority of the copies is the original wording. Even though the copies of the New Testament books were not written at the same time or in the same region, biblical scholars have several strategies that help them determine what the autographs said. Some take the numerous copies of the New Testament and reconstruct what was written by the "majority text" or what the majority of manuscripts would have said. Most use other, more complex and sophisticated methods than this, but comparing numerous manuscripts is a basic understanding of how the originals can be reconstructed. In fact, over five thousand manuscripts in Greek alone have been discovered, several dating before the year AD 300. With the abundance of New Testament sources, modern scholars are able to reconstruct 99 percent of the New Testament with extreme confidence.[6] In contrast, most reconstructions of ancient nonbiblical literature are based on only a few texts written many centuries after the original.

Besides the copies of the New Testament books and letters, there are the massive number of references that are made to these New Testament books by the writings of Christians. In fact, we could reconstruct most of the New Testament from these writings alone. Dr. Dan Wallace, one of the foremost New Testament scholars of our day, has confirmed this:

Now, if you were to destroy all those manuscripts, we would not be left without a witness. That's because the ancient Christian leaders known as church fathers wrote commentaries on the New Testament. To date, more than one million quotations of the New Testament by the church fathers have been recorded. "If all other sources for our knowledge of the text of the New Testament were destroyed, [the patristic quotations] would be sufficient alone for the reconstruction of practically the entire New Testament."[7]

THE SIGNIFICANCE OF THE DEAD SEA SCROLLS

In 1947 a fifteen-year-old was shepherding with his cousins in Qumran, Palestine, near the Dead Sea. He threw a rock into a cave and heard the sound of pottery cracking. When he entered the cave to investigate the unusual sound, he found several clay jars containing writings that went back to the second century BC. Documents in this and similar caves included at least fragments of every book of the Old Testament, except the book of Esther. These copies were a thousand years older than any Hebrew manuscript of the Bible discovered at that time.

The scrolls gave scholars the remarkable ability to compare how much the writings had changed over the years. Some were essentially the same. In particular, the entire book of Isaiah was identified. Amazingly, the text was 95 percent identical to that in Bibles today, and most of the differences were simple spelling errors or easily identifiable slips of the pen.[8]

WAS IT WRITTEN BY MEN?

The question is often posed, was the Bible written by men? Absolutely. Many of these books have the names of the writers as their title: Isaiah, Jeremiah, Job, Mark, Jude. But that's not the whole story. These books bear the marks of divine inspiration and, ultimately, divine authorship. That is why they are referred to as the Word of God, not just in a metaphorical sense but in a very real one. Not just inspirational but authoritative. Jesus unambiguously spoke of the Scripture as completely authoritative and trustworthy, even down to the smallest markings (Matthew 5:18). His rising from the dead confirmed that He was God, so His authentication of Scripture can be trusted.

The Bible contains commandments and laws commonly referred to as the "Thou shalt nots." They are not just prohibitions but statements of reality that function as moral laws. Just as gravity and relativity function in the physical world, breaking these moral laws has consequences. If you're driving down the road and see a warning sign that says "Danger Ahead! Bridge Out!" you don't resent the sign or the person who put it there. Its purpose is to protect you, not harm you. The harm comes from ignoring the sign. In the same way, harm comes from ignoring the commandments of God.

But there are also promises. God is a promise maker and a promise keeper. "I will bless you" (Genesis 12:2), He says. "'Honor your father and mother,' which is the first commandment with a promise: 'that it may be well with you and you may live long on the earth'" (Ephesians 6:2–3). There are more promises than commandments, over seven thousand in fact. There are actually promises that help us keep the commandments. "Having these promises, beloved, let us cleanse ourselves of all filthiness of the flesh and spirit" (2 Corinthians 7:1). God doesn't give commandments He knows we cannot keep, but we cannot keep them without His help.

It's like the Apple computer I'm using to write this manuscript (the analogy applies to PC users as well). To know how it works, I must consult the instruction manual Apple gave me. I must repair it with Apple parts and use a charge cord specifically made for Apple computers. I never consider those requirements exclusive or unfair. I focus more on the amazing things the computer can do, and I see the instructions for operating it properly as helpful, not as a hardship.

In the same way, because we are designed by God, we function best with His power and truth by following His instructions. Any deviation hurts us in the way that putting water instead of gasoline in an automobile's engine will hinder its function. God wants to empower us to live optimally in the world He made, so He gave us accurate instructions on how this happens. The Bible, in a real sense, is the instruction manual for life.

THE MOST POPULAR BOOK IN THE WORLD

There is no way to overstate the Bible's importance in terms of how it has shaped history, given value and dignity to mankind, defined good and evil, given rights to women and children, and shown that everyone who fears Him is welcome in His presence (Acts 10:35). It is safe to say that you cannot understand the world we live in without understanding the Bible. From the foundations of Western civilization to the Middle East crisis, the

Bible is the key to understanding the origins of these and other events.

The knowledge of God that comes through creation is *general revelation*. There is enough evidence of God in what God has created that we are "without excuse" to reject His existence (Romans 1:20). The Scripture is God's *special revelation* to man in that we are given greater clarity as to what God is like. Special revelation is like putting on glasses and seeing clearly what we can only see partially through general revelation.

Do You Read the Bible Literally?

Well, first of all, it is important *literally to read it* and not just own a Bible. Having a big one on your coffee table or at your bedside won't help you much. Many skeptics who dismiss the Bible have never really read it. Picking it up and skimming through it doesn't help your life any more than picking up a calculus book and skimming through it would help you build a rocket ship.

There are various types of literature in the Bible: poetry, allegory, parables, history, didactic, epistolary, apocalyptic, prophecy, and more. To say you read the Bible literally means you take it in the sense that the author intended to communicate the written message. There are many theories that critics have put forth to diminish the weight of the Bible's authority. Some of these arguments are sophisticated and nuanced. Others border on the absurd. On a university campus, it can get pretty funny.

A student approached me once and said, "I believe the Bible came here from outer space." I had just finished speaking at the University of Calgary in Canada and was answering questions at the campus pub where the meeting had been held. (The Christian leaders who invited me were worried that I wouldn't be comfortable speaking at a bar, which made me laugh when I recollected my days at university, working at a local bar. It was a much easier setting than a lot of churches I've been in. Certainly much easier to get the folks in the bar to sing along than it has been at some of the eight o'clock Sunday services I've attended.)

The young girl who told me she believed the Bible had been the product of aliens visiting our planet and beginning life was very sincere in her explanation. I tried to take her seriously and not burst into laughter. It was actually a fairly novel idea in terms of what I'd heard students say in the past. Usually I get the standard, "The Bible is full of contradictions," or *Da Vinci Code*–inspired conspiracy theories,[9] claiming Scripture was corrupted or contrived by priests with their own agenda or by Emperor Constantine around AD 325.

I stepped back, looked at a campus worker standing by me, and thought, *What am I going to say to her?* And then it hit me like a flash of inspiration from heaven: "If people from outer space went to the trouble of coming all this way to leave you the Bible, don't you think you ought to read it?"

The student was stunned at my answer and slowly nodded her head in agreement. I just conceded the UFO argument as if it were true. If she really believed the Bible had that kind of unusual origin, it should be motivation enough to at least read it.

Belief in the existence of God doesn't depend on whether someone embraces the truth that the Scripture is God's revelation to man. William Lane Craig, who most certainly believes the Bible is God's Word, offered me advice on how to navigate the debate about this vital topic. His strategy is to demonstrate the Bible as an historically reliable book that gives clear testimony that Christ lived, died, and rose again. In Craig's opinion it is important not to get sidetracked focusing on a defense for the inerrancy of Scripture, especially if someone doesn't believe in God. Dr. Dan Wallace agrees with this approach:

> The way I approach this is to recognize the primacy of Christ as Lord of my life, as sovereign master of the universe. And, as I look at the Scriptures, they first and foremost have to be those documents that I regard as relatively trustworthy to guide us as to what Christ did and what God has done in history. On that basis, on that foundation, I begin to look at it in more ways than that.[10]

In other words, the Bible gives us a reliable account of the life, death, and resurrection of Christ. His identity as the Son of God was verified by His resurrection. Our faith is first and foremost in Him, and because of His authority, we approach the Scriptures as true and trustworthy.

Some skeptics think they can dismiss the Bible as a witness for the existence of God by rejecting the possibility that God could use words to reveal Himself. It's obvious that if you don't believe in God, you won't believe it's possible that the Scripture could be divinely inspired. A typical tweet or blog post from the world of Internet atheists conveys a flippant attitude by the committed unbeliever: "Do you actually think someone could be persuaded to believe a god is real by quoting a religious book?" This question is the intellectual equivalent of a drive-by shooting. An absolutely random, irrational thought that will injure naïve bystanders. Could I not give someone an accurate picture of the history of America or any other country by reading its history from a book to you? Of course. Certainly there is a difference in fiction and nonfiction. The Bible doesn't begin, "Once upon a time," or "In a galaxy far, far away." It is rooted in history—verifiable history.

The phrase "Thus says the LORD" occurs hundreds of times in the pages of the Bible. This points to the divine origin of these sacred writings. The ultimate testimony of its authority comes from Jesus Himself. As His resurrection verified His identity as the Son of God, He stated, "Heaven and earth will pass away, but My words will by no means pass away" (Matthew 24:35).

To help you remember some of the important aspects that make the Bible trustworthy as well as unique, you can use the acronym SHARPER, inspired by Hebrews 4:12: "For the word of God is living and powerful, and *sharper* than any two-edged sword" (emphasis mine).

SAME

The Bible has been consistently transcribed and passed down to us for centuries. The notion that it has been corrupted to the point of obscuring what was originally said is simply not true. The autographs were written on perishable material and are no longer with us, but there are enough copies of those originals for us to reconstruct the original text to an accuracy of 99 percent. "Of the approximately 138,000 words in the New Testament only about 1,400 remain in doubt. The text of the New Testament is thus about 99 percent established. That means that when you pick up a (Greek) New Testament today, you can be confident that you are reading the text as it was originally written."[11] None of these differences in words, phrases, or verses affect any Christian claim or doctrine. "The great majority are spelling differences that have no bearing on the meaning of the text."[12] Likewise, the book of Isaiah was shown to be virtually unchanged through the centuries by the discovery of the Dead Sea Scrolls.

It's worth repeating that the Bible is a collection of sixty-six books written by forty different authors over a period of sixteen hundred years. In spite of the diversity of authors and contexts of each book, the theme of redemption or salvation is consistent. From Genesis to Revelation this is true. The different strands weave together into a beautiful tapestry representing God's redemptive story in history. Though many issues are covered in the Bible, an overarching consistent theme unfolds to reveal the ultimate salvation found in Jesus Christ.

HISTORICALLY ACCURATE

The names and places mentioned are real. Skeptics often claim that the New Testament is full of myths and misrepresentations of both Jesus' teaching and His ministry. They argue that Jesus' followers were so dismayed by His untimely death that they deluded themselves into believing that He rose from the dead. Naturally, such a scenario would result in their perceptions of Jesus after His death being radically different from the Jesus of history. However, as argued in the previous chapter, Jesus actually did rise from death. Why else would his followers have boldly proclaimed Jesus' resurrection at Pentecost and eventually die as martyrs defending their claims? Therefore, we know with confidence that Jesus' disciples carefully guarded His teaching and the stories about His ministry. Moreover, they regularly repeated them for decades to large numbers of early believers. Those who were taught by the disciples then retold the stories in other communities countless times. In fact, studies of oral traditions indicate that the similarities and differences between the Gospels match what would be expected if the core information were true.[13]

The Gospels and the book of Acts also present a consistent picture with each other and the writings of the apostle Paul of Jesus' life, ministry, and teaching. For instance, Luke and Matthew both use the gospel of Mark as a source and possibly another common source called Q. By comparing those three gospels, we can tell that both authors used their sources faithfully. Minor differences do exist between parallel accounts, but these tensions are usually explained in terms of the flexibility ancient authors had in rearranging material, paraphrasing teachings, and contextualizing stories for particular audiences.[14] Some differences are more challenging to harmonize, such as the accounts of Judas's death (Matthew 27:5; Acts 1:18). However, none of these tensions affect our understanding of the core message or events, and no unbiased historian would consider these differences as evidence that the books were fabrications.

Even more striking, descriptions of events in one gospel "interlock" with parallel descriptions in other gospels. For instance, Jesus asked Philip where they could buy food in John's account of a miraculous feeding (6:5), but no explanation is given as to why Philip was asked. In Luke we learn that this miracle occurred near Bethsaida (9:10), which was Philip's hometown (John 12:21). Jesus asking Philip, as described in John, makes sense with the additional information from Luke. These connections show that the gospel stories must have been based on real historical events.[15]

ARCHAEOLOGICALLY VERIFIED

Archaeology has verified the historicity of the Bible. The view that the New Testament authors were intimately involved in the stories they described is supported by numerous archaeological confirmations. For instance, the famed archaeologist William Ramsay confirmed that countless details in the book of Acts are correct. He originally expected his studies to disprove the book's reliability, but his work proved his theory wrong.

> The more I have studied the narrative of the Acts, and the more I have learned year after year about Graeco-Roman society and thoughts and fashions, and organization in those provinces, the more I admire and the better I understand. I set out to look for truth on the borderland where Greece and Asia meet, and found it [in the Book of Acts]. You may press the words of Luke in a degree beyond any other historian's, and they stand the keenest scrutiny and the hardest treatment, provided always that the critic knows the subject and does not go beyond the limits of science and of justice.[16]

More recent scholars have likewise confirmed the extraordinary reliability of Luke as a historian.[17]

Archaeologists have also confirmed countless details in the Gospels from the description of the pool at Bethesda (John 5:2) to details about the coin mentioned when Jesus was questioned about paying taxes to Caesar (Mark 12:13–17). Since many such details in the Gospels and Acts were not widely known outside the original locales, the authors must have been drawing from firsthand experience.[18]

The historical reliability of the Old Testament is a much more complex question since many of the recorded events take place in the distant past. Many of the details that were challenged by skeptics have been confirmed by recent archaeological evidence. In summary, the Old Testament has fared quite well where compared to other ancient documents.[19] Any remaining historical difficulties in no way threaten the Bible's reliability.

Reliable Manuscripts

The number of early manuscripts of the New Testament far exceeds any other ancient documents'. For instance, manuscripts of the early Greek writer Homer's *Iliad* are more than a half millennium later, with less than two thousand discovered. But there are more than five thousand copies of the New Testament, and more than one hundred were written within the first four centuries.

Let me repeat: the majority of the differences between manuscripts simply consist of differences in spelling, different synonyms, and summaries of sections. Very few differences represent significantly different understandings of the text, and none in any way alter any foundational Christian teaching.

The discovery of the Dead Sea Scrolls revealed startling evidence for the reliability and integrity of the Old Testament books. Claims that the manuscripts were somehow corrupted over the centuries by the hands of the rabbis and priests who copied them were shown to be spurious. If the scribes copying the Scripture in medieval times made even one error in a manuscript, it was destroyed immediately. The integrity and reverence of the Bible transcription is astounding and unparalleled.

Prophetic

Another startling dimension of the supernatural nature of the Scripture is the prediction of future events known as *prophecy*. Naturally, skeptical scholars have attempted to redate the prophetic books to years after the prophecies were fulfilled. However, internal evidence such as the vocabulary and languages used in the books suggest they were each written during the times of the claimed authors.

Numerous predictions made throughout the Bible were fulfilled in history. For instance, Isaiah predicted a century in advance that King Cyrus of Persia would enable Israel to return to their land and rebuild the temple (Isaiah 44:28). The prophet Ezekiel predicted several details about the falls of Tyre (Ezekiel 26) and Sidon (Ezekiel 28:22–23). Likewise, the prophet Daniel predicted the rise of the next three empires and the general timeframe for the coming of Jesus (Daniel 9:24–27).

Equally striking, dozens of prophecies were fulfilled by Jesus Christ Himself. The Old Testament authors predicted Jesus' birth in Bethlehem (Micah 5:2), ministry in Galilee (Isaiah 9:1–2), descent from King David (Isaiah 11:1), and triumphal entry into Jerusalem (Zechariah 9:9). Such predictions are divine fingerprints throughout Scripture.

One challenge to prophecy does need to be addressed. As mentioned, many Old Testament scriptures clearly point to Jesus, but some references by New Testament authors are more complex. In particular, gospel writers at times seem to take Old Testament scriptures out of their original context. For instance, Matthew references Jeremiah 31:15 in connection with Herod's slaughter of male children in Bethlehem while Jeremiah seems to be referring to the Jewish exile. While such tensions might appear problematic to modern readers, they vanish when the theological framework of the New Testament writers is fully understood. The authors did not simply see a scattering of Old Testament scriptures pointing to Christ. Instead, they saw Jesus as the fulfillment of Israel's entire history and divine calling. As such they often connected Old Testament scriptures, which related to events in the original author's timeframe, to Jesus since He in even greater fashion fulfilled their fuller meaning.

EXTRAORDINARY IMPACT

The Scripture has powerfully altered the lives of individuals and entire nations. Moral law is given specific clarity through the pages of the Bible. The Ten Commandments stand as the unsurpassed benchmark for civil law. The two great commands of Jesus to love God and love your neighbor are summaries of the Ten Commandments. To love God is to have a specific expression, and to love your neighbor is demonstrated not merely in a feeling or emotion but in our actions. If we love our neighbors, we won't lie to them or steal from them. As entire communities have embraced the teaching of Scripture, such transformation has spread throughout cities and even to entire nations. Examples of such cultural change are presented in chapter 9. In terms of personal impact, the Bible's teaching has empowered its readers to overcome addictions, restore families, experience peace and joy, and even forgive bitter enemies. Specific testimonies of such evidence of divine power are presented in chapter 10.

It is extraordinary that the Bible has survived all the attempts to discredit it. The Bible has been banned, burned, and belittled, and yet has outlasted all its detractors. Skeptics often challenge such evidence by saying that many individuals and societies have embraced the Bible without seeing positive results. A common example is Christian communities throughout history that have embraced racism and shown little concern for the poor and needy. This critique is certainly fair. However, it ignores the fact that Jesus Himself predicted that many who profess to follow Him would not faithfully obey His teachings. Just believing in the Bible or even just reading it does not transform lives. People must place their complete faith in Jesus' promise of forgiveness for their sins and in the power of the Holy Spirit to transform them from the inside. Then the Holy Spirit brings divine revelation causing the Scripture to reshape readers' hearts and minds. Reading the Bible without the Holy Spirit is much like watching a TV without a cable connection.

RELEVANT

The Bible gives timeless insight into the nature of God and humanity. Its commandments are still the best guide for human behavior. Skeptics have dismissed the laws as simple common sense, but history has shown our tendency toward evil and the need to restrain it.

The last *R* could just as easily stand for *real*. It's like looking in the mirror. It shows you exactly what you look like. The Bible has shown the real picture of humanity throughout history, good and bad. The most faithful of God's people who sinned have had their stories told just as they happened. No whitewashing of the ugly parts or retelling them to cover up the blemishes. The Bible tells the story of real people and real life. It's important to know that the various authors of Scripture wrote in the literary styles of their day and addressed the specific concerns of their audiences. God divinely guided this process to ensure that they wrote what He intended for their particular setting. But He also guided the authors to ensure their words connected to the larger story, which was intended for all people in all generations.

The different books of the Bible translate God's truth into a vast array of cultural contexts and situations: ancient Eastern nomadic (Exodus), Western cosmopolitan (Romans), Greek (Corinthians), faith-dominant (1 and 2 Samuel), faith-hostile (Esther), postmodern (Ecclesiastes), artistic (Psalms), and so on. Therefore, Christians from virtually any cultural context and perspective can deeply identify with multiple books of the Bible. Those books can jump-start understandings of the other books. As a particular notable example, modern Westerners often find the genealogies of Genesis completely irrelevant. They typically wonder why God would have even desired to include them. They connect much more strongly with the logical flow of Romans. In contrast, missionaries who translate the Bible into tribal languages often discover that the native readers do not find the stories credible until the genealogies are translated. Unlike most Westerners, tribal cultures often look to the past, so genealogies prove credibility.

Summary

During this project, I had the chance to sit down with one of the preeminent Bible scholars of our day, Dr. Dan Wallace, a professor of New Testament studies at Dallas Theological Seminary. Dr. Wallace also leads the Center for the Study of New Testament Manuscripts. He has debated Bart Ehrman three times and is as engaging as he is intelligent.

In my time with him I came away with three distinct principles.

First, the Bible is true in what it *tells*. When the Bible tells us about a person or place, it can be taken as true. Second, the Bible is true in what it *teaches*. The teachings of the Bible have changed the course of history for the good, and its principles remain the guiding lights for humanity in every way and in every culture. Third, the Bible is true in what it *touches*. Though it is not a science book, it doesn't contradict what we know to be true from a scientific standpoint. Even the first chapters of Genesis, though hotly debated in many circles, do not contradict what science has verified about the physical world. Though very narrow interpretations by both skeptics and believers alike can leave some with a sense of irreconcilable differences, there are clear answers to the objective mind.

All people are created in the image of God, and we are all affected by the fallen nature of creation. Therefore, the truth of the Bible speaks directly to the core issues of everyone's life. Christians from any background will experience a life of much greater abundance if they simply follow the core principles behind the teaching of Scripture. In fact, experience and several academic studies have shown that Christians who follow Scripture have greater health and other life benefits.[20]

All of the facts that have been mentioned here point definitively to the truth that the Bible is a divinely inspired work that serves as a trustworthy witness to the existence of God.

9

THE GRACE EFFECT

From the fullness of his grace we have all received one blessing after another. For the law was given through Moses; grace and truth came through Jesus Christ.

—JOHN 1:16–17 NIV

I have such a fantastic life that I feel an overwhelming sense of gratitude for it. . . . But I don't have anyone to express my gratitude to. This is a void deep inside me, a void of wanting someone to thank, and I don't see any plausible way of filling it.

—BART EHRMAN, *GOD'S PROBLEM*[1]

LIFE WAS CHEAP. THAT'S THE BEST WAY TO DESCRIBE THE world of two thousand years ago. It was not becoming less evil but becoming insidiously and callously more indifferent to human life. Children were sacrificed in pagan rituals, women had little more value than livestock, and slavery bound at least one-quarter of Rome's population. The world was covered in thick darkness in a spiritual sense.

Four successive empires had taken their turns dominating the human race: Babylon, Persia, Greece, and Rome. All four boasted emperors who acted as gods, brutally conquered all opposition, and used the full force of their strength to keep the world under their thumb. The might of their empire had no equals and few challengers—until they were conquered by the next empire.

Several years ago actor Russell Crowe starred in the movie *Gladiator,* set in the days of the Roman Coliseum, where contestants, mostly slaves and criminals, fought to the death. The blatant disregard for human life was on full display as the crowd's cheers or jeers determined life or death for the loser.

It was into this world that Jesus was born. The most unlikely Savior anyone could have imagined. A small child against the Roman Empire? Not very good odds. In a culture where only the strong survived, Christ would call His followers to "love their enemies" and "turn the other cheek." The statement of Jesus, "for God so loved the world" was also new to the pagan mind.[2] It was a revolutionary idea that God loved and cared for His creation, as opposed to the mythological gods of the Greeks and Romans who watched from their mountaintop.

Because of the compelling nature of its truth and message, Christianity prevailed against this powerful juggernaut of the Roman State, not by military force from without but by changing hearts and minds from within. Historian Will Durant, who wrote a classic series of works on world history, spoke of the triumph of the cross over the Roman Empire:

There is no greater drama in human record than the sight of a few Christians, scorned or oppressed by a succession of

emperors, bearing all trials with a fiery tenacity, multiply-
ing quietly, building order while their enemies generated
chaos, fighting the sword with the word, brutality with
hope, and at last defeating the strongest state that history
has ever known. Caesar and Christ had met in the arena,
and Christ had won.[3]

Contrary to the fictitious work of Dan Brown in *The Da
Vinci Code*, Christianity didn't gain its influence because the
emperor Constantine accepted it; it was accepted because of
the power of its message and the compelling lives of believers in
the three hundred years before Constantine. In fact, within the
first thirty years after Christ's resurrection, the world would be
turned upside down by this committed group of His faithful followers. As Michael Green wrote,

> Three crucial decades in world history. That is all it took. In
> the years between AD 33 and 64 a new movement was born.
> In those thirty years it got sufficient growth and credibility
> to become the largest religion the world has ever seen and
> to change the lives of hundreds of millions of people. It has
> spread into every corner of the globe and has more than
> two billion putative adherents.[4]

God's plan to overthrow such might and force was not sending a human army, but sending a child, born without privilege,
the son of a carpenter: "The Word became flesh and made his
dwelling among us. We have seen his glory, the glory of the One
and Only, who came from the Father, full of grace and truth. . . .
From the fullness of his grace we have all received one blessing

after another. For the law was given through Moses; grace and truth came through Jesus Christ" (John 1:14, 16–17 NIV).

The effect of this grace on the world has been colossal to say the least. Taking that grace away would be like removing the water from the human body and expecting it to survive. "Prior to the coming of Christ, human life on this planet was exceedingly cheap. Life was expendable prior to Christianity's influence. Even today, in parts of the world where the gospel of Christ or Christianity has not penetrated, life is exceedingly cheap."[5] That's why grace is often referred to as amazing. It doesn't just mean we are forgiven by God for our wrongdoing, but we are empowered to overcome the human tendency to be evil. Not only to commit evil acts but also to create evil cultures and structures to institutionalize and legitimize the evil people do.

GRACE AND RELIGION ARE TWO DIFFERENT THINGS

Skeptics are quick to confuse grace with religion and then rattle off every evil done by a religious group or religious person to prove their point. It is the classic case of broad-brushing practically 90 percent of the world's population (less than 10 percent are atheists/agnostics) based on the actions of relatively few people.

No one was better at confusing grace and religion than Christopher Hitchens, one of the most vocal atheists of our generation. In his book *God Is Not Great: How Religion Poisons Everything*, he painted a distorted picture of religion that is both scary and grossly unfair. To take all the worst parts of anything deemed religious and patch it together as reality is the tactic of a dirty politician, not someone attempting a serious historical commentary.

Educated at Oxford, Hitchens had a grasp of literature and a breadth of experience as a journalist that made him a formidable debating opponent to any would-be challenger from the Christian camp. Hitchens carried himself with the swagger of a boxing champion, toying with his opponents until he decided to dispose of them with a flurry of rhetoric and ridicule, aimed at his favorite target: the evils of religion. He went as far as calling Mother Teresa a fraud.[6] Hitchens's undefeated streak came to a screeching halt when he met William Lane Craig at Biola University in 2009. Craig may be the most formidable Christian apologist of our day. Craig opened his remarks by challenging Hitchens to a debate on philosophical grounds and not a debate about religion. "Mr. Hitchens obviously doesn't respect religion, maybe he'll respect philosophy," he challenged.[7] He proceeded to give the evidence for God from a philosophical and scientific point of view. Hitchens's railings against religion as his primary case against the existence of God were merely beating the air. Atheist magazines admitted, "Craig spanked Hitchens like a foolish child."[8]

Probably recognizing that he should not stray far from his antireligious theme, Hitchens found someone who was ready and willing to take him up on his challenge that religion had done more harm for the world than good. That challenger was Larry Taunton, director of the Fixed Point Foundation in Birmingham, Alabama. Taunton, a quintessential southern gentleman with an accent and an unassuming demeanor, could have led Hitchens to underestimate him as a debater. Instead, Hitchens met a formidable argument from Taunton on the evidence for the existence of God he calls the *Grace Effect*. Taunton's thesis is that the world has been dramatically impacted for good because of the influence of God's grace.

Taking seriously John Lennon's challenge to "Imagine" looks at not only the positive impact of the grace of God on society but also how life would be if these positive influences were removed. In the book *The Grace Effect*, Taunton explained it this way:

> It is, rather, my purpose to make a case for society's need of Christianity's gentling, inspiring, and culturally transforming power. I hope that through the narrative of our experience, readers will be given a glimpse into a world without faith in Jesus Christ and, as a consequence, have greater appreciation for what Christianity has given, is giving, and may give us still if we will mine the vast richness of it.[9]

Taunton tells the amazing story of Sasha, a young girl whom he and his family adopted from Ukraine. The grim condition of the godless society she was born into provides the contrast of what culture looks like when there are no signs of that grace. The oppression is palpable. On the other hand, grace can be palpable too.

> As one experiences grace in his own life, he extends grace to others. Through the inward transformation of the individual, there is a corresponding outward transformation of society. This is what I call the "grace effect." Simply defined, it is an observable phenomenon—*that life is demonstrably better where authentic Christianity flourishes.*[10]

Critics of Religion Have a Point

Make no mistake, regardless of the vast number of people claiming a belief in God and the enormous variety of religious expressions, the skeptics' aim is at the Christian faith. It's common to hear things like, "All Christians are hypocrites," to which I respond, "How many of these hypocrites do you personally know?" When they stop and count, they often realize they are taking the sins of a few people and marginalizing close to two billion others on the planet who would say they are believers in Jesus Christ.

The English reformer William Wilberforce, whose twenty-year campaign against slavery resulted in its abolition, wrote a book that shook his country in 1797. Its title was unusually long: *A Practical View of the Prevailing Religious System of Professed Christians, in the Higher and Middle Classes in This Country, Contrasted with Real Christianity*. It was later shortened to *Real Christianity*. He showed how the essence of Christianity had been replaced with mere moralism and religious obligation. This is exactly what Christ encountered during His earthly ministry. The prevailing religion had missed the point of the mercy and motive of God's laws. Jesus came to set the record straight by demonstrating the power of mercy and truth in action.

Therefore, the critics of religion are not always wrong in pointing out failures and deficiencies in Christianity. It is simply not the whole story. Just believing in God and knowing good and evil won't make you choose good over evil. That knowledge simply means you have no excuse. The Bible warns that even the demons believe in God and tremble (James 2:19).

But grace is the result of God's Spirit acting on the human

heart and empowering us to overcome evil. There are millions of real believers who are serving God faithfully as well as serving their fellow men through acts of kindness, integrity, and service. Through their lives, God has poured out His grace like a pipeline of fresh water into the desert. Because of this grace, life can arise from death.

AMAZING GRACE

One of the most well-known songs on the planet is "Amazing Grace," written by former slave trader John Newton and published in 1779:

> Amazing grace! How sweet the sound,
> That saved a wretch like me.
> I once was lost, but now am found,
> Was blind but now I see.

The reference to Newton being a "wretch" demonstrated the fact that he had seen how horrible his actions were in the light of God's grace and truth. You see, many accuse the God of the Bible of being hard or merciless. They point out acts of judgment, such as the flood of Noah, the ordering of the Hebrew armies to destroy the Canaanites when entering the promised land, or harsh penalties, such as stoning, for breaking God's law.

The accusation is that God couldn't be loving if He carried out such acts of judgment. First, God is a God of judgment as well as love. The two traits are not mutually exclusive. If God did not judge evil, then He wouldn't be truly loving. That is why the Bible says that "righteousness and mercy are the foundation of Your throne" (Psalm 89:14). Our hearts cry out for justice today. Think of TV shows such as *The People's Court* and *Divorce Court* where we witness the constant cry of men and women for someone to set the record straight and give them justice. When a crime of any kind is committed, we long for justice. The only Being in the universe who is wise enough to judge rightly and truly and knows the whole story is God. When we read of God acting in judgment toward a person, city, or nation, many fail to recognize the seriousness of the evil that was committed and the number of opportunities the wrongdoers had to change their ways before judgment came. God's mercy is more abundant than His judgments.

History records how debauched and depraved were the nations He ordered destroyed. The murder and disregard for human life through their detestable practices was only a part of how perverse they had become. When God acted in judgment, He was like a surgeon amputating a cancerous limb to save the entire body. These nations needed to be stopped as the Nazis of World War II did.

Even in the law of God where there were harsh punishments for evil, there were sacrifices that could be made to avoid the punishments. As always there was more mercy than judgment. Remember the story of Jonah? Most critics focus on whether he could have been swallowed by a whale and survived. Yet the real miracle was the grace God extended to a wicked city. God told Jonah to tell the city of Nineveh that they would be destroyed. Jonah ran away from this call, and that is how he found himself in the belly of that whale. When he finally obeyed and delivered the message from God to the people of Nineveh, they repented, and God spared them. Jonah was upset and said, "That is why I was so quick to flee to Tarshish. I knew that you are a gracious and compassionate God, slow to anger and abounding in love, a God who relents from sending calamity" (Jonah 4:2 NIV). In most cases severe warnings from God to mankind are balanced by the offer of grace. Amazing grace was demonstrated in the Old Testament as well as the New. That is why every year during Yom Kippur, the Jewish Day of Atonement, the book of Jonah is read in synagogues around the world.

You see, if you don't know how serious the consequences for your actions should be, you'll never really understand how amazing the grace is that God extends to you. That's why people today tend to minimize the sacrifice of Christ on the cross for our sins to pay for our salvation. They have never realized the eternal separation from God that we deserve for our sins and assume the reward of heaven is certainly theirs.

Take for example the belief in heaven or the afterlife. A majority of people will say they believe there is a place called heaven that exists beyond this physical life. They will also admit when you ask them that there are some who will probably not be in heaven because of their crimes here on earth. But who decides that? And furthermore, what is the criterion for getting into heaven? Being good? But how good is good enough?

No one *deserves* heaven. Our sins of pride, selfishness, lust, and rebellion have resulted in a separation between God and us. Only when we realize the punishment we deserve will we comprehend the magnitude of God's gift of salvation in Jesus Christ. Grace is God's unmerited favor toward us that He gave us through Christ's death and resurrection.

The Impact of Grace

The grace we have been talking about is the grace that is available to us as individuals. There is another type of grace called *common grace*. This describes the blessings that a culture receives because of God's blessing on an individual. It is why God causes the "sun to rise on the evil and the good, and sends rain on the righteous and the unrighteous" (Matthew 5:45 NIV). Many of the good things we take for granted are the result of God's grace that has mightily influenced the world we live in. Let's take a closer look at the Grace Effect upon our society.

1. Dignity of Life

The ancient world's devaluation of life logically follows from any worldview that rejects the true God as the author of life and reduces it to merely a natural explanation. Because God designed and created humanity, there is significance to our existence. We are more than chemicals and chance.

Can you place a real price on one human life? Remember the Chilean miners who were trapped twenty-three hundred feet below the earth for sixty-eight days? The world watched in amazement as the extensive efforts to rescue them paid off, as each one was extracted from a living nightmare and brought safely to the surface of the earth. Did anyone talk about how much those efforts cost or the man-hours spent to coordinate such an effort? There is no price too high when it comes to saving a human life. Where faith in God is present, so is this premium on human life. In the ancient world as today, abortion and infanticide were results of a materialistic view of life.

The impact of the grace that comes through the gospel is

clearly illustrated in the history of the Fiji Islands. There is no better before-and-after picture than this one.

> In 1844, H. L. Hastings visited the Fiji Islands. He found there that life was very cheap and that it was held in low esteem. You could buy a human being for $7.00 or one musket. That was cheaper than a cow. After having bought him you could work him, whip him, starve him, or eat him, according to your preference—and many did the latter. [Hastings] returned a number of years later and found that the value of human life had risen tremendously. One could not buy a human being for $7.00 to beat or eat. In fact, you could not buy one for seven million dollars. Why? Because across the Fiji Islands there were 1,200 Christian chapels where the gospel of Christ had been proclaimed, and people had been taught that we are not our own; that we have been purchased with a price, not with silver and gold, but with the precious blood of Jesus Christ.[11]

2. PROTECTION OF CHILDREN

It is difficult to imagine the world that a child faced two thousand years ago. "Roman girls married young, very often before puberty."[12] The most vulnerable had the fewest rights and least protection from the brutal world they entered. That vulnerability was exploited without backlash until Christ and His followers demonstrated the value of each child. Jesus warned of the harshest of judgments against those who would harm a child. "It would be better for him if a millstone were hung around his neck, and he were thrown into the sea, than that he should offend one of these little ones" (Luke 17:2).

Think about our world five hundred or even one hundred fifty years ago. Children worked in dangerous mines or in forced labor. Even today the sex-trafficking industry exploits millions of innocent children. Christ brought value to children by giving them honor and dignity and commanding that they be protected by the strong and not harmed.

A dismal fate awaited the youngsters of ancient Rome, Greece, India, and China. Herod slaughtered the innocents, but the advent of Christ was the triumph of the innocents. Jesus gathered the little children unto Himself, saying, "Let the little children come to Me, and do not forbid them" (Matt. 19:14a). His words gave a new importance to children, an importance that bestowed dignified treatment upon them.[13]

Abortion was normal two thousand years ago. The practices of the Greco-Roman world made killing the unborn or discarding newborns as common as discarding a bruised melon at the market. The grace of God released through the influence of His people on the culture made an enormous impact in that area. Both infanticide and abortion ended in the early church, which eventually led to its dramatic reduction in the entire Roman Empire.[14] The US Supreme Court justice who wrote the opinion on the landmark *Roe v. Wade* in 1973 that legalized abortion saw the connection between the value of human life and religious ideas: "If I were to appeal to religion, I would appeal to the religions of Rome and Greece."[15] Therefore, as a culture embraces the knowledge of the one true God, the respect for human life and the unborn rises. As that knowledge recedes, so does the attitude toward the protection of human life.

3. ELEVATION OF WOMEN

Jesus Christ was the unquestioned champion of women's rights and their value as joint-heirs of the grace of life (1 Peter 3:7). He ministered to women and lifted them up from subservience and gave them the dignity, value, and protection they deserved. This was certainly the opposite of how the ancient world saw them: "In ancient cultures, the wife was the property of her husband. . . . Plato taught that if a man lived a cowardly life, he would be reincarnated as a woman . . . Aristotle said that a woman was somewhere between a free man and a slave."[16]

The source of the change in this mind-set was the force of the Christian community and their view of women. "Although some classical writers claimed that women were easy prey for any 'foreign superstition,' most recognized that Christianity was unusually appealing because within the Christian subculture women enjoyed far higher status than did women in the Greco-Roman world at large."[17]

In nations where the gospel has not taken root, this low view of women is what you'll find. Adam Smith, writing in 1776, confirmed this in his book *The Wealth of Nations*: "In all great towns [of China] several [babies] are every night exposed in the street, or drowned like puppies in the water. The performance of this horrid office is even said to be the avowed business by which some people earn their subsistence."[18] This was just two hundred years ago, and it was before any influence of Jesus Christ was to begin to penetrate China.[19] In the twenty-first century, where the communist ideology still is embraced, the disregard for women is rampant in China. Its one-child policy places a premium on men as opposed to women. Young girls are many times unwanted, discarded, or turned over for adoption.

The Muslim world's treatment of women is at the center of an international debate. Women lack rights and are forced to keep themselves under a cloak of obscurity. While many Muslim women willingly accept this lifestyle, it is not an option for faithful adherents. During my teenage years when I lived for a short season with my parents in Algeria (a Muslim nation), we were told how the women had always been forced to walk behind their husbands. The only exception had been in times of conflict where land mines were hidden and posed a great danger to someone stepping on them. In those cases the women were allowed to walk in front.

4. ABOLITION OF SLAVERY

The abolitionist movement to free the slaves first in England and then in America was led by committed followers of Jesus Christ. William Wilberforce, an English parliamentarian, was influenced by John Newton and Methodist Church founder John Wesley to lead a twenty-year battle ending slavery in England. It was on his deathbed that he received the news that parliament had voted to outlaw completely this abhorrent practice. Thirty years later the United States would do the same.

Slavery was a fact of life in the ancient world. The slave population in ancient Athens reached eighty thousand, which was at least 40 percent of the population.[20] At least a quarter of the population of ancient Rome were slaves.[21] The Bible was the only source of opposition or restraint against the broad spectrum of human slavery. The book of Exodus records the radical deliverance of the Hebrew people from slavery in Egypt. Nothing like this had ever occurred in human history.

Slavery consisted of a broad spectrum of meaning in the Bible. It is used in different ways from economic slavery, to conquered peoples, to the idea of being a servant. Paul often referred to himself as a servant or slave of Jesus Christ. The gift of salvation is what Christ offers the world. Salvation from what, you ask? Slavery.

The Bible was definitive about the most insidious and harmful form of slavery, which is spiritual slavery. While abuse and man-stealing were condemned, there was the constant reference to redemption, or being bought out of slavery. Critics were upset with Jesus because He did not offer immediate political liberation from Roman oppression. He came, however, to liberate us in the spiritual sense. It is only when we are free internally from the bondage of sin that we are free indeed. All roads there lead back to the gospel since the gospel gives the promise of true freedom to the captives (Luke 4:18).

We find throughout the Bible the unfolding of God's plan for redemption. Even though it was a spiritual deliverance, a physical deliverance followed. God starts from the inside out. For instance, even though Hebrews were delivered physically from Egypt, they were still in spiritual bondage to sin. Jesus first liberated hearts, then the physical followed.

Most biblical slavery wasn't permanent and instructions were given on how someone's freedom could be obtained. The Bible also describes how slaves were to be treated humanely. These are some of the first examples of human rights in history! By the end of the New Testament, Paul would introduce the radical concept that slaves and masters were brothers (Galatians 3; Philemon).

Historian Rodney Stark summed it up this way: "And just as it was Christianity that eliminated the institution of slavery inherited from Greece and Rome, so too does Western democracy owe its essential intellectual origins and legitimacy to Christian ideals, not to any Greco-Roman legacy. It all began with the New Testament."[22]

5. EDUCATION

Of all the areas of life that the grace of God has touched, none is more obscured than the arena of education. The fact that the Bible is excluded from having any influence in much of the academic realm today may be one of the great ironies of history. The reason? It was the Judeo-Christian framework that emphasized glorifying God with all your mind as well as your heart. Skeptics argue that religion called people to retreat from study of the physical world, but the reality was just the opposite.

Universities in Europe were birthed out of the monastic schools in the Middle Ages and continued to serve Christian purposes.[23] The vast majority of colleges and universities in the United States also were started explicitly to promote the Christian faith. Most today, however, ignore their foundations and often teach against Christianity.[24] The very idea of the *university* is the concepts of *unity* and *diversity* being combined. The diversity relates to the numerous branches of knowledge from astronomy to zoology. What was the unifying factor that connected all these areas of study? An intelligent Creator.

With the invention of the printing press in the fifteenth century, books proliferated. Bible reading and study became the fuel that fired a reformation in the area of religion and education. Commoners now had knowledge within their grasps. Leaders of this reformation became known as *Protestants*, primarily because they believed that God's Word was the ultimate authority over popes and kings alike. Public education was largely birthed in Western Europe during the Protestant Reformation. Reformers Martin Luther and John Knox promoted universal public education since they saw it as indispensable to Christian faith.[25]

6. CHARITY

The generosity of the Western world is beyond dispute. In spite of the financial woes of late, the history of giving to those in need is a direct result of the Christian ethos that permeated the foundations of America and the free world. Christ didn't just bring salvation to the world; He taught that it is "more blessed to give than to receive" (Acts 20:35). This spirit of giving demonstrated that God was the ultimate source of wealth and that as people gave in His name they were honoring Him.

There may be some charities as of late that have been funded by skeptics due to the glaring omission of this kind of activity, but it does not logically follow their worldview. As Taunton explained:

> While atheists can perform works of charity or maintain high moral standards, history reveals that they *don't* with any degree of consistency. The statistics bear this out. According to a study by the Barna Group, Christians are the most charitable segment of the population. The same study indicates that the average evangelical gives almost *ten times* as much money to nonprofits as the average atheist.[26]

The movements in England to help the poor in the nineteenth century were prime examples of the motivation of Christians to demonstrate their faith through their benevolence. The drive to establish orphanages was led by believers in order to follow the instruction about what real religion is supposed to do. "If anyone among you thinks he is religious, and does not bridle his tongue but deceives his own heart, this one's religion is useless. Pure and undefiled religion before God and the Father is this: to visit orphans and widows in their trouble, and to keep oneself unspotted from the world" (James 1:26–27).

The very word *charity* actually comes from the Bible itself. In Greek it is the word *agape*, which is the term for God's love. This is distinct from the word *phileo*, which means brotherly love. To give from a heart of love, therefore, is a godly characteristic and demonstrates that a person is a true believer. To give without that kind of love is an empty, self-centered activity that has little value in an eternal sense: "And though I bestow all my goods to feed the poor, and though I give my body to be burned, and have not charity, it profiteth me nothing" (1 Corinthians 13:3 kjv).

7. Care for the Sick

The idea of helping the sick originated in the Old Testament and was expanded through the rise of Christianity. Jesus explicitly sent His followers to heal the sick (Matthew 10:8). He also commanded them to show great concern for the lowest and most vulnerable in society (Luke 14:13). Early Christians placed a great emphasis on hospitality (Romans 12:13), which even became a requirement for church office (1 Timothy 5:10).

For centuries large numbers of Christians have put this teaching into practice. "In homes, whole families adopted a style of life modeled on that of the Apostles; some devoted themselves to missionary works, others to Charitable deeds among the outcasts of Roman Society—lepers and others identified as 'unclean':

vagabonds, prostitutes, the homeless and destitute."[27] Christian homes and church meeting areas became primary care centers. When the persecution of Christians subsided in the fourth century, these efforts expanded into centers dedicated to the care of the sick, which were the forerunners of modern hospitals. "Churches everywhere took care of widows and orphans; tended the sick, the infirm, and the disabled; buried the dead, including indigents; cared for slaves; and furnished work for those who needed it."[28]

Other parts of the world offered similar care on a much smaller scale, but the extent of and emphasis on helping the poor, needy, and infirm were unprecedented in history. The witness of the church even drove the Roman emperor Julian to write in the fourth century, "Why then do we think that this is sufficient and do not observe how the kindness of Christians to strangers, their care for the burial of their dead, and the sobriety of their lifestyle has done the most to advance their cause? Each of these things, I think, ought really to be practiced by us."[29]

Looking around the world today, we clearly see that the building of hospitals and the care for the sick and dying are a part of the Christian mandate. Mother Teresa stepped into the hopeless situation of Calcutta, India, and sacrificially served the poorest of the poor. She explained why she felt this daunting task was her duty: "There is always the danger that we may just do the work for the sake of the work. This is where the respect and the love and the devotion come in—that we do it to God, to Christ, and that's why we try to do it as beautifully as possible."[30]

8. ETHNIC UNITY

One of the major story lines in world history is the conflict between ethnicities. Ethnic cleansing is still practiced as some nations attempt to eliminate minorities by force. Christianity introduced the idea that you be "brothers and sisters" with people from another ethnicity because of Christ. Noted historian Rodney Stark explained, "The natural tendency of man was to segregate into their own particular ethnic circles and exclude others on the basis of being lesser or even non-human. Christianity broke down the wall of division between ethnicities and promoted a message that all men could be brothers through Christ."[31]

The term *race*, in the way it attempts to define the distinctions between people groups, actually becomes twisted to the point of suggesting that people of different color are somehow different "kinds." When Darwin wrote *On the Origin of Species*, the subtitle was *By Means of Natural Selection, or The Preservation of Favored Races in the Struggle for Life*. Racism's roots are derived from this kind of naturalistic mind-set. The Bible on the other hand states clearly that God made the nations from "one blood" (Acts 17:26 KJV). This is why the Christian message offered hope to all nations through the gospel. Jew and Gentile, black and white, male and female were all equal in Christ (Galatians 3:28).

One of the most unique teachings of Christ is known as the parable of the good Samaritan. In response to His message of "love thy neighbor," He was asked, "Who is my neighbor?" (Luke 10:29). Jesus responded with a story of a man who was robbed and beaten and left for dead beside the road. He told how religious people as well as the man's own countrymen passed by and ignored him. The hero of the story was a man from Samaria, someone from a different, even despised ethnicity. He stopped and helped the man in need. We are told to imitate his actions and love others regardless of the color of their skin or their countries of origin.

9. Liberty and Freedom

Freedom and liberty are some of the most precious gifts of the gospel of grace. Kings, pharaohs, dictators, and tyrants fill the historical landscape with legacies of their oppression over those they ruled. Certainly they were not all bad. Many of these leaders were just and righteous. But the concept of these leaders themselves being subject to a higher law came from the revelation of Scripture. Christ is revealed as King of kings and Lord of lords. Every knee will bow and every tongue confess that Jesus Christ is Lord (Philippians 2:9–11), even the knees and tongues of kings. Everyone is accountable to God's law. This is the foundation of freedom from the arbitrary tyranny that was commonplace throughout history. Personal freedom had been born. Indeed, liberty is a God-given idea.

Rodney Stark wrote about John Locke, one of the key foundational thinkers whose writings shaped America's founding fathers. Locke put the spotlight on the real source of the freedom and liberty that distinguished America from every nation before it.

Many also express admiration for John Locke's seventeenth-century works as a major source for modern democratic theory, seemingly without the slightest awareness that Locke explicitly based his entire thesis on Christian doctrines concerning moral equality. Most textbook accounts of the birth of our nation now carefully ignore the religious aspect, as if a bunch of skeptics had written these famous lines from the Declaration of Independence: "We hold these truths to be self-evident, that all men are created equal, that they are endowed by their Creator with certain unalienable

Rights, that among these are Life, Liberty, and the pursuit of Happiness."[32]

10. STRONG SERVING THE WEAK

The overarching impact of the grace of God on civilization is that the weak are to be protected by the strong, not trampled or exploited. Some of the strongest judgments in Scripture come from oppressing the poor and the helpless. This is far from a view of man simply being another animal and wired by DNA to behave in such a primal manner. The Bible calls humanity to live another way, not to act like animals. Skeptics claim that a loving God couldn't have been responsible for the violent struggle that is so evident in the animal world. Think about it—what is normal for animals is abominable for humans. "We inescapably believe it is wrong for stronger human individuals or groups to kill weaker ones. If violence is totally natural why would it be wrong for strong humans to trample weak ones?"[33] This is another way of demonstrating who we are as human beings by contrast. We are not animals and are not to act like them. The strong serving the weak is the antithesis of evolution and natural selection, but it is the heart of the teaching of Jesus Christ.

By the grace of God our hearts as humans are marked by God's inward law. There is a sense of right and wrong that is communicated to us through the faculty of conscience. Without this sense of conscience, humanity reverts to the darkness so evident in the ancient world. Grace brought about a deep sense of civility and compassion for one another. To serve the elderly and give them honor instead of seeing them as possessing little use because they are no longer physically strong. To lack this kind of grace results in cruelty, which may be the defining trait of the culture that rejects God.

SUMMARY

Jesus told His followers, "You are the salt of the earth . . . You are the light of the world" (Matthew 5:13–14). As salt is a preservative necessary for our existence, the grace of God coming through the lives of believers is indispensable as well. Grace also flows to society at large through the truths of Scripture. This is what is known as the Grace Effect.

As we look back in history, we can see how grace has made a substantial difference in institutions as well as the lives of people. It is a distorted view of the past that paints religious faith as destructive or a deterrent of progress. Science rose out of a Christian worldview and so did education, hospitals, charity, and the concept of individual liberty. One of the most significant areas of influence of this amazing grace is in the area of human rights. Children were given their proper value and not treated as objects to be abused or discarded. People of faith have offered the loudest voices of opposition against the horrible practice of abortion as well. Grace has been the only refuge for the unborn. Women's rights have been advanced because of the principles of Scripture that defined women as joint-heirs with men of the grace of life. Jesus lifted women from the obscurity of a permanent underclass to their rightful place of dignity that is equal to men. Our world would be a dark place without the light of God's truth overwhelming the emptiness of unbelief.

10

LIVING PROOF

My God's not dead,
He's surely alive.
He's living on the inside,
Roaring like a lion . . .

—Newsboys, "God's Not Dead"[1]

One poll in 2006—fifteen years after the fall of the
Soviet regime—discovered that 84 percent of the
Russian population believed in God while only 16
percent considered themselves atheists.

—John Micklethwait and Adrian
Wooldridge, God Is Back[2]

IF YOU BELIEVED THE MAYAN CALENDAR, 2012 WAS SUPPOSED
to be the year that life on earth came to an end. That prediction
was obviously wrong and takes its place in infamy along with
the other countless guesses as to when the world would end.
Many people have made wild predictions of this sort and

that Christianity would eventually disappear. From Vladimir Lenin, the cofounder of communism, to John Lennon of the Beatles, who shared his views with Maureen Cleave in 1967: "Christianity will go. It will vanish and shrink. . . . We're more popular than Jesus now."[3] What history has shown is quite the opposite. The Christian faith is surging globally. In fact, some of the most remarkable growth is coming in places such as China and Russia where Christianity was once outlawed and atheism was institutionalized. Secular journalists such as John Micklethwait, editor-in-chief of *Economist* magazine, and Adrian Wooldridge, also of the *Economist*, confirmed this in their book *God Is Back*:

> Today an unsettling worry nags at Western liberals: what if secular Europe (and for that matter secular Harvard and secular Manhattan) is the odd one out? They are right to be worried. It now seems that it is the American model that is spreading around the world: religion and modernity are going hand in hand, not just in China but throughout much of Asia, Africa, Arabia and Latin America.[4]

What's so ironic about that quote is that there has been phenomenal growth of Christianity in every city that is described as a truly secular city. Tony Carnes, who has studied the trends in religion in New York City for the last thirty years, is the editor of the website *A Journey Through NYC Religions*. Tony said emphatically, "This is the time of the rise of faith—it is determining our headlines both good and bad."[5]

I sat with Tony for several hours and heard the amazing progress of the gospel in the city. "In 1979 there were only around eight evangelical churches in Manhattan, and most of them were fairly weak. Today there are over two hundred churches, and most of them are vibrant." The overall presence of various religious groups has prompted him to call New York, "The Post-Secular City." A truly remarkable turn of events. This turnaround is taking place as individuals of all ages, educational levels, and cultural backgrounds encounter the truth and reality of the gospel and consider its claims objectively.

I must mention that as I write this I'm sitting in a hotel in the heart of Times Square. It's the very hotel where I stayed on Sunday nights for most of 2002, as we were beginning our outreach to New York in the wake of 9/11. Over the last decade, I have had a front-row seat to watching people find faith in a city that common knowledge says God has abandoned. It reminds me that no one is ever too lost, and it is never too late for any person, city, or nation to turn to God. After all, because He is the Creator of the nations, they will indeed flourish when they recognize Him.

> All nations whom You have made
> Shall come and worship before You, O LORD,
> And shall glorify Your name. (Psalm 86:9)

AFRICA

The growth of Christianity is particularly explosive overseas. Africa is a prime example. In 1900, Africa was 8 percent Christian. In 2000, it was at 45 percent and is still growing.[6] Frans Olivier, who works as a campus minister in Cape Town, South Africa, sees this rise in faith among university students. "Hundreds of students are coming to Christ each month in South Africa. These are people who have heard the arguments both for and against God and are choosing to believe."[7]

Nation after nation in Africa is experiencing a spiritual awakening. From the small, such as Burundi and the Central African Republic, to the large, such as Nigeria and Ethiopia, there is a great advance of the gospel taking place. Sam Aiyedogbon from Nigeria writes a regular column for a major newspaper in Lagos and is senior pastor of a church there. He described the phenomenal expansion of the gospel this way: "In Nigeria, the message of Christ is making the difference in the lives of millions. In spite of widespread corruption in every area of society. The gospel is giving people hope that real transformation is possible."[8] In one of the poorest nations of Africa, Sierra Leone, hundreds of new churches are being opened each year. Not only are churches being planted, but also hospitals and schools are being opened. Dramatic results are being seen as people embrace the grace of the gospel and refuse to become victimized by AIDS. There is no question that the abstinence movement is energized by the power of the Holy Spirit. I witnessed firsthand the growing faith among young people in Egypt. Though the nation has been shaken with political turmoil, Christianity continues to grow. Shaddy Soliman, one of the new generation of Christian leaders who took me to Egypt in 2008, explained, "You won't hear about the spiritual awakening in the media, but there is a growing movement of Christianity in Egypt and the entire Arab world."[9] Shaddy is a part of a media outreach to the Arab world called *Al Karma*. They are broadcasting throughout the Muslim world and are receiving massive traffic to their website requesting information, Bibles, and help in learning more about the Christian faith.

For the longest time geographic isolation helped Muslim governments keep their people from exposure to Christianity. Most Muslims in the Arabic countries never had access to the Bible or Christian teaching due to very strict laws. That forced isolation is faltering, and the freedom the gospel brings is rushing in.

ASIA

In 1984, my college roommate Steve Murrell and I, along with our new wives Deborah and Jody and my four-month-old daughter Elizabeth, journeyed to the Philippines to conduct a summer outreach. Accompanied by sixty American students, we conducted nightly meetings and daily discussions with the students in the University Belt of Metro Manila.

We contended with the anger and unrest of political upheaval against the oppressive regime of Ferdinand Marcos. The meetings we held would witness an abundance of tears, not from a spiritual experience, but from the tear gas that had been released in the streets to disperse the crowds. In the midst of the turmoil, hundreds of students turned to Christ. The openness was so compelling that Steve and Deborah decided to stay and minister in this needy city. In 2013, that small group has grown to more than sixty thousand attending Victory Christian Fellowship.[10] As Ferdie Cabiling, a pastor and senior evangelist in VCF, described: "Each year thousands of students are turning to God because of the overwhelming evidence that Christ is indeed the truth. From the richest to the poorest, our nation is being touched by God."[11]

In the 1950s, China kicked out all Western missionaries, and the communist dictator Mao Zedong exchanged Bibles for his *Little Red Book* of communist teaching. Millions of people lost their lives as any potential opposition was eliminated. In spite of the brutal persecution, Christianity thrived. Once again dismissing the myth that faith in God is a crutch, millions of people suffered greatly rather than deny the living Christ. David Aikman, author of *Jesus in Bejing*, attests to this extraordinary explosion of faith in this unlikely place. "The growth of Christianity in China has been astounding. From numbering just a few million in the 1950s to estimates between 80 million and 120 million today."[12]

The same year we journeyed to the Philippines, we also began an outreach to the nation of Korea. It was a very special year in that nation's history, marking the centennial of evangelical Christianity. In 1900, Korea had no Protestant church, and the country was deemed impossible to penetrate. Today Korea is 25 percent Christian[13] with seven thousand churches in Seoul alone.[14]

In fact, more than one million people gathered in Yoido (the Manhattan Island of Seoul) in 1984 to celebrate the advance of the gospel in that once predominately Buddhist nation. I had the honor to speak for a few moments in front of that vast audience. It is still one of the highlights of my life. If you have ever been in a giant stadium to witness a sporting event, chances are the crowd didn't exceed one hundred thousand. Imagine more than 1.2 million people in one place, fervently praying, singing, and listening to messages all day about the power and love of Jesus Christ.

Those who attend gatherings of skeptics, which draw a few thousand, have no concept of the great number of believers around the world. Singapore contains multiple Christian congregations with tens of thousands of members. Its neighbor Indonesia, the largest Muslim nation in the world, has experienced tremendous growth as well. The number of Christians in that country has grown from 1.3 million, forty years ago, to more than 36 million today.[15] Massive churches with membership numbering in the tens of thousands are common.

The majority of the world has no idea of the magnitude of these numbers. With all the fears of potential acts of terror from the ranks of radical Islam, God has raised up a people who are praying for His hand of intervention as well as fearlessly proclaiming the gospel of Christ in the face of this very real threat. In fact, in virtually every part of the world where the perception is overwhelmingly negative, such as Iran, God is still working and building His church that He promised the "gates of hell shall not prevail against" (Matthew 16:18 KJV).

EUROPE

Signs of spiritual renewal are also appearing in Europe. "Nevertheless there are signs that the same forces that are reviving religion in America—the quest for community in an increasingly atomized world, the desire to counterbalance choice with a sense of moral certainty—are making headway in Europe."[16] In the UK, though attendance in the Church of England may be in decline, there are churches popping up all over the kingdom. This year I spent several days training students at Imperial College in London to share the gospel with *The God Test*. Possibly the foremost Christian apologist of our

time, William Lane Craig who holds two PhDs in both philosophy and theology, challenged Richard Dawkins to debate
his book *The God Delusion* at Oxford. Dawkins was a no-show.
Instead Craig spoke to a full house at the Sheldonian Theater at
Oxford and laid bare the empty arguments of the book. Dawkins
had spearheaded a bus campaign a few years before with signs
that read, "There's probably no God." In the days following
the scheduled challenge at Oxford, buses had a different sign,
"There's probably no Dawkins," referring to Dawkins's refusal
to debate Craig.[17]

Pastor Wolfgang Eckleben, who oversees six congregations
in the London area, told me recently, "After almost twenty years
in London, I see an unprecedented openness to the gospel. As
Jesus said, 'the harvest is plentiful but the laborers are few.' We
simply need more people who can come here and help us reach
out."[18] Over 2.5 million people have taken the Alpha Course,
which was developed at Holy Trinity Church in Brompton by
Nicky Gumbel.

Gareth Lowe, a young South African living in Berlin and
leading an outreach to the university students in that historic
city, sees the beginnings of spiritual openness in Germany:

> While there has not been an abandonment of rationalism
> and secularism in Germany, there is a growing awareness
> that it has not and cannot answer the deepest questions of
> life. There is a growing hunger for spiritual experiences, for
> meaning and purpose, and for deep relationships. It could
> be that Germany is at the early stages of a great spiritual
> awakening.[19]

South America

Though South America has historically been predominately Catholic, there has been a dramatic rise in evangelical Christianity. There are conservatively one hundred million evangelical believers, as well as millions of Catholics. In Brazil more than one million have gathered for concerts featuring Christian artists conducting massive worship services. Churches with ten thousand or more members are commonplace in Brazil, Argentina, Chile, and Colombia.

In Mexico, Bob Sanders and David Angulo conduct an outreach in the Baja peninsula. They have distributed over 100,000 Bibles and Purple Books (a Bible study guide) throughout the area. They have seen the crime rate fall as the knowledge of God's Word saturates the hearts and minds of the people.

In nations throughout Latin and South America, millions of Christians are experiencing powerful, life-changing encounters with God. As a result many churches are growing dramatically and driving cultural renewal in their cities.

North America

The prediction of the end of Christianity is proving to be wishful thinking on the part of secularists who want to see all public displays of faith eliminated. Though America was founded on the principles of freedom of speech and religion, many want freedom *from* religion. There has been a decline in North America in overall church attendance, but the numbers are misleading.

Nominal Christianity is fading, but evangelical Christianity is thriving. Ed Stetzer of LifeWay Research has confirmed this: "Mainline Protestantism and nominal Christianity are in decline, but robust evangelicalism is growing and is the future of the North American Church. In the years to come, evangelical Christianity will continue to be marked with committed Christians."[20]

A Barna research poll indicated that the percentage of Americans who fall under the category of Born-Again Christians has actually increased from 31 percent in the early 1980s to 45 percent today.[21] Theological moderates have transitioned to theological liberals or evangelicals, who both have clear messages and convictions. Members of mid-sized churches have migrated either to small spiritual communities or to megachurches.[22] The church in America is still strong and vibrant. Thirty years ago there were relatively few congregations that exceeded one thousand in attendance. Today there are over seven thousand. From the enormous conferences that fill stadiums to massive displays of faith at the Washington Mall, the Christian faith continues to flourish in this land. America is a nation that firmly believes in God as the book *God Is Back* confirms: "The most thorough study of American religious beliefs, the U.S. Religious Landscape Survey by the Pew Forum on Religion and Public Life, demonstrates clearly that the world's most powerful country is also one of the most religious."[23]

Let's look beyond the numbers into the very lives of people who have been impacted by the message of the gospel. There are literally millions with testimonies of how they came to faith from unbelief. Many even testify to experiencing supernatural miracles.[24]

Though many throughout history have turned their backs on God, many more have turned to Him. The majority of those who turn from Christ do so not because of a lack of evidence, but because of a lack of effort. They simply quit trying, or others stop trying to reach them. Living in darkness is much easier than living in the light; so are apathy and indifference toward others. That's why nominal Christianity is diminishing, but the real faith is growing. This kind of faith is not a particular church or denomination but consists of genuine believers who have yielded themselves to following Christ.

PERSONAL STORIES OF ATHEISM TO FAITH

Each story is unique, each life important from the poor to the wealthy, from the educated to the illiterate. The stories I highlight here are, for the most part, not of people who were brought up as Christians. In these testimonies we see how faith can grow in the most challenging of circumstances.

MING WANG: A CHINESE ATHEIST AT HARVARD
Graduate of Harvard and MIT

The existence of God is demonstrated powerfully in the amazing journey of a dear friend of mine, one of the world's foremost laser eye surgeons, Ming Wang, MD, PhD. He is a Harvard and MIT honors graduate and one of a small number of cataract and LASIK surgeons in the world who holds a doctorate in laser physics. He has performed well over fifty-five thousand cataract and LASIK procedures, including over four thousand on fellow doctors. Dr. Wang performed the world's first 3-D LASIK and was one of the first surgeons in the United States to perform laser cataract surgery.

Growing up during the tumultuous Cultural Revolution in China, Ming was denied the opportunity of going to school. Instead, he played the Chinese violin, called the *er-hu*, in an effort to avoid deportation to a poor part of the country, where he would have faced a life of poverty and hard labor. This devastating fate fell upon millions of youth in China during that time. A chance meeting with a visiting American professor helped Ming come to America. He arrived in the United States in 1982 with fifty dollars, a Chinese-English dictionary in his pocket, and a big American dream in his heart. Ming truly appreciated the freedom and opportunity to learn in this country, and he worked hard, becoming one of the world's most renowned laser eye specialists today. "God is not dead. He is alive and well and more powerful than ever before, including in the scientific community." Dr. Wang continued:

> I came to know Jesus Christ because I did not find in science the answers to life's questions for which I was searching. Actually, the more I learned about science, the more—not less—evidence that I saw of God's creation and design. For example, as I was becoming an ophthalmologist and learning about the inner workings of the eye, the amazing and logical arrangement of photoreceptors, ganglion cells, and neurons, I realized that there is absolutely no way that an intricate structure such as a human eye could ever evolve from a random compilation of cells. The very complexity of a human eye is, in fact, the most powerful evidence of the existence of God.

While Ming was at Harvard Medical School and MIT, a Christian pediatric professor sensed the opportunity to influence then-atheist Ming and took him out for lunch. "What is across the street?" he asked.

"A car," Ming responded.

"What is the difference between a car and human brain?"

Ming answered confidently, "A brain is much more complex."

The professor then made this critical point: "Can you imagine a random pile of scrap metals assembling themselves into a car?"

"No!"

"Then, how about a human brain? Could it assemble itself?"

To this day, Ming feels deeply indebted to the professor, whom he admired scientifically and who cared enough about young Ming, sensed his struggle with science, and pointed out the way to Jesus Christ. Ming says now that he has found the Lord for himself, he needs to do what the professor did years ago in helping him, namely, use his scientific influence and medical reputation to encourage the next generation of young doctors to search for truth and find answers in Christianity. "As a Christian and a scientist, I do believe that faith and science are compatible and can work together. Actually it is through uniting rather than separating them and through perseverance and believing that God has created this world, and it is without contradictions, that we can actually find new, unexpected, and more powerful solutions to the problems in our lives."[25]

Joe Marlin: An Atheist with Compassion
MD and PhD Candidate at New York University

Joe is one of those people who simply wants to make a difference in life. More specifically, he wants to help others. He dispels the myth that atheists are all angry people who care about nothing but themselves. After graduating from Cal Berkley, he was accepted at New York University into a program that allowed him to earn his PhD and MD simultaneously. Though an atheist, his philosophy on creation was simple: "something happened." He describes his beliefs as rooted in the *chaos theory*, the idea that all life's occurrences are interconnected, though the cause-and-effect link between them is often obscured or unknown.

It was in a classroom at NYU where he started questioning his atheism. "Sitting in class one day there was this deep sense of the reality of God that swept over me. It was as if God were speaking to my mind, 'I am real.'" Months would go by before he told anyone of this experience.

After a series of conversations about God and spiritual things, he was invited to a Manhattan church, Morningstar New York. There he met Bruce Ho, a pastor who had relocated from Honolulu after the 9/11 tragedy. "Bruce met with me every week for two months. He listened to me and would give me straightforward answers. What really touched my heart was that he would tell me every time we completed a session together, 'Joe, I'm really excited about the things God is doing in your life.' Even though I wasn't a Christian yet, I knew that there was more to our existence than 'something happened.' There is actually a Someone."

Joe had read *The God Delusion* by Richard Dawkins and other books that talked about the Bible being merely a book of myths. He started reading the Gospels for himself and found them completely opposite from how the skeptics portrayed them. "One day I started praying and sensing that same presence I felt in the classroom months before. This time, I knew that it was Jesus. So I spoke to Him and said, 'Hello, I'm Joe.'"

I asked him in the interview if Jesus said anything back to him. He said, "No, He didn't. But I knew that He knew me."[26]

BRIAN MILLER: A PHYSICIST WITH FAITH
Graduate of MIT and Duke

Dr. Miller began his undergraduate education at MIT wanting to understand how the universe works and to pursue the deepest questions about human existence. To fulfill the first goal, he majored in physics. To pursue the second, he had lengthy discussions about the meaning of life with his friends, signed up for a freshman course on the Bible, and read Richard Dawkins's book *The Blind Watchmaker*. The Bible professor claimed that the stories in Scripture were mostly fictional accounts written to advance the agendas of the authors. Dawkins's book claimed that the apparent design in nature was an illusion and the result of the blind forces of evolution. As a consequence, God most likely was a myth.

One night Brian confessed he did not know if God existed, but if God did exist, He needed to show him clearly what was true. Brian further explained to me in our interview that as a scientist, he could believe only what was proven true with clear-cut evidence. That night began a long journey that led him through a careful study of science, philosophy, history, archaeology, anthropology, and a few other disciplines. Through his studies, he learned that science plainly pointed to God's existence and His care for humanity. Brian also realized the Gospels are well supported by historical evidence, and the resurrection of Jesus is virtually undeniable by any rational standard. God not only satisfied Brian's need for clear evidence but also performed miracles: Brian saw his Christian friends supernaturally heal the sick in

Jesus' name, and at times he heard God's voice in subtle yet transformative ways. He was personally experiencing God's love.

Since finishing his PhD in physics, Dr. Miller has spoken to hostile crowds on university campuses across the world on the evidence for the Christian faith. Through these experiences, he has increasingly understood that the beliefs of skeptics are typically based more on blind faith in naturalistic philosophy than on hard evidence.[27]

Dr. Jo Goodson: A Childhood as an Atheist
Graduate of Imperial College, London

It has been my privilege to reach out to campuses in London, England, since 1981. It has been challenging, to say the least, but the testimonies of the transforming power of the gospel have been amazing. None of those stories is more encouraging than Joanna Goodson; here it is in her own words:

> I was brought up in an atheist household. It wasn't overly spoken about; we simply didn't bother going to church. We didn't talk about God—why would we? We understood that other people believed in God and felt that was fine if it helped them get through life. Luckily we were well educated and financially stable and perhaps believed we were a little smarter than others, so we didn't need to invent some "fantasy God" to help us get through life. We were happy, good people, and we believed that was enough.
>
> Looking back, I can see times in my childhood when my siblings and I were actually curious about God. I remember finding a Gideon Bible in a hotel room and making a decision to read it from beginning to end in one night.

I was about twelve at the time. I fell asleep halfway through Deuteronomy and never thought anything more of it. Was this intellectual curiosity, or God trying to communicate with me? Even now, I'm not sure. I remember my brother coming home from school at the age of seven and saying he believed that every word of the Bible was true. My parents didn't have to take him to the side and explain how foolish this was; my sister and I did a fine job over dinner of beating it out of him with ridicule and insult, calling him "naïve." He now considers himself a Buddhist, so I guess you could say we weren't able to make him a skeptic when it came to spiritual things.

The change for me happened when I went to university at eighteen, an arrogant undergrad who had it all figured out, both life and religion. I met a dynamic Christian with dreadlocks and a winning personality. Everyone loved him and wanted to hang out with him. He was open about his faith and didn't drink, although he did go clubbing and danced for fun. What's more, he didn't sleep around. That didn't make sense to me. He was well educated, well liked, and not in need of a crutch. He was an anomaly in my understanding of life.

We discussed religion a lot. I thought I could convince him that he was being silly and obviously clinging to something he had been taught in childhood but never really critically assessed. He was an adult who still believed in Santa Claus, and I would show him the truth; because at his age it was cruel not to know. As our discussions progressed, I was shocked to find that I was the one who had never really thought things through. I was the one who had never challenged what I had been told in terms of the atheistic view of life. This didn't automatically make me a Christian; it just opened my eyes to the possibility that God was real.

It was when Natty, my dynamic Christian friend, took me to church that things fell into place. I wasn't convinced by any fancy arguments; I was challenged to consider the possibility that Christ had indeed died for me. Eventually God met me where I was, hiding at the back of a church service in London, asking, *Is there anybody really up there?* I knew when I finally came to a place of faith that God had indeed done so much for me that I had simply ignored. A deep sense of gratitude has been in my heart since that day.

My life changed instantaneously, and it would take many volumes to explain how. It wasn't about stopping the drugs and the sex and simply becoming a good person. It was about living for God, sincerely wanting to change as well as to see the world changed for Him and His honor. Ten years later I am married with a son and a daughter on the way. I am a doctor and a mathematician. My thesis at university was on proving the existence of God through mathematical logic. I really only proved that you can't prove it either way. That's good enough for me; it forces people to take a step of faith, one way or the other. I hadn't realized I had taken that step in the wrong direction until someone challenged me on it.

I am content, at peace, and can trust others because God puts His trust in me. I can forgive others because God has forgiven me. I am strong because God gives me His strength. I can deal with the bad times because I have something to put my hope in. I smile because I know that whatever my world may look like, God is working all things for my good. My family has yet to believe in God, but amazingly they want to. They tell me they want the faith that I have. My mother has often expressed a wish that my brother and sister would find a nice church like I attend. She thinks the happiness, friendliness, and the ability to deal with the challenges of life come from church. I know they really come from Jesus. When she sees this, she will believe too.[28]

Brant Reding: An Atheist Who Took His Doubts Seriously
Canadian Student

Brant Reding is one of the brightest minds I have ever met. He was a young business leader in Calgary, Canada, and a very sincere follower of Christ when we met in the early 1990s. It was hard to believe that this guy had been an atheist.

I asked him to explain the story of his journey from unbelief to faith. He began by telling me of a conversation he had his freshman year with a person of faith while attending the University of Calgary, where he was challenged to take his doubts seriously.

I was presenting my best arguments against belief in God, and yet this man threw it back in my face. He said, "I can't answer all your objections, but I think you should do one thing: why don't you take some time and disprove the existence of God. Whatever you determine, live your life in that truth."

"That should be easy," I responded. "Every university

and academic in the world would agree with me: religion and God is simply a crutch, an opiate of the masses, an ancient superstitious attempt to explain life."

This was the conversation that prompted me to take a semester off university. I set out to settle this issue, to disprove the existence of God and live with a clear conscience. The intellectual wrestling proved longer than a semester, however. Disproving God's existence was not as simple and as "logical" as I had first assumed.

On campus I had evolved from a simple skeptic into a strong cynic, describing myself as an atheist who simply wanted to have fun and be a nice guy. By second year I had successfully talked a number of nice people out of their so-called faith. It was easy; no one had any substantial proof for their beliefs.

I had not been raised in religion; I had never opened a Bible or a Qur'an. I had never attended a religious gathering up to that point in my life. I was not angry or bitter with religious people, just perplexed by their blind-faith ignorance that seemed archaic and devoid of reason. Any childlike wonderings of God I may have had as a child were firmly filed away under the weight of reason, science, and individualism.

I began my quest reading and researching, and I began to discover there where two viewpoints: the skeptics I expected but also many respected academics, scientists, and philosophers who had no problem integrating faith in God within pure intellectual pursuit. Frankly it confused me. How could intellectuals suggest that God exists when our five rational senses confirmed otherwise? You cannot *see* God or *hear* God; you can't *touch* or *taste* or *smell* God. It seemed obvious to me: He, therefore, could not exist.

At one point in my research, a wise academic kindly dropped a pencil into my hand from a foot high. "What caused the pencil to fall?" he asked.

"Gravity," I replied.

"What does gravity look like? Can you see it?" he pressed. "What's its texture? Can you feel it? What odor does gravity have, what sound does gravity make, what does it taste like? This force that holds the entire universe together is invisible, undetectable to your five senses, and yet you live your life subject to its reality, even if you can't prove it with your five human senses."

I honestly had to admit the possibility of a creative force in the universe was feasible and reasonable. Logically that meant there might even be a reason for the universe, a purpose for life and consciousness; and if that was possible, then there might even be a reason and purpose for me. That thought was honestly very unnerving. I had lived twenty-three years in my "matrix"; life was simply the product of evolving genetic processes—lucky mud—and we make life what it is. There is no grand purpose or reason; just live and let live.

It became clear there was no conclusive evidence to disprove God scientifically; rather, the circumstantial evidence was stacking up in the other direction. I shifted to look at the world's religions. They claimed God was real, so why not look into them? It seemed obvious to me: all the God-centered belief systems would, in fact, prove my understanding: they were all concocted, man-made belief systems rooted in superstition.

I chose to focus on the key individuals, not the pot-
pourri of confusing religions. The obvious characters
included Muhammad, Joseph Smith, Siddhartha Gautama,
and Jesus, among others. It was soon evident that the person, life, and teachings of Jesus floated to the top of all the
others. Most of the other groups pointed either directly or
indirectly to Him.

I dug further. A turning point for me came after reading C. S. Lewis's *Mere Christianity* and Josh McDowell's
Evidence That Demands a Verdict. The weight of evidence
and the sincere people I was now accustomed to watching
live their faiths were impossible to ignore. On a cold, minus-
thirty-degree winter day, sitting in my car, I took a step and
out loud asked God, "If You are real, if all this is true, make
Yourself real to me." The invisible became tangible immediately. Everything changed inwardly. The words of Blaise
Pascal, the famous mathematician, came true for me: inside
of every man there is a God-shaped vacuum that nothing
can fill except the Creator. I was a skeptic turned believer.
What I had set out to disprove had in fact been proved. It
took a few years, but now I would not change those years of
searching for anything.[29]

Jim Munroe: The Illusion of Unbelief
Professional Illusionist

Jim Munroe is a psychological illusionist and a self-proclaimed
"skeptic from birth." From a very young age, Jim had a unique knack
for making people believe something was happening when it really
wasn't. His ability to create false belief in his audiences as an illusionist left Jim skeptical about all forms of religion and spirituality.

While studying psychology and philosophy at the University of Texas, he decided that he'd answer the God question for himself, once and for all. He studied the claims of all major world religions and philosophies. His one question for God, through all of his study, remained the same: "God, if You are real, You need to make Yourself so real that You can't be ignored." Little did he know, his prayer was going to be answered, probably in the way he least desired or expected.

In 2009, he was diagnosed with a rare blood cancer. At one point the doctors told Jim that the leukemia would kill him in only two months. He started treatment at MD Anderson Cancer Center in Houston and had to undergo a bone-marrow transplant. The catch to this transplant was finding someone who matched Jim's blood perfectly and who would be willing to donate his marrow on Jim's behalf. After searching for a match in a nine-million-person international database, there was only one who could save him from this biological disease. Jim explained that he could see a direct comparison to the gospel message of Jesus Christ. Jesus was the One with the perfect blood who could substitute His healthy blood (in a spiritual sense) for our hopelessly diseased condition.

Upon completion of his successful cancer-curing bone-marrow transplant, Jim saw that God had indeed answered his prayer and revealed Himself in an undeniable way. "The doctors told me that I had been given a second birthday. The nurses told me that I was like a baby inside the womb all over again." Through his amazing journey, Jim claims his skeptical nature "was overwhelmed by the realities of Christ." Now Jim leads thousands to the Lord and to the bone-marrow donor registry through his remarkable story.[30]

Dr. Augusto Cury: Intense Atheism Implodes
Psychiatrist and Author

I met Dr. Augusto Cury, a Brazilian, while he was in the United States writing a book. A world-renowned psychiatrist and a prolific author, he has written thirty books with more than forty million copies sold worldwide. His teachings and insight have impacted people in more than sixty nations. It is my honor to call him a friend.

I was one of the most committed atheists who ever walked this earth—maybe more than Nietzsche, who wrote about the death of God; or Karl Marx, who wrote that religion is the opium that numbs humanity; or Freud, who wrote that seeking for God is to seek for a father protector. The great majority of atheists, in reality, are antireligious. In contrast to them, I was a scientific atheist.

By theoretically researching one of the latest scientific frontiers, the nature and limits of the process of building thoughts, God was to me fruit of the highest engineering complexity of thought, produced by a brain impassioned by life that would resist its chaos in the solitude of a tomb. It is probable that I arrived at the ultimate stage of atheism. Nevertheless, since my theory contemplated not only the construction of thought but also the training process of thinkers, I studied the minds of great men and women to see how they broke out of the prison of the routine and fanned their intelligence and what tools they used to produce their great ideas.

As a psychological atheist I decided to study a man called Jesus. I began with His biographies, called the

232

Gospels, in various versions. I expected to find an ordinary person without great intellect or emotion, produced by a group of Galileans who needed a hero to free them from the oppression of Tiberius Caesar, the Roman emperor. But my detailed analysis left me perplexed, astonished, and fascinated because, clearly, I understood that no mind could concoct an individual with His personality characteristics. He didn't fit into human imagination. Hundreds of the examples I investigated confirmed this thesis. I cite just two.

First: the psychological and sociological phenomena occurring at His Last Supper. He chose one of the worst classes of young men as His students or disciples to form an excellent breed of thinkers. It was a very risky choice. They had grave personality defects, such as the neurotic need for power and control over others and the social attitude of always being right. At the Last Supper, knowing that He would soon be dead, Jesus still needed to teach them important lessons about generosity, altruism, and social tolerance. Then, to my psychological, sociological, and psycho-pedagogical astonishment, He controlled His dramatic stress, opened the portals of His mind, got some water and a towel, and began to wash the feet of those young men who had given Him only headaches. With unique intelligence He bombarded their neurotic needs, causing them to re-edit the film of their unconsciousness and rewrite their histories. *Never has anyone so great made Himself so small in order to make the small great.*

Second: when Judas Iscariot betrayed Jesus, one would expect that He would close the circuit of His memory and react instinctively, aggressively, succumbing to attacks of rage or fear. But to the perplexity of human science, He governed His intense frustration, gazed upon His traitor, and had the courage to say, "Friend, why are you here?"

In the first place, Jesus called Judas *friend*, which is notable, indicating that He was not afraid of being betrayed but feared losing a friend. In the second place, He asked a question—*a question is the beginning of wisdom in philosophy.* Jesus didn't give a quick answer, but by His question made Judas internalize, question himself, and find his own answer. He wanted minds that think, not slaves. He solemnly showed that a person is more important than his error. *Never in history has a betrayed person treated the traitor with such dignity.*

There is no historic precedent for the characteristics displayed in Jesus' personality. Freud, one of the most brilliant minds of humanity, reacted completely differently. He banished Jung and Adler from the psychoanalytic family for contradicting his ideas.

I was so fascinated by Jesus' intelligence that I wrote one thousand pages in five volumes about it. One of Christianity's greatest errors was to study Jesus Christ only from the angle of spirituality and not the complex functions of His mind. World education would be different if it incorporated the tools that He used to train thinkers. I don't defend any religion, but the science that has led many to atheism convinced me fourteen years ago that there is a God found behind the curtains of time and space.[31]

Summary

The living proof of God's existence is the continued testimony of His working in the lives of people around the world. Regardless of age, ethnicity, or even cultural context, the message of Jesus Christ continues to be the hope of the nations.

As Christians live out their faith amid the confusion, boredom, and fear of the twenty-first century, there has never been a better time to demonstrate the reality of God through His presence that empowers us to go through the toughest of times with the greatest of hope. The unbelieving world attempts to dismiss people's positive testimonies as admissible evidence for the existence of God, yet they are quick to use the painful stories of others as proof God doesn't exist. There are countless stories of those who went through painful experiences that would cause others to point a finger toward the sky and ask, "Where was God?" But, instead, these believers found great grace and comfort through God in the midst of their trying circumstances.

In May 2011, tornadoes rampaged through Alabama. In the wake of the crisis, hundreds of people descended on the state to provide food, water, and aid to the victims of these tragic events. I went to the home of an elderly couple who had survived a direct hit from a tornado while cowering in a closet. When they opened the closet door after the tornado had passed by, their entire house was gone. I actually stood in the very closet they had hid in and marveled at the sight of their home and their neighbor's home being swept away in a moment. This precious couple looked at me with a smile and said, "When people ask us, 'Where was God during those tornadoes?' we say, 'He was in that closet with us.'"

CONCLUSION

SEEKING GOD

There is enough light for those who desire only to
see and enough darkness for those of a contrary
disposition.

—BLAISE PASCAL[1]

God . . . is a rewarder of those who diligently seek Him.

—HEBREWS 11:6

GOD'S NOT DEAD. WE HAVE LOOKED CLOSELY AT REAL
evidence for His existence, at nine key proofs covered in chapters 2 through 10 that present a solid foundation for believers of all ages and educational backgrounds. Any one of these proofs is enough to demonstrate that God exists.

The atheist and skeptic must tear down every single one of the proofs and then establish their own evidence that all of life and existence is not a product of intelligent planning and is therefore ultimately an accident. If any one of these points is left standing, then the case for unbelief fails. The burden of proof that God doesn't exist is enormous. Even Richard Dawkins, in a debate with the archbishop of Canterbury, said that on a scale of one to seven, he was a six in terms of his certainty that God did not exist.[2] This technically makes the world's most famous atheist an agnostic, though he may obviously call himself whatever he'd like.

We have, however, been given enough evidence for God to keep us from languishing in perpetual uncertainty. Science is certainly giving us a clear look at the enormous order and expanse of the universe, causing the open-minded to acknowledge God.

My sincere hope is that you will go beyond believing merely that God exists to developing the relationship with Him that is available. Believing He exists is step one; believing He rewards those who diligently seek Him is step two.

What Should We Do Now?

The Bible says we are to seek Him. Jesus said, "Ask, and it will be given to you; seek, and you will find; knock, and it will be opened to you" (Matthew 7:7). The power of God is freely given to those who are humble enough to ask, desperate enough to seek, and bold enough to knock. He isn't just a force to be analyzed or a formula to be worked; He is a Person to be known. Look closely for a moment at the message the great teacher of Christianity, the apostle Paul, gave at Athens, Greece, to a diverse, highly educated audience. Strong links exist between the needs of the ancient world and ours today. The way he boldly spoke in the face of a fairly hostile crowd reminds me of how we should speak in the twenty-first century.

"The God who made the world and everything in it is the Lord of heaven and earth and does not live in temples built by hands. And he is not served by human hands, as if he needed anything, because he himself gives all men life and breath and everything else. From one man he made every nation of men, that they should inhabit the whole earth; and he determined the times set for them and the exact places where they should live. God did this so that men would seek him and perhaps reach out for him and find him, though he is not far from each one of us. 'For in him we live and move and have our being.' As some of your own poets have said, 'We are his offspring.'

"Therefore since we are God's offspring, we should not think that the divine being is like gold or silver or stone—an image made by man's design and skill. In the past God overlooked such ignorance, but now he commands all people everywhere to repent. For he has set a day when he will judge the world with justice by the man he has appointed. He has given proof of this to all men by raising him from the dead."

When they heard about the resurrection of the dead, some of them sneered, but others said, "We want to hear you again on this subject." (Acts 17:24–32 NIV)

The audience's reactions reveal many of the same sentiments we face today in presenting the gospel while addressing the obstacles in people's minds. Paul saw that the Greeks had an expression of every idea imaginable—religious, philosophical, and scientific. They entertained all new ideas and considered them equally valid (Acts 17:22–23). Paul stepped up to the microphone (so to speak) and spoke out in the marketplace of ideas with clarity and conviction, unafraid to expose erroneous beliefs.

Paul specifically addressed the Epicureans and the Stoics, two notable schools of philosophical thought (Acts 17:18). The Epicurean ideal was "eat, drink, and be merry, for tomorrow we die," and the Stoics faced all of the ups and downs of life with unflappable emotions. Each group was diametrically opposed to the other's belief system, yet they united in a common unbelief in a real God. What was Paul's message to these groups and the numerous others just shopping in the market that day?

1. GOD MADE THE WORLD

He started with presenting God as the Creator. This is the beginning of faith. As science today has confirmed a beginning of the universe, Paul spoke to a culture that believed in many gods and a variety of stories of how things came to be. He said to them simply, the one true God made the world. This belief is not a side issue but the foundational truth in coming to understand and know God.

2. GOD DOESN'T LIVE IN TEMPLES BUILT BY HANDS

Buildings are useful in terms of facilitating gatherings for worship and teaching, but the human heart is the real temple God desires to inhabit. Paul challenged the expressions of faith and corrected the mistaken views of God and worship. He exploded the myth that a person's religious beliefs are off-limits for any critical evaluation. Atheists who rail that people of faith hide from such cross-examination many times hold their own views above such scrutiny. This is the complete opposite of how the life of faith is depicted in Scripture.

3. God Is the Author of Life

The answer to the mystery of the origin of life was not conceded to the domain of philosophers and scientists; Paul credited God as the Author of life. Science can tell us how systems and processes function, but it never will be able to tell us from where life comes. God as the Creator is the possessor of the patents and copyrights for life. By explaining that God is the Author of life, Paul was establishing the right of God to speak to the condition of our souls, to be trusted as the Source of all wisdom. Just as the manufacturer of a product gives the most dependable instructions for its proper use, the Creator of life is the most reliable expert on how life should be understood.

4. God Is the Creator of Both Men and Nations

Paul then ventures into the area of human origins and tells his listeners that God created humanity. He made us to be humans and animals to be animals. He created us in His image that we might have fellowship with Him. God, though infinitely higher than humans, created us with the capacity for real relationship with Him.

5. God Did This So We Would Seek Him

Paul gives the secret away right there: all of life was designed so that humans would desire and seek after God. Think about yourself. Who do you let become your friend? Are there certain types of people whom you like and don't like? Could God have the same type of feelings? Could He reveal Himself to those He wants to and conceal Himself from others?

French philosopher and mathematician Blaise Pascal spoke directly to this: "He so regulates the knowledge of Himself that He has given signs of Himself, visible to those who seek Him, and not to those who seek Him not."[3] That's how we as humans function. Many may see us or know we exist, but that doesn't mean we allow everyone to build a relationship with us. We reveal ourselves to those we trust. In essence, this idea and trait came from God Himself. The reward for diligently seeking God is to come to understand who He is and what He is like.

He has given us enough evidence to know He exists but waits for us to seek Him. Why wouldn't we? Scientists seek answers, philosophers seek wisdom, doctors seek cures, businessmen and businesswomen seek profit and opportunity. Believers should seek God. Because God is indeed alive, that knowledge should inspire us to press through the obstacles and seek Him with all our hearts. That's what we do as people when we are told we have an opportunity to meet someone rich, famous, or influential.

If we were told the president of the United States or queen of England had issued an invitation for us to meet him or her, wouldn't that be an honor not to be disregarded? Even tickets to a U2 concert with an all-access pass backstage to meet Bono would be a highlight in some people's lives. You could substitute any example you like, but the point should be clear: you have been given an open invitation to meet the Creator of the universe and even become His friend, which is without question the highest possible honor imaginable. It is from that kind of relationship with God that the blessings of compassion, wisdom, and knowledge flow into your life. He wants to make you an outlet of that grace to the world.

START THE CONVERSATION

If you are able to grasp the basic nine proofs for God's existence, then you are more than ready and capable to engage unbelievers and believers confidently in a dialogue on the critical areas of faith, skepticism, and the meaning of life. Sure, there are some sophisticated arguments skeptics use that may be beyond your ability to answer. I face this all the time. Many times, though, those who default to the highly technical language of science and philosophy have found an easy place to hide from the implications of an intelligent Creator and the expectations He has for us as human beings.

Sooner or later everyone has to seriously ponder the questions "What is the meaning of life?" and "Does God exist?" These are the great questions of our time. The answers to these questions will define and direct your life like no others. They are not questions that can be ignored forever. As you simply open your eyes to the people around you, you will find there is an enormous openness to start conversations that will have eternal significance.

NOTES

Introduction

1. William Wilberforce, *Real Christianity*, ed. Beb Beltz, rev. ed. (Ventura, CA: Regal, 2006), 20.
2. Greg Graffin and Steve Olson, *Anarchy Evolution: Faith, Science, and Bad Religion in a World Without God* (New York: HarperCollins, 2010), 61.
3. Richard Dawkins, *The Blind Watchmaker: Why the Evidence of Evolution Reveals a Universe Without Design* (1986; New York: Norton, 1996), 5.
4. Stephen Hawking, *A Brief History of Time: The Updated and Expanded Tenth Anniversary Edition* (New York: Bantam, 1996), 146.
5. "Partisan Polarization Surges in Bush, Obama Years," Pew Research Center, June 4, 2012, http://www.people-press.org/2012/06/04 /section-6-religion-and-social-values (accessed October 30, 2012).
6. "Most Twentysomethings Put Christianity on the Shelf Following Spiritually Active Teen Years," Barna Group, September 11, 2006, http://www.barna.org/barna-update/article/16-teensnext-gen/147 -most-twentysomethings-put-christianity-on-the-shelf-following -spiritually-active-teen-years (accessed September 18, 2012).
7. Sam Harris, *The End of Faith: Religion, Terror, and the Future of Reason* (New York: W. W. Norton, 2004), 221.

Chapter 1: God's Not Dead

1. *Richard Dawkins vs. John Lennox: The God Delusion Debate*, University of Alabama at Birmingham, October 3, 2007 (Birmingham: New Day Entertainment, 2007), DVD.
2. Although often attributed to G. K. Chesterton, the exact

provenance of this quotation is unknown. See "When Man Ceases
to Worship God," The American Chesterton Society, http://www
.chesterton.org/discover-chesterton/frequently-asked-questions
/cease-to-worship (accessed September 18, 2012).

3. "Is God Dead?" *Time*, April 8, 1966.

4. Karl Marx, "A Contribution to the Critique of Hegel's Philosophy of
Right," *Deutsch-Französische Jahrbücher* [German-French Annals],
February 1844.

5. "God: After a Lengthy Career, the Almighty Recently Passed into
History. Or Did He?" *The Economist*, December 23, 1999.

6. John Micklethwait and Adrian Wooldridge, *God Is Back: How the
Global Revival of Faith Is Changing the World* (New York: Penguin
Press HC, 2009).

7. C. S. Lewis, *Mere Christianity* (1952; New York: HarperCollins,
2001), 35.

8. Ibid., 16.

9. Andrew Sullivan, "Christianity in Crisis," *Newsweek*, April 2, 2012.

10. Stephen Hawking and Leonard Mlodinow, *The Grand Design* (New
York: Bantam, 2010), 5.

11. Daniel C. Dennett, *Darwin's Dangerous Idea: Evolution and the
Meanings of Life* (New York: Touchstone, 1995), 21.

12. David Aikman, in discussion with the author, September 12, 2012.

13. Malcolm Muggeridge, *A Third Testament: A Modern Pilgrim
Explores the Spiritual Wanderings of Augustine, Blake, Pascal,
Tolstoy, Bonhoeffer, Kierkegaard, and Dostoevsky* (New York:
Ballantine, 1983), 32.

14. Richard Dawkins, *The God Delusion* (New York: Houghton Mifflin,
2006), 15.

15. Richard Dawkins, interview by Tony Jones, *Q&A*, ABC Australia,
April 9, 2012.

16. Greg Graffin and Steve Olson, *Anarchy Evolution: Faith, Science, and
Bad Religion in a World Without God* (New York: HarperCollins,
2010), 5–6.

17. Plato, *Republic*, 394d.

18. John Lennon, "Imagine," *Imagine* (Apple Records, 1971).

19. Bill Maher, *Religulous*, directed by Larry Charles (Santa Monica:
Lionsgate, 2008), DVD.

20. Rice Broocks, *Finding Faith at Ground Zero* (Nashville: Every Nation, 2002), 10.

Chapter 2: Real Faith Isn't Blind

1. *Richard Dawkins vs. John Lennox: The God Delusion Debate*, University of Alabama at Birmingham, October 3, 2007 (Birmingham: New Day Entertainment, 2007), DVD.
2. William Lane Craig, *Reasonable Faith: Christian Truth and Apologetics* (Wheaton, IL: Crossway, 1984), 48.
3. *Dawkins vs. Lennox: The God Delusion Debate.*
4. Ibid.
5. Timothy Keller, *The Reason for God: Belief in an Age of Skepticism* (Ontario: Penguin, 2008), xviii.
6. Dan Cray, "God vs. Science: A Spirited Debate Between Atheist Biologist Richard Dawkins and Christian Geneticist Francis Collins," *Time*, November 13, 2006, http://www.time.com/time /magazine/pacific/0,9263,503061113,00.html (accessed September 16, 2012).
7. Ibid.
8. John Polkinghorne, quoted in Dean Nelson, "God vs. Science," *Saturday Evening Post*, September/October 2011, http://www .saturdayeveningpost.com/2011/08/16/in-the-magazine/features /god-vs-science.html.
9. C. S. Lewis, *Miracles: A Preliminary Study* (London: Fontana, 1947), 110.
10. Albert Einstein, *Physics and Reality*, trans. Jean Piccard (Lancaster, PA: Lancaster, 1936).
11. Johannes Kepler, *Defundamentis Astrologiae Certioribus*, Thesis 20 (1601).
12. Richard Dawkins, speech at the Reason Rally, Washington DC Mall, March 24, 2012, quoted in Charlie Spiering, "A Rally Without Faith," *Crisis Magazine*, March 27, 2012.
13. Peter Hitchens, *The Rage Against God: How Atheism Led Me to Faith* (Grand Rapids: Zondervan, 2010), 12–13.
14. David Albert, "On the Origin of Everything: *A Universe from Nothing*, by Lawrence M. Krauss," *New York Times*, March 23, 2012.

15. Joe Marlin, in discussion with the author, August 15, 2012.

16. C. S. Lewis, *Mere Christianity* (1952; New York: HarperCollins, 2001), 140–41.

17. Stephen M. Barr, "Retelling the Story of Science," Sixteenth Annual Erasmus Lecture, Institute on Religion and Public Life, New York, November 15, 2002, cited in Melanie Phillips, *The World Turned Upside Down: The Global Battle over God, Truth, and Power* (New York: Perseus, 2011), 79.

18. Leon Wieseltier, "The God Genome," *New York Times*, February 19, 2006.

19. "Science in the Dock: Discussion with Noam Chomsky, Lawrence Krauss & Sean M. Carroll," *Science & Technology News*, March 1, 2006.

20. William Lane Craig, debate with Peter Atkins, Georgia, April 1998, http://www.youtube.com/watch?v=3vnjNbe5lyE (accessed September 16, 2012).

21. Eugene Wigner, "The Unreasonable Effectiveness of Mathematics in the Natural Sciences," *Communication on Pure and Applied Mathematics* 13, no. 1, February 1960, 1–14.

22. Phillips, *The World Turned Upside Down*, 321.

23. Richard Dawkins, interview by Tony Jones, *Q&A*, ABC Australia, April 9, 2012.

24. *Dawkins vs. Lennox: The God Delusion Debate.*

25. Stephen Jay Gould, *Rocks of Ages: Science and Religion in the Fullness of Life, The Library of Contemporary Thought* (New York: Ballantine, 1999), 4–6.

26. Polkinghorne, quoted in "God vs. Science."

27. Ibid.

28. Albert Einstein, *Out of My Later Years* (New York: Citadel, 1956), 26.

CHAPTER 3: GOOD AND EVIL ARE NO ILLUSIONS

1. Richard Dawkins, interview by Tony Jones, *Q&A*, ABC Australia, April 9, 2012.

2. Francis Schaeffer, *How Should We Then Live? The Rise and Decline of Western Thought and Culture*, L'Abri 50th Anniversary Edition (1976; Wheaton, IL: Crossway, 2005), 145.

3. Larry Alex Taunton, *The Grace Effect: How the Power of One Life Can Reverse the Corruption of Unbelief* (Nashville: Thomas Nelson, 2011), 6.

4. Ibid., 21.

5. Hugh Ross, *Why the Universe Is the Way It Is* (Grand Rapids: Baker, 2008), 169.

6. Cornelius van Til, *The Defense of the Faith*, ed. K. Scott Oliphint (Phillipsburg, NJ: P and R, 1955).

7. C. S. Lewis, *Mere Christianity* (1952; New York: HarperCollins, 2001), 38.

8. Sam Harris, *The End of Faith: Religion, Terror, and the Future of Reason* (New York: W. W. Norton: 2005), 67.

9. William Lane Craig in debate with Sam Harris, "Is the Foundation of Morality Natural or Supernatural?" University of Notre Dame, April 2011.

10. Melanie Phillips, *The Spectator*, "Welcome to the Age of Irrationality," April 28, 2010, http://www.spectator.co.uk/features /5951248/welcome-to-the-age-of-irrationality (accessed December 20, 2012).

11. Lewis, *Mere Christianity*, 8.

12. Sam Harris, *The Moral Landscape: How Science Can Determine Human Values* (New York: Free Press, 2010), 28.

13. David Hume, *A Treatise of Human Nature* (1739; Brisbane: Emereo, 2010), 335.

14. Harris, *The Moral Landscape*, 39.

15. Immanuel Kant, quoted in *Wiener Zeitschrift* [Vienna Journal], February 1, 1820.

16. Immanuel Kant, *Grounding for the Metaphysics of Morals*, trans. James W. Ellington (1785; Indianapolis: Hackett, 1994), 30.

17. Kant, *Metaphysics of Morals*, 22.

18. Friedrich Nietzsche, "Twilight of the Idols," *The Portable Nietzsche*, ed. and trans. Walter Kaufman (New York: Penguin Books, 1976), 515–16.

19. Herbert Spencer, *The Principles of Biology* (New York: D. Appleton, 1866), 1:444.

20. Thomas Huxley, "Evolution and Ethics," *Evolution and Ethics and Other Essays* (New York: D. Appleton, 1899), 83.

21. Richard Dawkins, *River Out of Eden: A Darwinian View of Life* (New York: Basic, 1995), 133.

22. Dawkins, *Q&A*.

23. Aldous Huxley, *Ends and Means: An Enquiry into the Nature of Ideals and into the Methods Employed for Their Realization* (London: Chatto and Windus, 1946), 273.

24. Jean-Paul Sartre, *Existentialism Is a Humanism*, trans. Carol Macomber (1945; New Haven: Yale, 2007), 28–29.

25. Malcolm Jones, *Dostoevsky and the Dynamics of Religious Experience* (London: Anthem, 2005), 7.

26. *Richard Dawkins vs. John Lennox: The God Delusion Debate*, University of Alabama at Birmingham, October 3, 2007 (Birmingham: New Day Entertainment, 2007), DVD.

27. Christopher Hitchens, *Letters to a Young Contrarian* (New York: Basic, 2005), 64.

28. Lewis, *Mere Christianity*, 69.

29. Gottfried Wilhelm Leibniz, *Theodicy: Essays on the Goodness of God, the Freedom of Man and the Origin of Evil*, trans. E. M. Huggard, ed. A. Farrer (1951; LaSalle, IL: Open Court, 1985), 228.

30. Christopher Hitchens, *The Portable Atheist: Essential Readings for the Nonbeliever* (Cambridge, MA: Da Capo Press, 2007), 394.

31. Lewis, *Mere Christianity*, 47–48.

32. Ross, *Why the Universe Is*, 159.

33. Revelation 21:1–4.

34. Ravi Zacharias, *Can Man Live Without God* (Nashville: Thomas Nelson, 1994), 189.

35. William Lane Craig debate with Sam Harris, "Is the Foundation of Morality Natural or Supernatural?"

Chapter 4: There Was a Beginning

1. Sir Fred Hoyle, "The Universe: Past and Present Reflections," *Engineering and Science*, November 1981, 12.

2. Malcolm W. Browne, "Clues to Universe Origin Expected; The Making of the Universe," *New York Times*, March 12, 1978.

3. Stephen W. Hawking and Roger Penrose, *The Nature of Space and Time* (Princeton: Princeton University, 1996), 20.

4. Carl Sagan, *Cosmos* (New York: Ballantine, 1980), 1.

5. Bertrand Russell and Frederick Copleston, "A Debate on the Existence of God" in *The Existence of God*, ed. John Hick (New York: Collier, 1964), 175.

6. P. C. W. Davies, "Spacetime Singularities in Cosmology," in *The Study of Time III*, J. T. Fraser, ed. (New York: Springer Verlag, 1978), 78–79.

7. Robert Jastrow, *God and the Astronomers*, 2nd ed. (New York: Norton and Norton, 1992), 9.

8. Arthur S. Eddington, "The End of the World: From the Standpoint of Mathematical Physics," *Nature* 127 (1931): 450.

9. Stephen Hawking, *A Brief History of Time: The Updated and Expanded Tenth Anniversary Edition* (New York: Bantam, 1996), 49.

10. Sir Fred Hoyle, *The Intelligent Universe* (New York: Holt, Rinehart and Winston, 1983), 237.

11. J. P. Moreland and William Lane Craig, ed., *Philosophical Foundations for a Christian Worldview* (Downer's Grove, IL: InterVarsity, 2003), 465.

12. Ibid., 468.

13. William Lane Craig and J. P. Moreland, eds., *The Blackwell Companion to Natural Theology* (Chichester: Blackwell, 2009), 130.

14. Ibid., 192.

15. G. W. Leibniz, "On the Ultimate Origination of Things," in *Leibniz: Philosophical Writings*, ed. G. H. R. Parkinson, trans., M. Morris and G. H. R. Parkinson (London: J. M. Dent, 1973), 136–44.

16. *Richard Dawkins vs. John Lennox: The God Delusion Debate*, University of Alabama at Birmingham, October 3, 2007 (Birmingham: New Day Entertainment, 2007), DVD.

17. Lawrence M. Krauss, *A Universe from Nothing: Why There Is Something Rather than Nothing* (New York: Free Press, 2012), xiv.

18. http://www.reasons.org/articles/universe-from-nothing-a-critique -of-lawrence-krauss-book-part-1.

19. Victor Stenger, "Why Is There Something Rather Than Nothing?" *Skeptical Enquirer* 16, no. 2, June 2006, http://www.csicop.org/sb /show/why_is_there_something_rather_than_nothing (accessed September 20, 2012).

20. Michael Shermer, "Nothing Is Negligible: Why There Is Something

Rather Than Nothing," *eSkeptic*, July 11, 2012, http://www.skeptic.com/eskeptic/12-07-11/#feature (accessed September 20, 2012).

21. Allan Sandage, quoted in J. N. Willford, "Sizing up the Cosmos: An Astronomer's Quest," *New York Times*, March 12, 1991, B9.

22. Stephen Hawking and Leonard Mlodinow, *The Grand Design* (New York: Bantam Books, 2010), 180.

23. *Curiosity*, "Did God Create the Universe?" YouTube, http://www.youtube.com/watch?v=jcrRyK4uO8g.

24. *The Wizard of Oz*, directed by King Vidor (1936; Burbank, CA: Warner Home Video, 1999), DVD.

25. Sean Carroll, "The Pointless Universe," in John Brockman, ed., *This Will Make You Smarter: New Scientific Concepts to Improve Your Thinking* (New York: HarperCollins, 2012), 9.

26. Krauss, *A Universe from Nothing*, 142.

27. Richard Dawkins, *The Blind Watchmaker: Why the Evidence of Evolution Reveals a Universe Without Design* (1986; New York: Norton, 1996), 15.

28. Alvin Plantinga, "The Dawkins Confusion: Naturalism 'ad absurdum,'" *Christianity Today*, March/April 2007, http://www.booksandculture.com/articles/2007/marapr/1.21.html (accessed September 20, 2012).

29. Richard Swinburne, "Argument from the Fine-Tuning of the Universe," *Physical Cosmology and Philosophy*, ed. John Leslie (New York: Macmillan, 1991), 160.

30. John D. Barrow and Frank J. Tipler, *The Anthropic Cosmological Principle* (New York: Oxford University Press, 1986), 40.

31. Hugh Ross, *Creator and the Cosmos: How the Latest Scientific Discoveries of the Century Reveal God* (Colorado Springs: NavPress, 2001), 150.

32. For a detailed description, see Hugh Ross, *Why the Universe Is the Way It Is* (Grand Rapids: Baker Books, 2008).

33. John C. Lennox, *God's Undertaker: Has Science Buried God?* (Oxford: Lion Hudson, 2009), 71.

34. *The New Encyclopedia of Unbelief*, Tom Flynn, ed. (Amherst: Prometheus, 2007), s.v. "Anthropic Principle, the," by Victor Stenger.

35. Freeman Dyson, *Disturbing the Universe* (New York: Harper and Row, 1979), 250.

36. Hoyle, "Universe: Past and Present Reflections," 8–12.

37. Paul Davies, "Yes, the universe looks like a fix. But that doesn't mean a god fixed it," *Guardian*, June 25, 2007, http://www.guardian.co.uk/commentisfree/2007/jun/26/spaceexploration.comment (accessed September 20, 2012).

38. John Horgan, "Clash in Cambridge: Science and religion seem as antagonistic as ever," *Scientific American*, September 2005, http://www.scientificamerican.com/article.cfm?id=clash-in-cambridge&page=2 (accessed September 20, 2012).

39. Edward Harrison, *Masks of the Universe: Changing Ideas on the Nature of the Cosmos* (New York: Collier Books, 1985), 252, 263, 286.

40. William Lane Craig, *Natural Theology*, 142–44.

41. C. S. Lewis, *Mere Christianity* (1952; New York: HarperCollins, 2001), 31–32.

42. *Dawkins vs. Lennox: The God Delusion Debate.*

43. Jastrow, *God and the Astronomers*, 9–10.

44. *Dawkins vs. Lennox: The God Delusion Debate.*

CHAPTER 5: LIFE IS NO ACCIDENT

1. Darwin, *On the Origin of Species: By Means of Natural Selection*, ed. Thomas Crawford (New York: Dover Thrift, 2006), 119.

2. Richard Dawkins, "The Illusion of Design" in *Biological Anthropology: An Introductory Reader*, ed. Michael Alan Park (New York: McGraw Hill, 2007), 30.

3. Anthony Flew, *There Is a God: How the World's Most Notorious Atheist Changed His Mind* (New York: HarperOne, 2008), 75.

4. Ibid.

5. Bill Gates, *The Road Ahead*, rev. ed. (New York: Penguin, 1996), 228.

6. Dan Cray, "God vs. Science: A spirited debate between atheist biologist Richard Dawkins and Christian geneticist Francis Collins," *Time*, November 13, 2006.

7. Francis S. Collins, *The Language of Life: DNA and the Revolution in Personalized Medicine* (New York: HarperCollins, 2010), 6.

8. Julian Huxley, "At Random: A Television Preview" in *Evolution After Darwin*, ed. Sol Tax (Chicago: University of Chicago, 1960), 45.

9. *Richard Dawkins vs. John Lennox: The God Delusion Debate*, University of Alabama at Birmingham, October 3, 2007 (Birmingham: New Day Entertainment, 2007), DVD.

10. Albert Einstein, *The World as I See It*, trans. Alan Harris (1948; New York: Wisdom Library, 2000), 29.

11. Jared Diamond, "Foreword," in Ernst Mayr, *What Evolution Is* (New York: Basic, 2001), vii.

12. Jerry A. Coyne, *Why Evolution Is True* (New York: Penguin, 2009), 3.

13. Richard Dawkins, *The Blind Watchmaker: Why the Evidence of Evolution Reveals a Universe Without Design* (1986; New York: Norton, 1996), 29.

14. Hugh Ross, personal interview with author, October 26, 2012. Used by permission.

15. Darwin, *On the Origin of Species*, 305.

16. *Dawkins vs. Lennox: The God Delusion Debate.*

17. *Richard Dawkins vs. John Lennox: The God Delusion Debate*, University of Alabama at Birmingham, October 3, 2007 (Birmingham: New Day Entertainment, 2007), DVD.

18. Dawkins, *Blind Watchmaker*, 1.

19. Francis Crick, *What Mad Pursuit: A Personal View of Scientific Discovery* (New York: Basic, 1988), 138.

20. Fred Hoyle and Chandra Wickramasinghe, *Evolution from Space* (London: Granada Publishing Ltd., 1981), 20.

21. Fred Hoyle, in "Hoyle on Evolution," *Nature*," vol. 294, 12 November 1981, 105.

22. Hoyle and Wickramasinghe, *Evolution from Space*, 28.

23. Richard Dawkins, *The God Delusion* (New York: Houghton Mifflin, 2006) 147.

24. Daniel Came, "Richard Dawkins Refusal to Debate Is Cynical and Anti-Intellectual," *The Guardian*, October 22, 2011, http://www.guardian.co.uk/commentisfree/belief/2011/oct/22/richard-dawkins-refusal-debate-william-lane-craig?CMP=twt_gu.

25. Alvin Plantinga, *Where the Conflict Really Lies: Science, Religion, and Naturalism* (New York: Oxford University, 2012), 27.

26. Richard Dawkins, "Militant Atheism," Monterey, California, February 2002, http://www.ted.com/talks/lang/en/richard_dawkins_on_militant_atheism.html (accessed September 20, 2012).

27. Jerry M. Mendel and Dongrui Wu, *Perceptual Computing: Aiding People in Making Subjective Judgments* (Hoboken, NJ: John Wiley and Sons, 2010), 20.

28. Richard Dawkins, *Climbing Mount Improbable* (New York: W. W. Norton, 1996), 77.
29. Michael J. Behe, *Darwin's Black Box: The Biochemical Challenge to Evolution* (New York: Free Press, 2006), 69–72.
30. Edgar Andrews, *Who Made God? Searching for a Theory of Everything* (Maitland, FL: Xulon Press, 2012), 76–77.
31. Ming Wang, personal conversation with author, June 5, 2012.
32. *Calvin and Hobbes* copyright 1990 Watterson. Distributed by Universal Press Syndicate.
33. Hugh Ross, interview with author.
34. William A. Dembski, *The Design Revolution: Answering the Toughest Questions About Intelligent Design* (Downer's Grove, IL: InterVarsity, 2004), 87–93.
35. Stephen C. Meyer, *Signature in the Cell: DNA and the Evidence for Intelligent Design* (New Your: HarperOne, 2009).
36. J. Madeleine Nash, "When Life Exploded," *Time*, December 4, 1995, http://www.time.com/time/covers/0,16641,19951204,00.html (accessed September 21, 2012).
37. Stephen C. Meyer, *Darwin's Doubt: The Explosive Origin of Animal Life and the Case for Intelligent Design* (New Your: HarperOne, 2013).
38. Nash, ibid.
39. Darwin, *On the Origin of Species*, 95.
40. G. M. Narbonne, quoted in Nash, "When Life Exploded."
41. For detailed discussion, see Walter Remine, *The Biotic Message: Evolution Versus Message Theory* (Saint Paul, MN: Saint Paul Science, publishers, 1993).

Chapter 6: Life Has Meaning and Purpose

1. Lawrence Krauss, lecture, "A Universe from Nothing," Oxford University, Oxford England, http://www.youtube.com/watch?v=EjaGktVQdNg (accessed September 21, 2012).
2. C. S. Lewis, *Mere Christianity* (1952; New York: HarperCollins, 2001), 39.
3. Carl Sagan, CBC interview, October 1988, http://www.youtube.com/watch?v=r5GFoFh4T2g.
4. William Lane Craig, *On Guard: Defending Your Faith with Reason and Precision* (Colorado Springs: David C. Cook, 2010), 30.

5. Harold S. Kushner, "Foreword," in Viktor E. Frankl, *Man's Search for Meaning* (New York: Beacon, 2006), x.
6. Frankl, *Man's Search for Meaning*, ix.
7. Friedrich Nietzsche, *The Anti-Christ*, trans. H. L. Mencken (New York: Alfred A. Knopf, 1923), 122.
8. For more information, please visit TheGodTest.org.
9. Richard Dawkins, *River Out of Eden: A Darwinian View of Life* (New York: Basic, 1995), 112.
10. Bertrand Russell, *Why I Am Not a Christian and Other Essays on Religion and Related Subjects* (New York: Simon and Schuster, 1957), 107.
11. Jean-Paul Sartre, *Truth and Existence*, ed. Ronald Aronson, trans. Adrian van den Hoven (Chicago: University of Chicago, 1992), 71.
12. Rick Warren, *The Purpose Driven Life: What on Earth Am I Here For?* (Grand Rapids: Zondervan, 2004).
13. Lawrence M. Krauss, *A Universe from Nothing: Why There Is Something Rather than Nothing* (New York: Free Press, 2012), xii.
14. David Robertson, letter 3. www.bethinking.org/science-christianity/introductory/the=dawkins-letters-3-respect.htm.
15. Francis A. Schaeffer, *The Church Before the Watching World: A Practical Ecclesiology* (Downer's Grove, IL: InterVarsity, 1971), 29.
16. Greg Graffin and Steve Olson, *Anarchy Evolution: Faith, Science, and Bad Religion in a World Without God* (New York: HarperCollins, 2010), 4.
17. *Richard Dawkins vs. John Lennox: The God Delusion Debate*, University of Alabama at Birmingham, October 3, 2007 (Birmingham: New Day Entertainment, 2007), DVD.
18. Francis Schaeffer, *Escape from Reason* (Downer's Grove, IL: InterVarsity, 2006), 32.
19. Christopher Tinker and Melvin Tinker, "Fifty Years On: The Legacy of Francis Schaeffer—An Apologetic for Post-Moderns," *Churchman* 119, no. 3, Autumn 2005, 208.
20. Stephen Jay Gould, quoted in David Friend, *The Meaning of Life: Reflections in Words and Pictures on Why We Are Here* (New York: Little Brown, 1991), 33.

21. "The True Core of the Jesus Myth: Christopher Hitchens @ FreedomFest," YouTube, April 11, 2009, http://www.youtube.com /watch?v=vMo5R5pLPBE.

22. Richard Dawkins, *A Devil's Chaplain: Reflections on Hope, Lies, Science, and Love* (New York: Houghton Mifflin, 2003), 23.

23. Jonathan Wells, "Survival of Fakest," *American Spectator,* December 2000 / January 2001.

24. Steven M. Stanley, *The New Evolutionary Timetable: Fossils, Genes, and the Origin of Species* (New York: Basic, 1981), 139.

25. Stephen Jay Gould, *Ever Since Darwin: Reflections in Natural History* (New York: W. W. Norton, 1977), 57.

26. Francis S. Collins, *The Language of God: A Scientist Presents Evidence for Belief* (New York: Free Press, 2006), 138–39.

27. Ann Gauger, Douglas Axe, and Casey Luskin, *Science and Human Origins* (Seattle: Discovery Institute, 2012).

28. Ravi Zacharias, *Can Man Live Without God* (Nashville: Thomas Nelson, 2004), 22.

29. "What Is Speciesism?" *The Ethics of Speciesism,* BBC, http:// www.bbc.co.uk/ethics/animals/rights/speciesism.shtml (accessed September 22, 2012).

30. Peter Singer, *Animal Liberation* (1975; New York: HarperCollins, 2002), 173.

31. Richard Dawkins, interview by Craig Ferguson, *Late Late Show,* RTC One [Irish television], September 18, 2009.

32. Noam Chomsky, *Language and Mind,* 3rd ed. (Cambridge: Cambridge University Press, 2006), 59.

33. Noam Chomsky, *New Horizons in the Study of Language and the Mind* (Cambridge: Cambridge University Press, 2000), 92.

34. Michael Denton, *Nature's Destiny: How the Laws of Biology Reveal Purpose in the Universe* (New York: Free Press, 2002), 241.

35. Ibid., 239.

36. Marcelo Gleiser, "We Are Unique" in John Brockman, *This Will Make You Smarter: New Scientific Concepts to Improve Your Thinking* (New York: HarperCollins, 2012), 4.

37. Harry G. Frankfurt, "Freedom of the Will and the Concept of a Person," *The Journal of Philosophy,* vol. 68, no. 1 (January 14, 1971), 5–7.

38. Michael Tomasello, "How Are Humans Unique?" *New York Times*, May 25, 2008, http://www.nytimes.com/2008/05/25/magazine /25wwln-essay-t.html?_r=0 (accessed September 22, 2012).
39. Merlin Donald, *A Mind So Rare: The Evolution of Human Consciousness* (New York: W. W. Norton, 2002), xiii.
40. Gary Habermas and J. P. Moreland, *Beyond Death: Exploring the Evidence for Immortality* (Eugene, OR: Wipf & Stock Publishers, 2004).
41. For a complete discussion of this and other examples, see Kevin Favero, *Science of the Soul: Scientific Evidence of Human Souls* (Edina, MN: Beaver's Pond Press, 2004).
42. Saint Augustine, *Confessions*, Book 1, 21.

CHAPTER 7: JESUS AND THE RESURRECTION

1. Josh McDowell, *More than a Carpenter* (1977; Wheaton, IL: Tyndale, 2004), 54.
2. Bart D. Ehrman, *Did Jesus Exist? The Historical Argument for Jesus of Nazareth* (New York: HarperOne, 2012), 7.
3. Naomi Schaefer Riley, "A Revelation: Civil Debate Over God's Existence," *Wall Street Journal*, October 12, 2007, http://online.wsj .com/article/SB119214767015956720-search.html (accessed December 20, 2012).
4. *Richard Dawkins vs. John Lennox: The God Delusion Debate*, University of Alabama at Birmingham, October 3, 2007 (Birmingham: New Day Entertainment, 2007), DVD.
5. Richard Dawkins and John Lennox, debate, University Museum of Natural History, Oxford England, October 21, 2008.
6. Ehrman, *Did Jesus Exist?* 5–6.
7. Tacitus, *Annals* 15.44.
8. Pliny, *Letters* 2.10.
9. Julius Africanus, *Chronography* 18.1.
10. Josephus, *Jewish Antiquities* 20.9.
11. Craig Blomberg, *The Historical Reliability of the Gospels* (Downer's Grove, IL: InterVarsity, 1987), 252–54.
12. E. M. Blaiklock, quoted in Josh McDowell, *Skeptics Who Demanded a Verdict* (Wheaton, IL: Tyndale, 1989), 85.
13. Richard Gordon, *Image and Value in the Graeco-Roman World* (Aldershot, UK: Variorum, 1996), 96.

14. Richard Carrier, "Kersey Graves and *The World's Sixteen Crucified Saviors*," Internet Infidels, http://www.infidels.org/library/modern /richard_carrier/graves.html (accessed September 22, 2012).

15. Craig S. Keener, *The Historical Jesus of the Gospels* (Grand Rapids: Wm. B. Eerdmans, 2009), 334–35.

16. Bruce M. Metzger, "Mystery Religions and Early Christianity, in *Historical and Literary Studies* (Leiden, Netherlands: E. J. Brill, 1968), 11.

17. Keener, *The Historical Jesus*, 336.

18. Ibid., 333.

19. Tryggve N. D. Mettinger, *The Riddle of Resurrection: "Dying and Rising Gods" in the Ancient Near East* (London: Coronet, 2001), 7, 40–41.

20. Dave Sterrett, *Why Trust Jesus? An Honest Look at Doubts, Plans, Hurts, Desires, Fears, Questions, and Pleasures* (Chicago: Moody, 2010), 141.

21. Lee Strobel, YouTube video, http://www.youtube.com /watch–v=6WGDfNlp2as.

22. William D. Edwards, Wesley J. Gabel, and Floyd E. Hosmer, "On the Physical Death of Jesus Christ," *Journal of the American Medical Association* 256, March 21, 1986.

23. John A. T. Robinson, quoted by William Lane Craig, in Lee Strobel, *The Case for Christ: A Journalist's Personal Investigation of the Evidence for Jesus* (Grand Rapids: Zondervan, 1998), 210.

24. James D. Tabor, *The Jesus Dynasty: The Hidden History of Jesus, His Royal Family, and the Birth of Christianity* (New York: Simon and Schuster, 2006), 230.

25. E. P. Sanders, *The Historical Figure of Jesus* (New York: Penguin Books, 1993), 279–80.

26. Bart D. Ehrman, *The New Testament: A Historical Introduction to the Early Christian Writings*, 3rd ed. (New York: Oxford University, 2004), 276.

27. John Dominic Crossan and Jonathan L. Reed, *Excavating Jesus: Beneath the Stones, Behind the Texts* (San Francisco: HarperCollins, 2002), 298.

28. Pinchas Lapide, *The Resurrection of Jesus: A Jewish Perspective*, trans. Wilhelm C. Linss (Minneapolis: Fortress Press, 1988), 125.

29. James A. Francis, *One Solitary Life* (Nashville: Thomas Nelson, 2005), 39. Mortimer J. Adler, *Great Ideas from the Great Books* (New York: Pocket, 1976), 274–75.

CHAPTER 8: THE WITNESS OF SCRIPTURE

1. Immanuel Kant, quoted in Friedrich Paulsen, *Immanuel Kant: His Life and Doctrine*, trans. J. E. Creighton and Albert LeFevre (New York: Charles Scribner's Sons, 1902), 48.

2. Abraham Lincoln, quoted in *Washington Daily Morning Chronicle*, September 8, 1864.

3. "The Great Isaiah Scroll," *The Digital Dead Sea Scrolls*, http://dss.collections.imj.org.il/isaiah (accessed December 20, 2012).

4. Wayne Grudem, C. John Collins, Thomas R. Schreiner, eds., *Understanding Scripture: An Overview of the Bible's Origin, Reliability, and Meaning* (Wheaton, IL: Crossway, 2012), 159.

5. F. F. Bruce, "Galatian Problems. 4. The Date of the Epistle," *Bulletin of the John Rylands Library Manchester* 54.2 (Spring 1972): 251.

6. Norman Geisler and Peter Bocchino, *Unshakable Foundations: Contemporary Answers to Crucial Questions about the Christian Faith* (Minneapolis: Bethany House, 2001), 257.

7. Robert Stewart, ed. *The Reliability of the New Testament: Bart D. Ehrman and Daniel B. Wallace in Dialogue*, 33–34. Augsburg Fortress - A. Kindle Edition. Referencing Bruce M. Metzger and Bart D. Ehrman, *The Text of the New Testament: Its Transmission, Corruption, and Restoration*, 4th ed. (New York: Oxford University Press, 2005), 126.

8. Gleason Archer, *A Survey of Old Testament Introduction*, rev. ed. (Chicago: Moody, 1974), 25.

9. Dan Brown, *The Da Vinci Code* (New York: Doubleday, 2003).

10. *The Reliability of the New Testament: Bart D. Ehrman and Daniel B. Wallace in Dialogue*, 55.

11. William Lane Craig, "Establishing the Gospels' Reliability," *Reasonable Faith*, April 5, 2010, http://www.reasonablefaith.org/site/News2?page=NewsArticle&id=5711 (accessed September 23, 2012).

12. *The Reliability of the New Testament: Bart D. Erhman and Daniel B. Wallace in Dialogue*, 39.

13. Craig Blomberg, *The Historical Reliability of the Gospels* (Downer's Grove, IL: InterVarsity, 1987), 55–62.

14. Ibid., 152–95.

15. Ibid., 203–04.

16. Sir William Ramsay, *The Bearing of Recent Discovery on the*

Trustworthiness of the New Testament (1915; Grand Rapids: Baker, 1975), 89.

17. Craig Keener, *The Historical Jesus of the Gospels* (Grand Rapids: Eerdmans, 2012), 85–94 and Colin Hemer, *Book of Acts in the Setting of Hellenistic History* (Winona Lake, IN: Eisenbrauns, 1990).

18. Blomberg, *Historical Reliability of the Gospels*, 206.

19. K. A. Kitchen, *On the Reliability of the Old Testament* (Grand Rapids: Wm. B. Eerdmans, 2003).

20. For detailed discussion, see Harold Koenig, *The Healing Power of Faith: How Belief and Prayer Can Help You Triumph Over Disease* (New York: Simon and Schuster, 2001).

CHAPTER 9: THE GRACE EFFECT

1. Bart D. Ehrman, *God's Problem: How the Bible Fails to Answer Our Most Important Question—Why We Suffer* (New York: HarperColliins, 2008), 128.

2. Rodney Stark, *The Rise of Christianity: How the Obscure, Marginal Jesus Movement Became the Dominant Religious Force in the Western World in a Few Centuries* (Princeton: Princeton University, 1996), 211.

3. Will Durant, *Caesar and Christ: A History of Roman Civilization from Their Beginnings to A.D. 325* (1944; New York: Simon and Schuster, 1972), 652.

4. Michael Green, *Thirty Years That Changed the World: The Book of Acts for Today* (1993; Grand Rapids: Wm. B. Eerdmans, 2004), 7.

5. D. James Kennedy and Jerry Newcombe, *What If Jesus Had Never Been Born? The Positive Impact of Christianity in History*, rev. ed. (Nashville: Thomas Nelson, 2001), 9.

6. Christopher Hitchens, interview by Dennis Miller, *The Dennis Miller Show*, Westwood One, October 30, 2009.

7. William Lane Craig, debate with Christopher Hitchens, Biola University, La Mirada, California, April 4, 2009, http://www.youtube.com/watch?v=4KBx4vvlbZ8.

8. Luke Muehlhauser, "The Craig-Hitchens Debate," *Common Sense Atheism*, April 4, 2009, http://commonsenseatheism.com/?p=1230 (accessed September 23, 2012).

9. Larry Alex Taunton, *The Grace Effect: How the Power of One Life Can Reverse the Corruption of Unbelief* (Nashville: Thomas Nelson, 2011), xii.

10. Ibid., 22.

11. Kennedy and Newcombe, *What If Jesus Had Never Been Born?* 27.

12. Stark, *Rise of Christianity*, 105.

13. Kennedy and Newcombe, *What If Jesus Had Never Been Born?* 12.

14. Stark, *Rise of Christianity*, 124–28.

15. Justice Harry A. Blackmun, quoted in Kennedy and Newcombe, *What If Jesus Had Never Been Born?* 27.

16. Kennedy and Newcombe, *What If Jesus Had Never Been Born?* 14–15.

17. Stark, *Rise of Christianity*, 95.

18. Adam Smith, *An Inquiry into the Nature and Causes of the Wealth of Nations* (Chicago: William Benton, 1956), 30.

19. Kennedy and Newcombe, *What If Jesus Had Never Been Born?* 14–16.

20. Siegfried Lauffer, "Die Bergwerkssklaven von Laureion," *Abhandlungen* 12, 1956: 916.

21. Keith Bradley, "Resisting Slavery in Ancient Rome," *History*, BBC News, February 17, 2011, http://www.bbc.co.uk/history/ancient /romans/slavery_01.shtml (accessed September 23, 2012).

22. Rodney Stark, *The Victory of Reason: How Christianity Led to Freedom, Capitalism, and Western Success* (New York: Random House, 2005), 76.

23. Paul Johnson, *The Renaissance: A Short History* (New York: Modern Library, 2000), 9.

24. George Marsden, *The Soul of the American University: From Protestant Establishment to Established Nonbelief* (New York: Oxford University, 1996).

25. Michael S. Horton, *Where in the World Is the Church? A Christian View of Culture and Your Role in It* (Phillipsburg, NJ: P and R, 2002), 29–31.

26. Taunton, *The Grace Effect*, 34.

27. Judith Herrin, *The Formation of Christendom* (Princeton: Princeton University, 1987), 57.

28. E. Glenn Hinson, *The Early Church: Origins to the Dawn of the Middle Ages* (Nashville: Abingdon, 1996), 171.

29. Julian, quoted in D. Brendan Nagle and Stanley M. Burstein, *The Ancient World: Readings in Social and Cultural History* (Englewood Cliffs, NJ: Prentice Hall, 1995), 314–15.
30. "Mother Teresa Quotes," *Brainy Quote*, http://www.brainyquote .com/quotes/quotes/m/mothertere158114.html (accessed September 23, 2012).
31. Stark, *Rise of Christianity*, 215.
32. Stark, *Victory of Reason*, 76.
33. Timothy Keller, *The Reason for God: Belief in an Age of Skepticism* (Ontario: Penguin, 2008), 155.

CHAPTER 10: LIVING PROOF

1. "God's Not Dead (Like a Lion)," written by Daniel Bashta, performed and recorded by Newsboys. © 2010 worshiptogether .com Songs (ASCAP), sixsteps Music (ASCAP), Go Forth Sounds (ASCAP) (adm. at EMICMGPublishing.com). All rights reserved. Used by permission.
2. John Micklethwait and Adrian Wooldridge, *God Is Back: How the Global Revival of Faith Is Changing the World* (New York: Penguin, 2009), 13.
3. John Lennon, quoted in Maureen Cleave, "The John Lennon I Knew," *Telegraph*, October 5, 2005, http://www.telegraph.co.uk /culture/music/rockandjazzmusic/3646983/The-John-Lennon-I -knew.html (accessed September 23, 2012).
4. Micklethwait and Wooldridge, *God Is Back*, 12.
5. Tony Carnes, interview with the author, August 19, 2012.
6. "The Explosion of Christianity in Africa," Christianity.com, http://www.christianity.com/ChurchHistory/11630859/ (accessed September 23, 2012).
7. Personal conversation with Frans Olivier, May 20, 2012.
8. Personal conversation with Sam Aiyedogbon, October 12, 2012.
9. Personal conversation with Shaddy Soliman, September 11, 2012.
10. William Murrell, "Manila's Mega-Move," *Charisma*, September 1, 2012, http://www.charismamag.com/spirit/church-ministry/15495 -manila-s-mega-move (accessed September 23, 2012).
11. Ferdie Cabiling, personal conversation with author, September 1, 2012.

12. David Aikman, in discussion with the author, September 12, 2012.

13. http://www.indexmundi.com/south_korea/demographics_profile
.htmlhttp://www.indexmundi.com/south_korea/demographics
_profile.html.

14. Samuel H. Moffett, "What Makes the Korean Church Grow? The Simple Secrets of Its Remarkable Explosion," *Christianity Today*, January 31, 2007, http://www.christianitytoday.com/ct/2007/januaryweb-only/105-33.0.html (accessed September 23, 2012).

15. Jason Mandryk, *Operation World: The Definitive Prayer Guide to Every Nation*, 7th ed. (Colorado Springs: Biblica, 2010), 447.

16. Micklethwait and Wooldridge, *God Is Back*, 14.

17. "There's Probably No Dawkins" Bus Campaign (William Lane Craig vs. The God Delusion), YouTube, http://www.youtube.com/watch?v=SGWr9qpeKpE&playnext=1&list=PLF30F88D1B4A47EFC&feature=results_main (accessed December 20, 2012).

18. Wolfgang Eckleben, personal conversation with author, August 15, 2012.

19. Gareth Lowe, personal conversation with author, August 1, 2012.

20. Ed Stetzer, e-mail correspondence with author, August 22, 2012.

21. "Barna Survey Reveals Significant Growing in Born Again Population," Barna Group, March 27, 2006, http://www.barna.org/barna-update/article/5-barna-update/157-barna-survey-reveals-significant-growth-in-born-again-population (accessed September 23, 2012).

22. Chad Hall, "Leader's Insight: The Disappearing Middle," *Leadership Journal*, July 2007, http://www.christianitytoday.com/le/2007/july-online-only/cln70716.html?start=2 (accessed September 23, 2012).

23. Micklethwait and Wooldridge, *God Is Back*, 139.

24. For a detailed study of miracles, see Craig Keener, *Miracles: The Credibility of the New Testament Accounts*, Baker Academic (November 1, 2011).

25. Ming Wang, personal interview with the author, June 5, 2012. Used by permission.

26. Joe Marlin, personal interview with the author, August 15, 2012. Used by permission.

27. Brian Miller, personal interview with the author, August 10, 2012. Used by permission.
28. Joanna Goodson, personal interview with the author, September 20, 2012. Used by permission.
29. Brant Reding, personal interview with the author, September 15, 2012. Used by permission.
30. Jim Munroe, personal interview with the author, September 20, 2012. Used by permission.
31. Dr. Augusto Cury, www.augustocury.com.br.

CONCLUSION: SEEKING GOD

1. Blaise Pascal, *Pascal's Pensées* (Radford, VA: Wilder Publications, 2011), 120.
2. Richard Dawkins, interview by Tony Jones, *Q&A*, ABC Australia, April 9, 2012.
3. Blaise Pascal, *Pascal's Pensées*, 120.

INDEX

ACKNOWLEDGMENTS

THE PROCESS OF WRITING THIS BOOK TOOK ABOUT TEN months from beginning to end. During this time, Jody, my wife of thirty years, and all of my five children have been a constant source of encouragement, inspiration, and constructive criticism. Having children whose ages range from thirteen to twenty-eight has given me a built-in focus group of the age demographic I'm most concerned with in the writing of this book. My deepest thanks to all of them: Charlie, Wyatt, William, Louisa, and Elizabeth (from youngest to oldest). No one is happier that I finished this project than my wife, who will be relieved to have her dining room free from the clutter of paper, books, articles, and coffee cups.

I am indebted to Dr. Brian Miller, a graduate of MIT and Duke in physics, who served as my technical consultant as well as a fantastic research assistant. It was a privilege to bounce ideas off such a brilliant mind as well as benefit from his guidance in the critical scientific commentary covered in the book.

I had a dream team of friends and advisors who read the manuscript, gave comments, and added strategy and insight to this project. Stephen Mansfield, David Aikman, Larry Taunton, Dr. Hugh Ross, Dr. Dan Wallace, Dr. William Lane Craig, and Dean Diehl are all accomplished writers and thinkers and did me a great service by taking time to help. My thanks also go to Elizabeth Broocks and Georgia Shaw for helping with various aspects of this project.

I must also say thank you to my friends and ministry partners at Bethel World Outreach Church in Nashville and Every Nation Ministries for their friendship and partnership: Ron and Lynette Lewis, James and Debbie Lowe, Kevin York, Steve Murrell, Jim Laffoon, Russ Austin, and many more I wish I could name.

Thanks to Troy Duhon who had the idea to turn the book into a movie and has been a faithful source of encouragement to keep the message of the book and movie spreading around the world. I also want to thank Russell Wolfe and Michael Scott from PureFlix for all the effort they put forth to incorporate the evidence for God presented in this book into the movie, *God's Not Dead*. I enjoyed working with Chuck Konzelman and Cary Solomon, the screenwriters for the movie. I look forward to future projects with this creative, faith-filled team.

I am deeply grateful as well for the daily encouragement from Dale Evrist of New Song Christian Fellowship in Nashville. He believed in the importance of this book and is a constant source of inspiration.

I'm grateful for the Engage 2020, Campus Harvest, and God Test team plus many others who are dedicated to seeing effective evangelism and apologetics as a part of every local church and campus ministry: Steve and Cindy Hollander, Frans Olivier, Jerret Sykes, Don Bush, Greg Chapman, Louisa Broocks, and Gene Mack.

There are also several families that have taken an interest in my life and have been there as supporters for me, my family, and my many projects. Deepest thanks to Kelly and Joni Womack, and Danny and Diane McDaniel, and to Bob and Candy Majors, and Mark and Melinda Flint for their love and generosity.

I appreciate Matt Baugher, Paula Major, Andrea Lucado, and the entire Nelson team for their genuine interest and enthusiasm about this book. It is an honor to be in partnership with you in this project.

ABOUT THE AUTHOR

RICE BROOCKS is cofounder of the Every Nation family of churches, which currently has more than one thousand churches and hundreds of campus ministries in more than sixty nations. He is also the senior minister of Bethel World Outreach Church in Nashville, Tennessee, a multiethnic, multisite church.

Rice is a graduate of Mississippi State University and holds a master's degree from Reformed Theological Seminary, Jackson, Mississippi, as well as a doctorate in missiology from Fuller Theological Seminary, Pasadena, California.

The author of several books, including *Every Nation in Our Generation* and *The Purple Book (Biblical Foundations)*, Rice lives in Franklin, Tennessee, with his wife, Jody, and their five children.

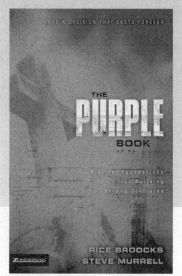

978-0-310-93600-8

THE PURPLE BOOK

Biblical Foundations for Building Strong Disciples

Rice Broocks and *Steve Murrell*

Have you done *The Purple Book*? From students and scholars to parents, kids, rock stars, and professional athletes, people all over the world are doing *The Purple Book*. Why? Because they're looking for a foundation that no storm in life will prevail against—and a heart that's shaped and guided by the knowledge of God's Word. *The Purple Book* is a twelve-part Bible study designed to help new believers and longtime followers of Jesus stand firm and grow strong in the Christian life. Take the challenge to build the foundation of your life on the Word of God. Do *The Purple Book*.

AVAILABLE IN STORES AND ONLINE!

◢ ZONDERVAN®